CROCHET SAVED MY LIFE

The Mental and Physical Health Benefits of Crochet

By Kathryn Vercillo

Cover photography by Julie Michelle
http://juliemichellephotography.com/

First Printing, July 2012

ISBN-13: 978-1478190455
ISBN-10: 1478190450

Table of Contents

Meet the Crafters

Introduction

Crochet saved my life.

I realize that this sounds completely absurd … or at the very least like a great exaggeration. I assure you, however, that it is the truest way I can possibly describe the role that crochet played in assisting me in moving through the deepest period of depression I had ever experienced. Without it, I may not have lived.

Prior to this terrible period, I had suffered with undiagnosed, sometimes debilitating, always untreated depression for nearly fifteen years. I didn't know that depression was the problem and I certainly didn't know how to deal with it. The delay in diagnosis was due in large part to stubbornness. I was very anti-medication, mostly anti-psychologists and believed that whatever was wrong was something I could solve on my own. The delay also had to do with my youth (I was a young teen when the problem started), a lack of self-awareness and an abundance of intelligence and creativity that made me generally keep going in some form despite many tough battles with deep sadness. In later years, I did try to reach out for help but the professionals I worked with didn't properly diagnose me or help me in any way.

All of this is to say that by the time that I reached the desperate stage of readiness where I would accept any help of any kind (despite feeling certain that nothing could ever help) the problem was nearly out of control. I was barely functioning. I cried most of the day every day. I could hardly move. I could hardly breathe. The idea of trying to make doctors' appointments or hold down "real" jobs was so far-fetched it may as well have filtered into my mind in another language. I couldn't do almost anything and yet the one thing that I could do was to move a crochet hook back and forth through yarn, repeatedly pulling one loop through the next to create fabric out of air so thin I could barely breathe in it. Since it was one of the only things that I could do, it became imperative to my mental health that I go ahead and do it. When I first started to crochet, that feeling of temporary relief from the muted chaos of depression was the only reason I was crocheting.

Of course, crochet alone could never have taken me out of that desperate place. It is a craft, not a cure-all for serious illness. And yet I am also fairly certain that I could never have loosened myself from the grip of that depression without crochet. I was stuck in between that proverbial rock and a hard place and my crochet hook served as a crowbar to begin prying me out of that difficult space. I hardly knew that it was happening and yet that hook dug deep down into the core of my being and lifted me into a space where I could once again begin to breathe. In the most basic and obvious way possible I was creating a life for myself simply through the act of creating.

A year later, breathing and healing, I was not only crocheting but also beginning to live my life again. I was beginning to meet other people who also enjoyed literally crafting a life for themselves. I had been a professional blogger/ freelance writer for approximately ten years and found the medium comfortable so I decided to start a crochet blog where I found an expansive community of like-minded crafty people. As I began to share my thoughts and feelings with this community, I began to see that I was not the only one who felt that crochet had been critical to saving one's mental health. In fact, it became obvious to me that it is more often than not the case that crocheters feel that they experience some personal health benefits from the craft although that may not be their main motivation for crocheting. Crochet heals. Crochet saves lives.

This realization dawned on me slowly. It started with just a few signs here and there that I wasn't alone. I was posting daily crochet quotes on my blog and in my research I came across several quotes about the mental health benefits of crochet. I liked them and would share them on the blog. Readers responding to those posts gave me insight into the possibility that crochet can be a tool to deal not only with depression but also with anxiety, OCD, PTSD, schizophrenia and other mental health issues. Crochet can serve as a form of meditation. It provides you with a focused task that distracts you from the drama that sometimes takes over the brain and tries to wreak havoc there. And it allows you to feel like you are producing and creating something even when you can't get out of bed and you can barely open your eyes to notice the passing of one day into another. This may seem like a small thing to someone who has never dealt with depression or a related mental health condition but I assure you that it is lifesaving.

People who don't really know about crochet often think of it as a craft for grannies in nursing homes. I dispute this stereotype, knowing from experience that crochet can be a healthy creative outlet for men, women and children of any age. That said, it is certainly true that there are a lot of elderly women who enjoy crochet and the more I pondered and researched this, the more I realized that they turn to the craft in large part to relieve the symptoms of some basic mental health issues that commonly afflict the elderly in our society. The elderly often suffer from feelings of uselessness. Women in particular spent their lives caring for others and now they are the ones that need to be cared for. To be able to spend time crocheting something for a family member, a loved one or a good cause allows these women to feel valuable in a time of their lives when society has discounted their value. Crochet can help build and maintain self-esteem for people of all ages and that is supremely important for the elderly who often lose dignity in small daily ways. And crochet is a way to pass the long hours when loneliness, boredom and apathy could otherwise set in, problems in and of themselves and also things that have the potential to lead to a variety of health problems.

As I began digging deeper into my research about the mental health benefits of crochet among the elderly, I learned that many older people who crochet feel that it helps to keep their hands limber. This helps them to stave off or deal with arthritis. Learning this got me started wondering whether there are other physical benefits to crochet in addition to the numerous mental health benefits that the craft offers. And of course I quickly learned that there are. Specifically crochet has been used as an occupational therapy tool for children and the disabled who need to develop their fine motor skills and build the muscles in their arms and fingers. Coming full circle, these same individuals may gain valuable mental health benefits from learning how to complete a task that ends with a finished product to show off.

You can trust me when I say that crochet saved my life. However, you don't have to trust just me. I was lucky enough to have the opportunity to interview nearly two dozen people suffering from varying conditions who all say that crochet has helped them improve their physical and / or mental health and I will share their stories with you here. You will meet amazing, strong women like Aurore who used crochet as a touchstone to help ground her in reality as she suffered hallucinations. And Laurinda who crocheted for charity as a way to get through the grief of losing a child. And Marinke who crochets to ease the stress of social isolation caused by Asperger's Syndrome. And Tammy who crochets to cope with the symptoms of Chronic Lyme Disease. We will all tell you about how we used crochet to help us with our problems, and I will do my best to support what we've shared with the professional research that's been done that backs up our experience with some science and math.

A note on format: I've placed everyone's individual stories throughout the book in the spots where they seemed most relevant. After the book's Table of Contents you can find a list of all of the crafters and a page number that will take you to their complete story. These stories are written in such a way that you can read them individually, separate from the text of the book, if you so desire. Quotes and references to these women are also interspersed throughout the entire text. In some cases, it may seem a little bit redundant to have the story told in the text and again on the individual's own page but it was important to me to have each woman's story told intact in addition to referencing it in the content of the book. I hope you find this format pleasing.

What I've outlined here in these first pages is the journey that I will be taking you on throughout this book, beginning with how I came to crochet. This book begins with my story because I think that's where every book begins, fiction or non-fiction. My story is about depression and that section covers a large portion of the text. What you'll find there, though, is that many of the reasons given for why crochet is healing to people with depression will hold true in later chapters when we look at the role crochet can play in healing other mental health conditions. Depression is a part of many illnesses and the cures for depression often help alleviate other issues as well. So even if depression isn't something you specifically relate to, I hope you enjoy that part of the book for the insight it can offer into the other conditions discussed herein.

I'll close this introduction with an author's note to say that I am not a doctor or a psychologist or even an art therapist. I have a college education and work experience background that provides me with some foundation in basic psychology. I have done extensive reading of various psychological texts in order to both educate and heal myself, but at this time I do not have the kind of professional training that legally qualifies me to tell you how to use crochet to improve your own mental health. I certainly don't have the experience to speak authoritatively about using crochet for improving physical health issues. The studies that I did were informal and I don't claim to have the definitive word on this issue. I didn't do background searches to find out if the stories that were told to me were "true"; I took them at face value as they came from the mouths and hearts of the people who shared them with me. (Incidentally, some names have been changed, while others kept the person's true name, sometimes first name only, all at the discretion of the individual who was interviewed.) This research wouldn't pass any professional test, I'm sure. I'm well-studied in the health benefits of crochet but I am not necessarily an "expert." What I am is a person who has dealt with mental health issues myself and who has experienced firsthand how the craft of crochet can be a benefit during tough times. And I am someone who has done extensive research into this topic because I am passionately interested in how crochet has helped people.

So I can't provide answers or definitive data on the issue but what I can do, and what I have done, is share my story and the stories of others who were kind enough to open up their hearts, homes and minds to me in my quest to better understand just how it could be that the craft of crochet is a potential life-saver. And in doing so I did meet people who had done more formal scientific studies on the role of needlearts in health so I have included references to them throughout the book as well. I hope something here resonates for you and I encourage you to share your own stories of healing through craft with others. Sometimes just knowing you are not alone in your solitary activities is healing.

Finally, I want to say that I am always happy to hear from my readers. You can visit my blog at www.crochetconcupiscence.com and reach me via email using the contact page on that site. Now, let's get into the meat of this book ...

Wielding A Crochet Hook Against the Demon of Depression

Depression is one of those things that we talk about often and yet you can't really understand it if you haven't been through it. Heck, it's hard to understand it even if you have been through it. When you aren't in the darkest phases of it you can scarcely remember why you ever felt as horrible and hopeless and haunted as you did then. What you remember is that the feeling was so incredibly terrible that you are desperate to never go back to that place because you really don't know if you could survive it again.

I won't try here to explain depression to you in clinical terms. There are numerous books and movies and journals that deal with that topic in great depth. What I will do is share my story, the abbreviated memoir of a real woman with a real experience of battling serious life-threatening depression in the 21st century. And what I'll say first is that it took me a decade and a half before I could even comfortably write that last sentence down for the world to see.

Get to Know Me: My Depression Story

Depressed? Me? No way.

I had read the books. I knew the stories. You see; the very best and very worst thing about me is that I have always been a voracious reader. I have often been overexposed to ideas when I was too young in my own experience to fully understand them. I have often over-thought my own feelings and experiences because of all that I read that related to them. As a result, I had a lot of opinions and ideas on what depression was and what it meant and how to deal with it, opinions that were based on what I thought and not on my real experience of the world. Because my teenage bookshelf was cluttered with the dangerous minds of every depressed woman from Sylvia Plath to Elizabeth Wurtzel (as well as the thoughts of many men about these women) I had a comprehensive picture of the experience of depression. And while I felt like some of the details of the depressed experience resonated within me, I didn't feel like it all fit into a neat label of depression. What I didn't realize then was that my story wasn't complete ... and therefore it couldn't be told like a story, couldn't be read like a story, couldn't mirror these women's lives completely because it was human experience and not just a chapter-by-chapter account of who I was.

What I am trying to say is that I denied being depressed, or truly depressed, or depressed in a way that could be solved by medication, or depressed in a way I couldn't control myself, or suicidally depressed ... I denied it vehemently and I denied it quietly and I denied it for about fifteen years.

Today I can look back through the tunnel of depression from the other side. From here, I can see that my first obvious battle with depression began when I was 14. What you will learn about me as I continue on with my personal story is that I often dealt with, acted out and ultimately worsened my depression in direct relationship to the man in my life at the time. It is a classic story for women dealing with depression but obviously I didn't see it as such at the time. I'll foreshadow the future of my story by saying that there's a lot of strength in being a girl alone with a crochet hook instead of a girl alone in someone else's bed.

At 14, I did not know how to crochet and I did not know that trying to solve your own problems by loving someone else would only make you feel more alone. What I knew was that I was living inside of a terror-filled situation and I didn't know if things were worse in the external halls of my junior high school or the internal halls of my increasingly unhappy mind. I'll save the details of my middle school unhappiness for another time and place. Suffice to say that the accounts of bullying that I read about in the news today make my stomach turn, not because I can relate to those stories but because the supposedly lurid details of those stories seem so pale and soft and simple in comparison to what I went through that I am sick with envy for people who had such a mild experience of life in middle school.

Take the frightening daily experience of a tortured junior high school existence, add some discontent in the home, pour on a little bit of normal teenage hormones and then strike a match and what you have is the perfect conflagration for a mind probably already prone to depression to enter its first serious experience of the condition. So I did what I would do for the next dozen years: I lost myself in the reflection of my soul seen in the eyes of an even-more-lost boy.

As you'll see, it wasn't only boys I turned to when I needed to escape the depression in my mind. In addition to boys I found suitable chaos in codependent friendships, attempting to parent my own siblings, taking on increasingly stressful jobs, moving to new places, exploring a diverse array of random interests in occasionally sketchy settings and essentially doing whatever I needed to do to get outside of my own head. It is as if the depression was an itch inside of my head and the only way to scratch it was to find something outside of myself that was even itchier. I'm not sure quite why this worked for me. Maybe what I needed was for the crazy pain inside of my own head to be externalized in front of me in the form of something else so that I could tangibly deal with it. Maybe I desperately needed a distraction loud enough to quiet my own thoughts. Maybe taking care of someone or something else made me feel competent in a way that I couldn't feel when I was just doing nothing, just being. I'm not sure. What I know is that it worked and the first time I really saw that it worked came during middle school.

So that's why at 14 I was deeply immersed in a chaotic relationship with a drug-selling gang member that I was initially attracted to because he "looked like a lost puppy" (according to my seventh grade journal). That is not the best way to start a relationship. It is, however, an ideal way to escape the prison of crazy depression in your own mind because instead those feelings are mirrored by someone else and acted out in a space external to yourself.

This boyfriend and I shared turbulent feelings about the pointlessness of life. He was suicidal. I should admit that almost everyone I was friends with at this point was either actively suicidal or passively suicidal (by which I mean that they were extremely unhappy and engaged in very reckless behavior with a high likelihood of death). It is shocking to me to look back and see that none of us actually died. The love of my fourteen-year-old life fell squarely into the actively suicidal category. I remember that he would call me in the middle of the night, telling me that he had just cut his wrists and was bleeding onto the kitchen floor. I remember being in my own kitchen at the time, a 2am teenager back in the days when phones all had cords and you talked in family spaces.

Sometimes my dad would get up, come into the kitchen for some water, and tell me to go to bed although I don't remember him ever actually doing anything that indicated that he meant it. I also don't remember ever feeling like I should tell him that there was a boyfriend with slashes up and down his arms on the other end of the line. I do remember thinking that this was my boyfriend who needed me and it was my job to make sure that he didn't die on the kitchen floor while I paced my own similar kitchen floor across town. And so I took it upon myself to try to convince this man-child to stop the bleeding, to bandage up his arms, to get help, to let me love him completely until he was okay.

And here is where it happened, where I first showed those initial signs of being astoundingly skilled at locating, latching on to and loving men who were far more obviously depressed than I was. As a result, I didn't feel like I really had that much of a problem. I was functional. I was fine. Never mind that I cried every night with worry about that boyfriend. Never mind that my best friend and I talked frequently about the possibility of suicide and that the only reason that I didn't consider it more seriously was because I felt an obligation to take care of my younger siblings as we grew up in our own chaotic household. Never mind that I engaged in seriously risky behavior like unprotected teenage sex and walking alone in questionably revealing clothes in dangerous areas of town. In comparison to the frenzied, aggressive depression of this person I was obsessed with, this boy who had gunshot holes in his front door, parents with lines of cocaine on broken mirrors in the next room and a knife pressed against a large vein in his arm, I really wasn't depressed at all.

Until I was of course. The thing that you need to know about depression is that if it is ignored, it gets bigger and bigger. It grows monstrous. And it always wins. It will get your attention no matter how insanely time-consuming your obsession with other things is. I could focus my depression outward into caring for the boyfriend bleeding on his kitchen floor, the siblings starting to get into neighborhood trouble, the best friend who became pregnant and didn't tell her parents until she was eight months along but in the end the depression demanded more attention than they did. Something in me knew that I desperately needed to deal with my own self because there was a downward spiral happening. Oh how I wish I knew then about the healing wonder of stitching a million single crochets until an afghan of comforting safety grows around you.

The thing about my youthful depression was that I could always pull myself out of it with a change. I could tell myself that the problem was the external craziness and if I changed the circumstances around me then I would not be unhappy anymore. To an extent, this seemed true. When things are so desperate around you and then you stop the desperateness, life feels calm and okay for a moment despite the problems inside your own brain. So I broke up with that boyfriend and I started a new school and met people who weren't constantly figuring out the best way to die ... and for awhile I was okay. I would even say that I was happy.

But depression never left me far behind. It was there at 16 when I was screaming and clinging on to a different boyfriend, sobbing every day and blaming him for my unhappiness. Depression again gave me a brief reprieve after that breakup when I was enjoying new friendships, but it was there at 18 when I dropped out of high school, citing numerous well-thought-out arguments against the institution of education but really just not capable of waking up each day and going to that place and sitting still while people talked because my head was raging too loud with unhappiness and I just wanted to stay in bed all day and read dark poetry.

When I dropped out of high school, I worked at a bookstore and I started taking massage therapy classes and I was okay for awhile, again. When the depression itched a little, I amped up the drama in an intense friendship I had or immersed myself in a brief fling that was dramatic enough to take my mind off of my own mind. The series of boys that I distracted myself with during this time included a brooding writer who fueled his poetry with vodka, a few guys going through intense conflicts with religious issues, and a women's studies major that my journal reminds me I did not have sex with because he only had sex with lesbians. Wait, what is that, is my life getting so quiet that I can actually hear the chemical pain inside my own brain? I had better go ahead and start dating my friend's little brother while also having a secret fling with her on-again-off-again boyfriend of sorts. Okay there, my problems have been externalized so that I don't have to cope with the depression inside.

But of course, depression crept back in despite these valiant efforts. So I changed my circumstances, again. I started a job traveling around the state doing photography. And I was okay again, for awhile. Until I suddenly found myself curled in a ball on my bed, ignoring the phone and the door because the ever-present companion of depression made me want to hide from everyone else. So I got a new job at a trophy shop and that change was okay for a little while.

Until it wasn't. One day in the midst of my brain starting to itch again a super attractive man walked into the trophy shop. By super attractive I don't mean that he was objectively good looking. I mean that my brain somehow knew instantly that this character was definitely trouble enough to distract me from my own depression. I took him home with me and he never left. That is to say that he never left until a few months later when he was arrested after robbing several of my neighbors. I was depressed enough at this point that I think the very idea of being alone inside of my own mind was so incredibly terrifying that instead of breaking things off at that point I visited him regularly at the prison and immersed myself in the drama of being a sort-of-girlfriend to an inmate. Yes, I knew that I didn't want to be nineteen and spending my weekends in a prison. But I was coping. If I could go back in time I would march my teenage self straight to a yarn store and load her arms with skeins of cashmerino, silk bamboo and baby alpaca fibers. I would give her hooks made of aluminum and plastic and wood and even glass. I would explain that the real prison was in the mind and that a stitch or two could begin to break down the barriers.

But I did not have crochet then. All I had was a suspicion that yet another change of scenery was required. I started back to college and was okay for awhile, again ... until I wasn't. The next few months were a doozy of trying to drown myself in the drama of others in order to escape my own depression. There was escalation in the drama between my then-best-friend and I, an even greater chasm of chaos opening up in the dysfunctional relationship we'd already been carrying on for years. It didn't help that she ended up sleeping with an acid-tripping musician friend of mine who had a serious crush on me and in this weird twist of complicated relationships I didn't mind the situation since I didn't like him but she was angry at me because she regretted sleeping with him. It also didn't help that I was secretly sleeping with her sixteen-year-old brother who had a girlfriend at the time. Oh boy how I wish I knew about anti-depressants and crochet at this point in my life. I would say a nice and pleasant "let's part ways" to that friend, get out of her brother's bed, take my Celexa, make an extra appointment with my therapist and then make granny squares in every color of the rainbow.

But I didn't know to do those things. What I knew was that even all of this crazy-making drama was not quite enough to scratch the intensifying itch of my troubled brain. So when I met a seventeen-year-old runaway with the worst drug habit of anyone I'd ever known I clearly thought that the best solution to my life was to have him move in with me. This was not a conscious thought mind you. The conscious thought was more along the lines of, "gee, he's cute in this lost puppy dog kind of way."

I didn't do any drugs myself. I didn't even drink socially at the time. Sometimes I wished I did because let me tell you that an out-of-control teenager with a drug habit can wreak considerable havoc on an otherwise sober home. I wished that I did do drugs to have a viable mental escape from dealing with things. Things like the time that I came home and found him having sex with a half-passed-out fifteen-year-old girl in my living room. Or the time I returned from an out-of-town trip exhausted but could not crawl in between the sheets of my bed because the kid had robbed my entire house including the sheets on the bed. It is hard to even think about the fact that you might have a problem inside of your own brain when you have someone like this as a glaring example of what life is like when you have "real" problems.

I needed more distraction. I needed a change. So when I met a man who was quitting his job to live in his car and bum around the country I instantly fell into a haze I thought was love. I officially dropped out of college, sold most of what I owned and ran away with this man I'd just met. We put a camper shell on my pickup truck and hit the road, each trying to outpace our own depression by leaving it a state line behind. The change of scenery helped a little bit. I felt happy sometimes. But don't worry. When the itch in my brain threatened to twitch I could always focus on the fact that he occasionally did things like pull over at a rest stop, stare off into space and say, "sometimes I just go to dark places" or listen intently when he would angrily talk about all of the ways he'd been wronged by the bisexual strippers he'd dated in the past. Don't worry; he was still a little more sick than I was.

By this time I was 21, more than half a dozen years into my depression, and the distractions were clearly helping less and less. This new man and I fought constantly, made up energetically and then fought more violently. Only later would I realize that the significant problem in our relationship wasn't anything that we ever actually fought about but rather simply the fact that we were both incredibly unhappy people wishing desperately for one another to solve that unhappiness. When we ran out of money we moved into my parents' house, the two of us living together in their living room, and I staggered through another year of depression. I tried a few odd jobs, lasting anywhere from half a shift to two weeks, before I landed a job at a group home helping to care for foster children in need of therapeutic level emotional care.

This was a new level of positioning myself around people who were far worse off than me emotionally. I never did this consciously, of course. I think it was just the best built-in coping mechanism that I had for denying and sublimating my own depression. If I could find people who were unhappier than me and then take care of them then it made me feel happier (for awhile). Or so I thought. In truth I guess I never felt happy but I did feel useful and functional and relatively mentally healthy in comparison to my environment. The problem with using this method of dealing with depression is that eventually there aren't worse situations. I read once in a memoir about drug addiction that you only get high the first few times and every time after that the drugs just bring you back to "normal" (your new normal). It was like that for me except that my drug was finding people in bad situations to "help." My suicidal boyfriend at fourteen was my marijuana, the boyfriend in prison was my cocaine, and now if I wanted to get any sort of high I needed to move on to heroin. So I tried.

I did a year of taking care of the kids at that group home job and then went on to work in the sexual abuse unit of Child Protective Services while applying to get my own foster care license and doing mentoring of kids "in the system." I was a foster parent for two years, holding myself together with the distraction of taking care of other people and being mostly unaware of my own depression. During the same time I launched my own through-the-mail non-profit program supporting arts and writing of incarcerated adults. I was going to save the world and somehow that was going to save myself. I wasn't depressed, damn it, but if (somehow, possibly, maybe) I was depressed then I was going to win the arm wrestling competition and flatten depression to the table with a million good deeds for others. I was going to get so high on fixing things that I would never have to come down off of that high.

At 25, I burned out. To the outside world it looked like I was simply trying to do too much. I can see how it would look that way, what with the foster kids and the non-profit and the four-year-college degree that I got in two years. But the real issue was entirely different. It was not that what I was doing was too much; it was that all that I was doing simply wasn't enough. It wasn't enough to cure the actual problem, which was the depression settling deeper and deeper into my life. I spent the next several months doing almost nothing. I got cable TV for the first time in my life and spent almost every day laying on my couch, eating gummy bears and Red Vines, watching endless pointless shows that I couldn't remember only days (okay, minutes) after watching them. I hadn't given up on the possibility of finding a new distraction because I knew I couldn't keep feeling the way that I was feeling. And yet, it was hard to think of any distraction that might work and most of what I tried rapidly proved itself inefficient against the darkness of my mind. Working with an artist at anime conventions. Doing more traveling. Trying to write a book. I started these things with urgent desire and quickly the enthusiasm faded. This is another time in my life when I could have used the hook – a nice middle-of-the-range G hook and some basic cotton yarn just to teach me that a normal, calm, non-dramatic, run of the mill life could be the best kind of life.

I did not have a hook … so I had to make another change. That's when I decided to move to San Francisco. I had fallen in love with the city on my first trip there when I was eighteen. I made up a reason to move there … telling myself that I was going to go to law school. I applied and got in and moved and started law school. The change of scenery helped for awhile (again) although I quickly realized I hated law school and dropped out to pursue writing (a job I'd been doing off and on for my entire adult life anyway). Moving to San Francisco was the best thing that I ever did for myself. It is a place where I feel creative and healthy and alive. But even this grand change couldn't stave off the depression for long because by this time I'd been fighting it off for more than ten years and I was getting weaker in the battle.

I'm sure you have heard the stories of someone trapped in the wild beneath a tree that has to cut off his own leg with a dull knife in order to get out and get to safety. Depression is not a limb that you can excise in order to start feeling better. If it were, I would have cut it off by this point, at any cost. But depression is an organ, stuck inside of you even when it is so unhealthy that it not only doesn't work properly but actually becomes toxic inside of you. Depression weakened my ability to function like a cancer weakens the body, like a flesh-eating bacteria spreads across the subcutaneous layer leaving holes in its wake and weakening the structure of the entire body.

All along I knew that I needed to find a support system and find some activities that I could enjoy. I tried. I have had Sunday dinners off and on at my home since my early twenties, trying to forge a family out of friends in ways that often didn't work. I have joined groups of all kinds. I have taken burlesque dance classes and art therapy classes and small business classes. I have met more people than I could ever possibly remember, trying to connect to others and to feel alive, to feel like I might actually want to be alive, for more than just a brief period. I promise you, I tried.

I share all of this (abbreviated) back story so that you can understand that by the time I reached the stage of depression that required the assistance of crochet, I had been through a lot. I had distracted myself from the torment of my own mind in every single way that I could think of doing. And still, the depression crept up on me and took over my entire life before I exactly knew what was happening. Somehow I found myself at 28 feeling entirely alone in the world despite having people I could call in the middle of the night if I needed to. I found myself feeling one hundred percent convinced that I would never find any activity or education or pursuit remotely interesting ever again. I found myself glued to my bed watching every episode of all twenty years of Law and Order over and over again because I could no longer leave my room. I found myself with such social anxiety that I often stood up even my closest friends. I recall one time when I agreed to go to dinner with a friend because I knew that I needed to be social but when he showed up I turned off the lights and ignored the door. He persistently stood outside for a long time, alternately ringing the doorbell and throwing pennies at my window, until he finally gave up and went away and I felt guilty relief, muted because all feelings are muted when you are depressed.

I found myself regularly in tears, showering three or four times per day because it seemed to be the only thing that stopped the sobbing for even a brief time. I still made occasional efforts to find a way to escape the depression yet again. This included efforts to do productive things like start new jobs as well as the familiar stand-by of negative efforts involving strange boys with puppy dog eyes. But these efforts were weak and failed. Finally I told my sister that she should come spend the summer with me. I thought the closeness and company and activity would be good for me, would "snap me out of it" again, for awhile.

But it couldn't save me despite how much we tried. I dragged myself out of bed, convinced that going to the beach with her would be a good idea. But the very process of trying to use my car share program, getting a car I wasn't familiar with, having to fill up the gas tank, navigating the traffic ... it was all too much and set me off into uncontrollable tears. I just wanted desperately to not have to wake up every day to keep dealing with this existence. I started really thinking actively about suicide for the first time in my life. And finally I mustered what I think might have been the last gasp effort I had in me and said, "I need help." I had my sister call my best friend (my real, ongoing best friend, not the "best friend" of the drama from years before) and he spent copious amounts of time with me while I tried to figure out how to find a therapist and how to get on medication and how to navigate the health care system. To this day I don't know where I got that puff of energy required to deal with these things. And although I won't jump on my high horse about the mental health system, I will say that even with health insurance and money enough to pay the bills, it is extremely, extremely difficult to find good mental health services especially when you need them most.

I met a psychologist and a psychiatrist, agreed to a light anti-depressant, threw myself into talking about what was wrong and tried to make things better. I didn't believe that it was going to help but I didn't know what else to do. Dragging myself to the appointments with these professionals took absolutely all of my energy. There was nothing left. The rest of every day was just stuck in my apartment, crying. My sister had spent several months with me and needed to go back home. I was lonely but relieved because even having someone else in the same room as me was exhausting. She would breathe and hearing the respiration would tire me out.

And still a voice nagged that I had to find a distraction, an activity that I could enjoy. I knew that I was supposed to do what was in my heart but the idea just angered me because I couldn't hear my heart. I honestly didn't think I would find any pleasure in anything. But I remembered a piece of advice from one of those many books that I had read – to go back to what you enjoyed doing in childhood. I remembered spending hours making friendship bracelets and somehow that led to a memory of my mom teaching me to crochet and I latched on to that and decided to try again because it was something I could do alone in my house in my pajamas with the TV droning on.

I wish crochet had immediately solved all of my problems but of course it didn't happen that way. What did happen was that crochet slowly became a positive replacement for some of my most destructive downtime. The thing is, even though I now finally had a therapist and a medication plan, I would still often find myself in the middle of the night crying on my bathroom floor, terrible sobs wracking my body. I was getting better but I didn't know it at the time. Because you see, getting better for me meant that I needed to finally deal with my own mind instead of going outside of it. And that did not feel better when I first started the process. On more than one occasion I found myself eyeing the vodka bottle and the pills I had, wondering if I had enough poison there to do myself in. I wrote goodbye letters to my family members although it will probably horrify them to read that since I didn't tell anyone about them at the time. And I sat crying on that bathroom floor with a knife pressed against my flesh ... until I would come to my feeble senses and realize that I needed to put the knife down and replace the empty space where it was with a crochet hook.

It is so difficult to describe the state that I was in. I did not want to die but I most definitely wanted to be dead. I did not see the point to life. All I saw was this endless cycle of having to continue waking up and feeling this horrible way forever. I knew from experience that no matter how much I tried to distract myself with men or friends or activities or social causes or jobs I was going to end up right back here on the bathroom floor with the tip of a kitchen knife poised to go into my arm. I hated hovering in this space. I did not want to kill myself but I wished desperately that I could just force myself to take that step. There were times when I would look at that knife in my hand and will myself to just press down. I never did. I never broke skin.

Looking back I can see that I did not want to die. To be honest, I don't know why that is. Maybe it is because I have younger siblings and parents and a best friend I've known for more than half my life ... and enough knowledge of human psychology to know that my death would irrevocably alter their lives. Maybe it is because I have always been a reader of stories and had an insatiable curiosity to know what lies on the next page of my own life tale. Or maybe it is because inside of most people is an instinct not to die.

I did not want to die. I also did not want to live. But somewhere deep inside of me I wanted to want to live. On the surface I was willing myself to just press the tip of that knife down and be done with it already. But deep down beneath that surface there was the spirit of a girl who had been fighting for years to craft a life for herself. The girl who was willing to try new boyfriends, new schools, new jobs, and new cities was still in there hoping that there was some new thing somewhere that would make waking up a joy instead of a burden.

For me, that place of indecisive hovering was the worst place I'd ever been. I did not want to live and I did not want to kill myself. I did not believe that I would ever find a life I didn't hate and yet I hoped that I would. I sat on that bathroom floor for months poised in between decisions, stuck in a position where a knife tip nearly entered my vein but never did. You can only hover there for so long. You have to choose a direction. I needed to locate yet another final puff of energy somewhere in my body and decide if I was going to use it to press that knife down and end things or drag myself up off of the bathroom floor and put the knife away. In the end, I used the little bit of strength I had left to pry my fingers apart, loosen my grip on the knife handle and put a crochet hook in its place.

That crochet hook became my lifeline. It was my go-to weapon whenever I felt like I needed to pick up another knife or a bottle of vodka or even a pen to write my goodbye letters. I picked up the crochet hook instead. I got books that teach kids how to crochet and I used YouTube videos to learn a few things and I started to make scarf after scarf. I did this at first because I had to, because I had to stop the desperation. It helped me to focus for even a few minutes on pulling a piece of yarn up with my hook to make a loop (and then a chain, and then a scarf). I would still sob but then I would stop sobbing and work on my crochet. The more I crocheted, the less I sobbed. I didn't know it was going to change my world but I knew that it changed that moment just a little bit.

So the initial phase of how crochet saved my life was very literal. It gave me something to do to prevent suicidal thoughts and actions. It gave me a bit of a distraction from the mess in my head that was making me simply not want to live anymore. But gradually it came to help with my depression in many other ways and for that reason I believe it can be a useful tool for people suffering from any stage or level of depression.

One of the key ways that crochet helped me was that it not only gave me something to do but it also gave me an end product that made me feel like a productive person again. After all, television was something to do, but the thing is that I felt bad about myself just being someone who stayed in bed all day watching TV. There was no point in feeling bad about this, I can see now, since I really physically and emotionally couldn't do much else. Nevertheless, I like to see myself as a creative, productive person and it was doing some serious damage to my self-esteem that I was stuck in this space where I couldn't do anything. To be able to make a scarf meant that I was finally doing something again, no matter how small that something would be. And now when I talked on the phone to my siblings I could describe something I was doing instead of just reiterating my own battle with the lack of desire to live. It didn't matter that the scarves weren't even all that special or great or that I was making far too many to actually keep and had no idea what I was going to do with them. I didn't ever think that far. I thought only about the fact that for that moment I was working on something. I was creating something.

Another key way that crochet helped with my depression is that it made me capable of making small decisions again. Indecisiveness had become a huge problem in my life as my depression worsened. Every single decision felt immense and important even if I knew intellectually that it was no big deal. For example, during that time that my sister was staying with me we talked about going horseback riding. I had ambivalent feelings. I wanted to but I didn't want to. Or maybe I didn't want to but I wanted to want to. I knew that it was something I used to enjoy and I wanted to enjoy something again but driving to get on a horse and staying on a horse for an hour sounded so incredibly tiring in those days. My sister didn't really care either way but I agonized over the decision for two days in tears until I finally felt so incapacitated by the decision-making process that I couldn't have physically made myself go if I'd wanted to, effectively making the decision for myself that way. Every single decision had become that way, from horseback riding to meal options. It was immobilizing.

Crochet requires some decisions but they felt manageable in large part because I didn't know enough about crochet to know just how many decisions there were to be made. For example, when I first decided I wanted to learn to crochet again, I went to the craft store with my mom to buy yarn. I immediately drifted over to a soft type of yarn that was wonderful to the touch. I chose blue and grey (a color theme I still love although I suppose it reflected my mental state more than anything at the time). Later I would learn that there are many different types of yarn and thicknesses of yarn and that these things should be taken into consideration when figuring out what yarn you want for a project but I didn't know that at the time so I just bought what I liked. And the fact that I could fairly easily decide what I liked was a really big deal for me at that time. I'll probably never know why choosing blue yarn felt easy when choosing between Ramen noodles and macaroni felt hard but it did.

Likewise I chose the crochet hooks that I did because they were the first set I saw in the store that I liked. (They were Boye hooks, if you're wondering, and they remain my favorite to this day. I'm a Boye girl at heart.) It was an easy enough decision. I chose the projects that I did because I needed beginner projects since I didn't know how to crochet yet. These decisions were small and yet being able to make them was crucial. And as time went on and I learned more about crochet and had to make more decisions I also learned that I was capable of much bigger decisions than what kind of yarn to buy. At the same time, I know now that if I ever slip back into that type of debilitating depression and feel like I can't decide anything at least I am capable of going to the yarn store and picking out yarn. That's something.

As a baby you must learn to wiggle your fingers and toes before you can learn to move your arms and legs. After that you learn to manipulate your body to a sitting position. You use what you've learned to pull yourself into a crawl and then into a standing position and then to become a walking human being. If someone told you as a newborn just how much effort would be involved in being able to walk you'd probably crawl back into the womb. And yet, for the rest of your life, walking will seem natural and easy, even though it was not always that way. Today I can wake up and get out of bed and make basic decisions that improve the quality of my day. I can assess my needs and the best way to meet them. I can set goals. It all seems fairly natural. But it was crochet that helped me learn how to wiggle my fingers and sit up before I could walk naturally through this life.

Having a personal community is a key part of dealing with depression. The more people that you feel tied to, the more reason you have to live. The more you see the world outside of yourself, the easier it becomes to get outside of your own depressed mind. I had to find myself before I could find comfort within a community. But having branched out and learned to walk, I have now found people who will walk alongside me. Not all of them are crocheters but the crochet community has supported me in an important way through this entire journey.

So that's a short glimpse into my personal story about depression and how crochet came to play a role in helping me through the toughest time of my life. It took about a year of therapy, medication and crochet to get to where I was once again living what looked like a normal life from the outside. It took another year before I could say that I was genuinely happy and carefree and relaxed and doing the craft of crochet purely out of love and not need. I believe that the worst of depression is behind me forever because I understand it better, have better coping skills and know how to treat it if it returns. But I know that life has many ups and downs and that depression is near at hand somewhere. If it does return, one of the many weapons in my arsenal for winning the fight will be my crochet hook. My newfound crochet community will also be there.

How Crochet Eases Depression

Now that you've learned my story, let's take a look at some of the research ...

As you will see throughout the rest of this book, crochet has the ability to assist people suffering from a diverse range of mental and physical health issues. In all of my research, though, the one issue that kept coming up again and again was the issue of depression. This is certainly due in large part to the fact that a high percentage of the population suffers from at least moderate depression at some point in their lives. It affects people as a condition on its own and is a side effect of many other conditions. However, the fact that depression and crochet come up together often in conversation is also due to the fact that crochet has many benefits that assist in alleviating depression. It does this through encouraging mindfulness and creating distraction from rumination, releasing serotonin, and allowing you to visualize a project and complete it, which in turn builds depression-combating self-esteem. Throughout the rest of this chapter we'll look more closely at each of those benefits and I'll share some other stories of people who have dealt with depression through the creative act of crochet.

Mindfulness

> *"Mindfulness is the state of mind where you are aware of yourself, your surroundings and relationship to those surroundings in the present moment. You are aware of pleasant and unpleasant sensations, which helps to put these feelings into context. Concentrating on the present moment means you're not worrying about the past or fretting about the future. It is being used to successfully manage depression."* (Corkhill, 2008).

Stitchlinks is a group that has done extensive research into the role that needlearts (specifically knitting but also crochet and cross stitch) can play in improving health. Mindfulness as a means to alleviating depression is one of the areas that this group has studied in depth. This makes perfect sense because of the fact that a rhythmic, repetitive craft like crochet can be a terrific tool for achieving mindfulness and also because there is a wide body of research indicating that mindfulness is a useful therapeutic approach to dealing head-on with depression. If mindfulness heals depression and crochet is a path to mindfulness then it makes sense to say that crochet heals depression.

So what exactly is mindfulness? Put simply, mindfulness is the act of focusing non-judgmentally on what is happening in the present moment both internally and externally. In Appendix A of this book you will find five mindfulness exercises for crocheters; here is another one to get you started so that you can see how this might work. Even if you don't do the exercise, go ahead and read through it because it will give you a sense of what mindfulness means.

Simple Mindfulness Exercise for Crocheters

> *If you are a crocheter interested in mindfulness then you may enjoy taking a break here to try out a mindfulness exercise. Read through the exercise first then find a quiet space in your home to practice the exercise.*
>
> *Select a crochet hook and yarn that are both easy to work with. Sit still with your work in your lap. All that you are going to be doing is making a long crochet chain. You will slowly work each loop of the chain, counting each loop as you make it. Focus all of your attention on making one loop at a time and not allowing any other thoughts to creep in. Every time that you notice a thought, frog the chain (meaning just take it apart) and start over.*
>
> *So, for example, you will start your chain ... One loop, two loops ... (I'm so annoyed that my check hasn't gotten direct deposited yet, I really need to go to the bank ... oops, I'm thinking, better start over.) ... Frog, re-start the chain ... One loop, two loops, three loops ... (I really like this yarn but it seems like such a waste to be using it for a mindfulness exercise. Damn. I'm thinking again.) Frog and start over.*
>
> *Try to continue this exercise until you have successfully focused on the loops at hand and let all other thoughts pass to the length of a ten-loop chain. When you are first learning mindfulness, you may only be able to achieve a chain length of five or six. That's okay. Cut yourself some slack. Mindfulness isn't easy. We have busy brains.*

One of the key things that mindfulness does, beyond just relaxing your brain, is that it teaches you to notice your feelings without becoming your feelings. For example, you learn to notice that you are feeling angry but then to breathe through that feeling rather than letting the anger take over your day. You make a concentrated effort not to judge the anger as good or bad, just to notice the feeling, the associated thoughts and how it is all affecting your body. (So when you get distracted on loop three you may notice that you're feeling angry. You don't need to judge the anger, give in to the anger or otherwise think about the anger. You just frog your chain and start over without the angry thought.) Mindfulness helps to regulate your emotions. That's why it is good for people dealing with depression and it is also used as a treatment for various other conditions ranging from borderline personality disorder to chronic pain issues.

How can crochet help with learning mindfulness? Crochet is terrific because it is a hands-on, focused activity that has repetitive (and therefore meditative) qualities. When you catch yourself ruminating on negative thoughts, you can learn to consistently bring yourself back to the work at hand. While the chain exercise is a great start, there are many other ways that you can use crochet meditatively to practice mindfulness. I'm sure you can come up with a few on your own to supplement the ones I've shared in Appendix A.

For the record, I also did a lot of yoga while I was going through my problems with depression. In yoga, your mind may wander but you keep telling it to come back to the breath, which is another variation on practicing mindfulness. I found crochet to be similar ... I'd come back to the stitch at hand again and again just like I'd come back to the breath in yoga. Crochet was more consistently helpful to me than yoga was, though. In the worst periods of depression, I couldn't bring myself to do yoga. Even doing it at home required far more physical energy than I could possibly exert and just made me want to go back to bed. Walk to a studio and do an hour with other people? Impossible. Pick up a crochet hook from its place next to my bed and try to pull up a few loops without thinking the kind of thoughts that were driving me crazy? Slightly more possible.

Basic forms of true meditation also didn't work for me at this time for the opposite reason that yoga didn't work for - meditation alone is too still. Whereas yoga required me to activate my too-tired body, meditation asked me to come to a place of total stillness that seemed equally impossible. Although mindfulness can be practiced even when just sitting quietly (in fact, it's a main feature of Buddhist meditation), my mind was way too far into so-called "monkey mind" to be able to handle this kind of stillness. My brain ate away at itself as I sat there and this made me uncomfortably incapable of truly reaching any restful place of mindfulness. At the time I blamed myself for not being able to sit through the meditation. I know from reading many spiritual memoirs that everyone struggles to sit still through meditation and that a racing mind is a part of the process. As a result, I felt bad that it didn't work for me, which made the depression worse instead of better. I have since realized that normal active thoughts that can be worked through with basic meditation are very, very different from the anxiety-ridden impervious thoughts of the depressed mind. It wasn't my fault that I couldn't do seated mindfulness meditation but I didn't know that at the time. All I knew at the time was that it didn't work.

Crochet worked for me for mindfulness. I could muster up the energy for it, which I couldn't do for yoga. And yet it required more activity than seated meditation and its easy physical repetition brought me personally to a place where mindfulness could sometimes be achieved. It also gave me a specific focus for my frustrated thoughts. It was immensely helpful to me at the time to remind myself that I could not solve THIS BIG PROBLEM (whatever I felt like the problem was) and that my only concern right then needed to be finishing the scarf in my hands because that was something I did have control over and could do. I could notice that I was thinking about something else or fretting or spiraling into negativity and then I could mindfully and intentionally let that feeling go in order to re-focus on the task at hand. I could make the scarf regardless of all of the other big life things that I couldn't do.

I won't lie, this wasn't always easy and it didn't always work. It was a skill that I gained over time as I continued to use crochet as a tool for dealing with depression. Sometimes I'd curl into a ball and get the scarf all wet with sobbing pointless tears. But at some point I'd eventually pick up the hook again, dry off the scarf and return to my focused activity. Sometimes I would have to say the stitch actions aloud as I worked them to bring my mind back. My "yarn over, yarn over, pull through, yarn over, yarn over, turn, yarn over" became a mantra that was more useful to me than "om." It brought me back to the vibration of my self, the yarn in my hands, the fact that even if I could never do anything else ever again I was right here doing this.

What is great about crochet compared to many other crafts is that the moments of frustration caused by the craft itself are typically brief and easy to remedy. First of all, crochet is a very easy craft to pick up. It may be a bit challenging at first to learn the basic stitches. The key thing is to find a method of learning that is easy for you – be that through YouTube instructional videos, book learning or taking a class with a local crocheter. Once you've learned the basics, you can make a lot of different types of products really easily without having to advance in the craft if you don't want to. More importantly, crochet mistakes are easy to fix compared to other crafts. If you make an error, you simply rip back the work (called frogging) and start over. Unless you're working with a really fussy yarn (mohair, for example), frogging the work is easy. (By the way, if you're not a crocheter and you wonder where this "frogging" business came from, the answer I've heard most often is that what you're doing is ripping back the stitches so you're doing "rip it, rip it, rip it" which sounds a bit like ribbit ribbit).

This all lends itself well to the practice of mindfulness. When you see a mistake you may get irritated and frustrated and overwhelmed. But you can easily bring yourself back to the project, reminding yourself that crochet is very easy to take apart and re-do the right way. Other crafts that are more difficult to master may prove too frustrating for someone dealing with the way that depression exaggerates small difficulties.

Nessa (whose story you can read on the page titled *Meet Nessa!*) does a great job of explaining about how the mindfulness aspect of crochet helped her when she says, "I would learn a pattern and spend hour after hour just playing out my life, one stitch at a time, moving forward. The act of learning how to just complete the stitch I was on, not looking too far ahead and not looking back, felt like it was teaching me a new way to live my life. Just one stitch, one moment, at a time, not allowing the huge overall pattern to overwhelm me, but to just keep going, and it would come to completion. Have faith that I would get there and I would ... but not if I skipped ahead and started thinking about a later stage of the pattern, which would make me forget how to complete the stitches I was making now."

Ann Hood, in her book *Comfort,* explains that knitting was a means to mindfulness for her in a way similar to crochet was for me. She writes, "For me, knitting is like meditation. It is not that my mind numbs or goes blank; in a way, the complete opposite happens. If I stop paying attention, I make a mistake. I confess that I love to knit while cooking shows play on my television. Knitters I know knit to all kinds of music, from classical to show tunes. But as soon as we pick up our needles, we enter that still place. Our attention becomes specific to what is in our hands and the outside world fades away."

For me, as I gained more control over my depression as well as more experience with both crochet and mindfulness, I came to notice that attention to my work could tell me a lot about what was going on with my mental health. If I was working on a fairly simple crochet project and making a lot of mistakes then it was usually because my mind was wandering. I could look at that big mess, ask myself what was going on and deal with the problem, not only making fewer crochet mistakes but also dealing head-on with the depression. Conversely, if I found my mind wandering constantly while I crocheted and I simply couldn't bring myself into mindful crochet then I might make a conscious choice to switch to a tougher project that would require more crochet attention and therefore give my mind a break from the other stuff happening in the larger world around me.

Breaking the Cycle of Rumination

Whether or not you "buy into" the act of mindfulness, it is difficult to disagree with the fact that ruminating on your problems makes them seem larger and more difficult to deal with than they often really are. There are times, particularly when dealing with difficult bouts of depression, when you need to just find relief from the ever-present thoughts that are circulating in your head. And crochet can provide that important distraction, giving you a focused activity to take your mind off of the pain. In fact, movement of any kind can help to interrupt the cycle of rumination, which leads to healthier options for dealing with issues in your life including things that are exacerbating your depression.

A June 2010 Whole Living article titled "DIY Therapy: How Handiwork Can Treat Depression" cites research by Yale University psychologist and author Susan Nolen-Hoeksema who specifically looked at the cycle of rumination in female depression. Hoeksema is quoted as saying: "We've found that doing a mentally absorbing task interrupts ruminations long enough for them to subside, and your thinking becomes more clear and less negative ... Then when you go back to your concerns, they seem less overwhelming and you're better able to see some action you could take to overcome them."

People who are dealing with mild forms of depression, or who have depression that's already being treated by medication and / or therapy may still find that they have cycling thoughts. Crochet is a motion-based activity that can help stop those thoughts in their tracks, re-focus them and put at least a temporary end to that oh-so-frustrating thought cycle. Stopping the cycle of rumination can be, at the very least, a source of reprieve from the pain of depression. At best, it may actually prevent the depression from continuing. A 2005 APA article also referencing Hoeksema's work explains that the psychologist completed multiple studies that draw a distinct link between rumination and depression. She looked at groups like the Bay Area residents who lived through the 1989 earthquake and adults of various ages who lost family members to terminal illness. Her studies found that people in these groups who ruminated on their problems were significantly more likely to experience both depression and Post Traumatic Stress Syndrome (PTSD). The APA article goes on to say: "In addition, a community survey Nolen-Hoeksema conducted on 1,300 adults, ages 25 to 75, backed those results. It found that ruminators develop major depression four times as often as nonruminators: 20 percent versus 5 percent. (The results were significant even for ruminators who weren't depressed at baseline.)"

Put more simply, Hoeksema's research shows that if you ruminate on your problems then you are more likely to suffer from depression. One can then conclude that finding a way to break the cycle of rumination, through keeping-busy activities such as crochet perhaps, can help curb depressive tendencies. In fact, Hoeksema went on to do research with Stanford University's Sonja Lyubomirsky that concluded that although it is difficult to get ruminators to stop ruminating on their problems, it is possible to distract them for a short period of time. Furthermore, once distracted, the ruminator is less likely to recall negative events and less likely to focus on problems. So yes, it may sound silly when I say that crochet can help you through depression but this research suggests that if you can set aside how silly you feel for a minute and immerse yourself in the craft then you may be able to stop ruminating on your problems and you will be less likely to be overcome by them even once you stop the actions of the craft.

The Whole Living article also talks about other professionals who agree with Hoeksema's findings. For example, it references Kelly Lambert, author and psychology department chair at Randolph-Macon College. Lambert may have a strong background in formal psychology but it was through reading fiction that she formed some strong opinions about the depression-alleviating benefits of crafting and completing domestic chores. According to the article, Lambert was reading *Little House on the Prairie* to her child when she began to notice just how much activity Ma Ingalls was required to do every day in order to keep her family going. From collecting rainwater for baths to sewing all of the family's clothing, Ma didn't get a moment of rest. That sounds tough to most of us in modern society but Lambert argues that perhaps all of that daily physical work might have been rewarding and even pleasurable for Ma. Lambert believes that we have an innate need to do hands-on work that produces tangible results and that this could actually be an antidote to many forms of depression.

Research may back up what Lambert is saying. The Whole Living article notes that "multigenerational surveys have shown that people born later in the 20th century, after the dawn of modern conveniences, suffer more bouts of depression than those born before World War II." Additionally, it cites research showing that Old Order Amish people have lower depression rates than the rest of society in modern times and of course those are people who are doing the same type of hands-on housework and crafting that Ma Ingalls was doing.

Undoubtedly there can be many, many explanations for the differences in depression rates other than the amount of hands-on housework being done by those surveyed. For example, maybe the Old Order Amish deal with just as much depression but don't express it in the same way that we do, particularly to the outside world; maybe it's a difference in cultural understanding and not a difference in their depression rates. But Lambert has done a variety of different types of research into this topic and stands by her theories and I can see how they hold some water. My father (who I personally believe has dealt with undiagnosed depression in his life) often says that you "just need to get your mind off of it" when things are bad. He fully acknowledges how impossible that sometimes seems and he can't always make himself do it but he will say it anyway because he has found it to be more or less true over the years. Early nineteenth century occupational therapist (and weaver) Mary E. Black once described the purpose of her work as literally to "keep people occupied" (according to author Erin Morton). And my own psychologist would also frequently suggest a variety of activities just to get the mind to stop that "cycle of rumination." So it seems that people from all walks of life and different backgrounds and approaches to dealing with depression often agree that there is a mental health benefit to doing something physical that gets the mind out of its rut for a moment or two at a time.

Serotonin Release

So we've talked about crochet as a means of helping out the mind but we haven't yet talked about how it may actually affect the brain. Let's get into that information now ... That means it's time to talk about serotonin. Without getting too deep into the medical details of it, serotonin can be explained as a neurotransmitter (or messenger) that assists in sending signals from one part of the brain to another. It is made in the brain but is also found throughout the body in blood platelets and other areas. Because serotonin is located throughout the body, it plays many roles in different aspects of our health. Problems with serotonin levels can affect everything from your muscles to your heart. However, what serotonin is best known for is the role that it plays in your mood and feelings of happiness.

A WebMD online article by Colette Bouchez explains that, "of the approximately 40 million brain cells, most are influenced either directly or indirectly by serotonin. This includes brain cells related to mood, sexual desire and function, appetite, sleep, memory and learning, temperature regulation, and some social behavior." Nearly all of those things have a relationship to depression. After all, if you aren't eating and sleeping right, don't feel like having sex and can't socialize properly then there is some depression issue going on, right?

Maybe that's over-simplifying it but much research has been done into the role that serotonin plays in depression with many researchers agreeing that an imbalance in serotonin levels may be a direct cause of depression for many people. Entire categories of psychiatric medication (SSRIs and SNRIs) have been created that are designed to improve serotonin levels for the specific purpose of reducing the symptoms of depression. People who need these medications should obviously always work with their doctors to get the right meds and the right levels of those meds. However, it is possible that crochet can be a supplement to such medications because it has actually been shown to help release serotonin in the body.

Princeton neuroscientist Barry Jacobs, PhD, is a leading researcher into causes of depression and the role that serotonin plays in depression. Although many researchers agree that serotonin levels play a role in mood and depression, they don't all agree about what that role is. Bouchez explains in the WebMD article that theories include "low brain cell production of serotonin, a lack of receptor sites able to receive the serotonin that is made, inability of serotonin to reach the receptor sites, or a shortage in tryptophan, the chemical from which serotonin is made." She goes on to explain that Jacobs has his own theory that "depression may occur when there is a suppression of new brain cells and that stress is the most important precipitator of depression."

Jacobs believes that the most common antidepressant medications, such as Celexa, Lexapro, Prozac, and Paxil (all of which are designed to boost serotonin levels) actually help kick off the production of new brain cells, which in turn allows the depression to lift. A Princeton website case study on Jacobs breaks it down to explain that all of his research has led to the conclusion that you need to generate new brain cells in order to fight off depression, that stress inhibits the body's ability to generate those new brain cells in certain parts of the brain and that serotonin helps to reduce that problem so that the brain cells can regenerate after all. He thinks that the reason that medications like Celexa take awhile to start working is because it takes time for those new brain cells to grow whereas natural activities that release serotonin, such as physical exercise or repetitive actions, work more quickly to regenerate the brain cells.

So what does that have to do with crochet? Well, in addition to his research into the role of medicine in improving serotonin levels, Dr. Barry Jacobs has also done research on animals about the role that repetitive movements play in releasing serotonin in the body. Betsan Corkhill's Stitchlinks article called Guide to Our Theories So Far references that research and also quotes Carol Hart (author of the popular book *Secrets of Serotonin)* as someone who personally believes that the repetitive movement of knitting (and therefore also likely of crochet) is something that may release serotonin in the body, creating a feeling of nearly instantaneous calm in the stitcher.

In *Secrets of Serotonin,* Hart says that literally “any rhythmic, repetitive movement can “drive up” serotonin system functioning.” She cites painting, woodworking, playing an instrument and even simply chewing gum as repetitive things that an individual can do to improve serotonin levels in small ways. Crochet is certainly a repetitive, rhythmic movement so if it is true that repetitive movements can enhance serotonin release and that increased serotonin levels can help alleviate depression then it is true that crochet has the potential to assist in alleviating depression symptoms for some people.

And there may be even more going on in the body than just the serotonin release to contribute to feelings of well-being related to physical and repetitive activities. Returning to the aforementioned Whole Living article, Kelly Lambert also discussed the role of serotonin as well as dopamine and endorphins in feelings of mental health:

> “As a result of her research, Lambert identified a network of geographically connected brain regions that appears to strongly influence well-being when activated by physical labor. This "effort-driven reward circuit," as she calls it, includes areas involved with not only reward (the nucleus accumbens) but also emotion (the limbic system), movement (the striatum), and higher reasoning associated with anticipation, planning, and problem-solving (the prefrontal cortex). In our contemporary age, when it's possible to Tweet one's deepest thoughts while waiting two minutes for dinner to warm in the microwave, this circuitry -- encompassing a vast amount of "brain real estate," as Lambert says -- isn't often called on to function in coordination and communication, as it seems evolutionarily designed to do. But when we activate our own effort-driven reward circuitry, it squirts a cocktail of feel-good neurotransmitters, including dopamine (the "reward chemical), endorphins (released with exercise), and serotonin (secreted during repetitive movement). When we knit a scarf, for instance, Lambert says, the brain's executive-thinking centers get busy planning, then the happy-

anticipation zone begins to zing with activity, talking back to the executive top brain and reaching out to other parts that make us dive our hands into the action."

All of this science talk can get confusing, I know. I like to think about it this way ... serotonin and other neurotransmitters have the job of telling different parts of the brain what to do, including to feel good. Sometimes, they get distracted and lazy and the job doesn't get done. You have to stimulate their interest with movement, taking an action like crochet to capture their attention so that they say, "oh yeah, I was supposed to tell the brain to chill out".

Healing Benefits of Visualizing and Completing a Project

Depression is a complex condition with a number of different possible causes. Person A may have depression primarily rooted in problematic serotonin levels. Person B may have depression caused by hormone imbalances. And there are different causes for Persons C – Z. Doctors and researchers have come a very long way towards identifying, understanding and treating depression in recent years but the truth of the matter is that we still aren't entirely sure what the causes are and therefore don't have one-off cures that can help everyone. Instead, depression varies from person to person and so the cures and treatments must vary as well. However, because crochet has such wide-ranging benefits and features, it can assist people who have depression rooted in diverse causes. My depression may be different from your depression and yet we can both treat the symptoms of the depression with crochet.

For example, not everyone has serotonin problems or a brain issue that causes the depression. Many people feel (rightly so) that their depression is situational and that they simply need to learn how to live and think differently in order to alleviate the symptoms of their depression. This is the reason that people dealing with depression may choose to solve it with a drastic life change or through talk therapy designed to provide greater insight into the person's feelings rather than by taking medication. So you might not feel that it benefits you to increase your serotonin levels by the repetitive act of crochet but crochet can still help you with this type of situational depression. This is due partially to the fact that crochet teaches you how to visualize a project and complete it, re-stimulating your creativity and imagination in an environment that allows you to succeed while also building your own self-esteem.

There are two parts to this process and both play an equally important role although some people will find one part more healing for them than the other. The first part is learning to visualize the project, getting the mind stimulated and acting creatively, planning for the future in the sense of how to create the project. The second part is actually finishing the project to completion, which brings its own depression-lifting benefit for many people who get a boost of self-esteem and a sense of reward from having completed the project.

Something I've experienced in my own dealings with depression and that I've seen mentioned often is a failure to visualize things in a positive way. You get rooted in a negative way of thinking and beyond that you truly have a difficult time imagining that things could ever be any different than they are. You are stuck with just that day's reality staring you in the face and that reality isn't pleasant so this stirs up feelings of hopelessness. When you learn to visualize again, even in a small way, you allow your imagination to work and this opens you up to new possibilities, stirring up hope instead of hopelessness.

In the Stitchlinks Guide to Our Theories So Far this idea is referred to as Mind's Eye. This describes the actual tangible ability to visually picture something that isn't right in front of you, imagining it more or less how it will look when it becomes realized. Stitchlinks' guide author Corkhill says, "I learnt that those suffering from depression have problems visualizing. As knitters and stitchers we're constantly referring back to pictures of the finished project, visualizing these and imagining the praise and reaction of others on the completed item. We're using our imagination all the time. So the question arose, "Could knitting and stitching be reawakening the Mind's Eye?" and "Is reawakening this ability to visualize, and to look forwards, crucial to recovering from depression?"

There may not be a specific researched answer to those questions about visualization and the Mind's Eye but many crocheters and knitters will tell you that their craft does help them to visualize things that aren't sitting right in front of them. I would argue that there is a correlation between being able to do this and being able to imagine a situation eventually being different than it currently is, something that helps immensely when dealing with depression. In my own life, I thought that there would never be anything that I would ever like doing ever again. In the rare moments that I could visualize a life in which I enjoyed an activity, the depression lifted.

One of the questions that I asked when interviewing people for this book was what part of the crochet process they felt was the most healing aspect of the craft. I broke it down by asking them to think about the anticipation and excitement of starting a new project, the actual experience of crafting a project and the satisfaction of having an end product to be proud of when the project is completed. The answers were different for everyone but what became clear to me is that each stage does play a role in the healing process and the fact that the crochet project is fairly easy to both imagine and achieve is important in the role it plays for helping people heal from depression.

Margaret Mills (whose full story can be read on the page titled *Meet Margaret!*) shared the following thought that helps explain that: "While all three stages work together, I think the part that really pulls me out of negative emotions is the planning stage. I can get absorbed in the "vision" of what I want to make. I can create a pattern or search through books or look on the Internet for a pattern and then I go in search of the perfect yarn, etc. I think that is the best part because it sets a goal and gives hope for the future. At the same time, it isn't rocket science or getting a graduate degree; it's a very achievable goal. Also, the anticipation when you are making a gift for someone really lifts the spirit. I designed an "alphabet" afghan for my four-year-old grandson, an afghan stitch blanket with the alphabet cross stitched on it, and I'm sure I got more fun out of making it than he did in getting it. Actually doing the work is a close second in healing for me. I think the work itself brings calmness and a sense of accomplishment."

Meet Margaret!

Margaret Mills is part of a three-generational household of women crafters. Her mom quilts, her daughter explores a variety of fiber arts and Margaret both crochets and sews. Crocheting has helped her feel better during a bout of depression.

I first learned about Margaret Mills from an article that she wrote for I Heart Art: Portland titled "The Healing Arts and Crafts." In late 2009 she was watching a lot of movies with her mother who was convalescing and she needed something to keep her busy so she dug out her old crochet hooks and some yarn and got to crafting. I loved her description in the article of what happened next:

> *"As the rhythmic work, the feel of yarn, and the misshapen poncho taking shape under my hands turned the world from black and white to Technicolor, I realized that I was also dealing with a bout of depression."*

I was moved by Margaret's vivid language as well as by my own connection to the experience that she went through and so I reached out to see if she would agree to an interview. She did. She explained that the depression kind of crept up on her and she really didn't realize that it was there until it was too late. She wasn't sad or crying all of the time or anything like that. She just had a series of things happen to her one on top of another and they added up.

In her own words, Margaret explains about this time:

> *"I had been through treatment for breast cancer and was just gaining strength after chemo when my mother became seriously ill. What started as a stay with me and my youngest daughter for her to recover from a heart procedure turned into a permanent move.*
>
> *There were other life stresses as well (financial, my daughter having trouble with school), and it just seemed like everything was about life, death, ambulances, hospitals. Serious stuff – and it just*

drained the joy out of living without me quite realizing what had happened."

Margaret didn't turn to crochet at this time specifically for its healing benefits but more because it gave her something to do. She says:

"It was a bit serendipitous that Mom moved in with all her craft stuff. Mom's main craft has been quilting, but in among the fabric was lots of yarn and crochet hooks. I wanted something to do with my hands while we watched movies in the evening – which is all Mom felt up to doing, and I wanted to spend time with her – so there was the yarn and the hooks. I had crocheted in years past, but it got lost in the pressures of life, divorce, raising kids, etc. Mom's yarn stash just sort of called my name – it was just a little nudge, a little thought: "I bet I could make a stocking cap or something while we watch movies."

Mom had been wanting to dump all the craft stuff, but she has such good stuff! My daughter and I couldn't bear to give it all away, and we have both been crocheting and sewing since. It really opened up a world for us, and helped us both emotionally, I think. Now I will deliberately use crochet to lift my mood, but at first I just wanted to keep my hands busy while watching TV and being with Mom. It was all backwards – I didn't realize I was depressed until I started to feel better, and I started to feel better when I started to crochet."

I asked people like Margaret to share with us what they feel are the most beneficial parts of the crochet process in terms of healing as well as how the yarn itself can heal. Margaret had a lot to say about that. First she talked about the process of crochet including the benefits of the planning stage, the actual crochet work and then having a finished product:

"While all three stages work together, I think the part that really pulls me out of negative emotions is the planning stage. I can get absorbed in the "vision" of what I want to make, and either creating a pattern or searching books and the Internet for one, then finding the perfect yarn, etc. I think that is the best part. It sets a goal and gives hope for the future. At the same time, it isn't rocket science or getting a graduate degree; it is a very achievable goal. Also, the

anticipation when you are making a gift for someone really lifts the spirit. I designed an "alphabet" afghan for my four-year-old grandson, an afghan stitch blanket with the alphabet cross stitched on it, and I'm sure I got more fun out of making it than he did getting it. Actually doing the work is a close second in healing. I think the work itself brings calmness and a sense of accomplishment."

Margaret then shared her thoughts about the healing aspects of the color and texture of yarn:

"It was the color of the yarn, the play of one color against another that really drew me. I've read fiction books, like Debbie Macomber's, that speak of "luscious" or "yummy" yarn colors. I do know color is thought to have an impact on emotions, and can be used in decorating to affect mood, so it makes sense. I think the colors are a huge part of the healing power of this type of craft."

"I tend to spend too much time inside my head (writing, researching, etc.), and find it helps to do "hands-on" work to balance that – crochet, of course, but also gardening or sewing or cooking."

Margaret finds special value in the relaxing and calming benefits of the repetitive nature of crochet. However, she believes it may also have other health benefits:

"I tend to believe the claims made for the health benefits of crocheting – it is good for stress management, strengthening the immune system, regulating blood pressure. I can only testify to its help with depression, but as a cancer survivor, I consider continuing to crochet part of my general health plan. I'm all for anything that strengthens the immune system! I have also found, as an unexpected bonus, that crocheting taps into an unrealized artistic vein. Creative ideas start with a new yarn project, then spill over into house decorating, gardening and even my writing."

Building Self-Esteem

So we've talked about how visualization is a very important reason that crocheting helps in healing depression but there's also another part of the equation and that's having a finished product that you've created yourself. When you see your crochet project through to the end, you've made something all your own and nobody can take that away from you. This offers several health benefits but the most important one, in my opinion, is that it helps to build your self-esteem.

You basically do not have self-esteem when you are depressed. I consider myself to be someone with fairly strong self-esteem. I am not easily swayed by what other people think about me. I generally feel confident about who I am and what I've accomplished in my life. I think I'm a cute girl and know that I am a good friend. But when depression takes hold, I sometimes believe that I am a terrible writer, a lazy person, a fat chick, and a worthless friend. When depression is holding the reins, I care very much what people think about me but only believe the negative things they say and often latch on to the smallest negative thing and magnify it. I'm embarrassed by this and don't really want to put it in writing because really, I am usually a confident girl, but this is what happens when depression gets control.

And I have seen it happen to so many other people in my life. I've seen it happen to a man who truly is one of the most wonderful people I've ever met and yet he thinks of himself as a terrible human being and regardless of what he says I know that it's just the depression talking. I've seen it happen to a new mother who isn't getting enough sleep and might have a little bit of post-partum depression and goes from being a confident person to feeling like she's the most terrible mother in the world who can't do anything right and is going to ruin her child. And I've seen it happen countless times in smaller ways when someone with a generally positive view of herself struggles with sad feelings that open up vulnerabilities and fears that eat at her self-esteem.

Nessa is an MS and depression sufferer who describes this so well: "Depression breathes lies to the person who possesses it, holding them back and telling them that they cannot do things and that they are worthless. Learning that these are lies, regardless of the feeling of their truth, and learning how to counter the lies over the years has, in a way, metaphorically led me home."

M.K. Carroll (see *Meet M.K. Carroll!)* puts it more succinctly when she says, "Depression is a lying liar that lies."

Most of us have experienced this to some degree on bad days or during difficult periods of time. You know that you aren't stupid but when you're having a tough time at your job or can't get a paper to go right then you might feel like you are truly incompetent. The feeling passes in most cases. With depression, however, it becomes an ugly cycle. You don't have positive self-esteem so you don't feel like doing anything and then you feel bad about yourself for not doing anything so you get worse self-esteem. Or you try to do something new to boost your self-esteem but it doesn't go well and you feel worse for having tried. It sucks. I know that "sucks" is not a fancy belongs-in-a-book word but it's true – depression sucks. Almost literally because it sucks any remaining self-esteem you have right off your bones and then you feel bad because even your bones don't look right.

As a result, it becomes very important for anyone dealing with depression to find ways to combat low self-esteem. You will find thousands of books on this topic but I'm here to argue only one point which is that I believe that creating something from scratch with your hands is a simple and direct route to building self-esteem. I choose crochet because it's simpler for me (and many people agree) than lots of other crafts and when you already feel like you can't do anything right you don't want to take on a complicated craft that can easily go wrong. I'm a terrible painter and don't have positive feelings about the craft so even though I know it's supposed to be something you do for fun I'd probably have felt badly about myself if I tried to "become a painter" during my bout of depression. Becoming a crocheter is simple, though, and you can easily have a fairly decent finished product in a short amount of time.

Now, here's another place where I refuse to lie ... if you're wrapped up in negative self-esteem and hating yourself critically in a multitude of ways then crochet may not break through that for you. You may be the exception to the rule who finishes that first crochet scarf and thinks only things like, "it's sloppy" or "I'll never get good at this" or "I chose a bad color" or whatever. If you are one of those people, there are three things I want to say to you:

1. **Go easy on yourself**. Yes, I know. This is easier said than done when you are depressed. I promise you that no matter what you think of your finished object, it looks decent. It's fine the way it is. You will get better at it because every single crocheter who ever stuck with the craft got better than their first finished object. And in the end, it's just yarn, so it doesn't matter that much anyway. Remember that depression is a lying liar and trust what I'm telling you about this instead.
2. **Find the good in it**. Again, I realize that this is easier said than done but it's something you need to learn to do to break the cycle of bad self-esteem and your crochet product is something easy to start with. Do you love the yarn you chose? Did you master a basic stitch? Do you at least have something warm you can wrap around your neck? Find something good about it. This is a quick trick to help battle those negative statements your depressed brain wants to say to itself.
3. **If you can muster the energy, find a local crochet group**. Alternatively, join an online community where you can show off your work. (Ravelry is a good crochet and knitting social networking site to get you started; you can find out more about this site and others in the Resources section at the end of this book.) Why do I suggest this? Because I can pretty much guarantee that your fellow crocheters will gush with enthusiasm for that first item that you have crocheted even if you think it's terrible and this will give you a nice little self-esteem boost that you may not be able to give yourself.

I like what Corkhill from Stitchlinks had to say on the benefits of completing creative works: "Finding something you can do and do well changes your outlook on life. The world begins to open up once more, reversing those downward spirals into that closed world where every detail of life is a worry. Success challenges those negative thought patterns and feelings of failure. After all how can you be a failure when you've created a beautiful piece of work? How can you be worthless when you give so much to others through gifts and charity?"

As that quote highlights, there are many different ways that finishing a crochet item can bring self-esteem. First of all, you've finished something. That's no small thing when you're dealing with depression. Second, you may even feel like it's something beautiful. My first crochet scarf isn't technically accomplished or even, looking back, all that pretty really but when I first completed that last stitch on it and held it up I felt like it was actually this really beautiful thing. I felt a tinge of awe and pride and a tiny little injection of self-esteem. I still have it. Third, you can give your work to others and their appreciation or just the fact that you've given to someone who needs it may also build your positive esteem.

Em of the Etsy store nothingbutstring was someone I interviewed who had the experience of crochet helping to build her self-esteem. (See her full story on the page titled *Meet Em!*) Em was over 50 in late 2008 when she was laid off from her job due to changes in the economy. She wasn't too worried about it at first but as the economy continued to her worsen, she found that too many strikes against her made it impossible for her to get a job. She wasn't as young as the other applicants. After the unemployment situation dragged on, her credit took a hit and that, combined with the now long absence from work, made her look bad to potential employers. Trying and trying to get a job and getting no response eventually took its toll and Em sunk into depression.

Em told me: "Needless to say there were days where I just didn't want to get out of bed. The depression was terrible. I'd cry all the time, I felt so worthless, and I had no idea what I was going to do if I couldn't get a job." She explained that, "that's one of the worst things about being unemployed; your self-esteem just takes a huge hit. You keep wondering: what's wrong with me, why doesn't anyone want me?" And of course this is where it cycles because the longer you're without a job, the more worthless you feel and that makes it harder to do what you need to do to get a job.

Luckily, with the support of her boyfriend, Em decided to take the reins into her own hands and create a job for herself on Etsy. She began crocheting items for the store, figured out how it all worked and slowly dragged herself out of depression through crafting in a way that helped to re-build her self-esteem. She explained that there was a two-tiered self-esteem boost with selling crochet items on Etsy. First she got a boost of self-esteem when she would complete a challenging crochet piece and have that finished item in hand. And then she would get another boost when someone would see it on Etsy and buy it or mark her store as a favorite. She says, "to actually create something and then have someone else praise it does wonders for the ego."

One of the things that I love about being a crafter today is that the Internet provides numerous opportunities to share your work with others and receive that kind of praise that helps to boost the self-esteem when you need it most. You can start a blog. You can join an online social group. You can participate in forums for crochet or for people dealing with depression or other illnesses. You can share photos of your work on sites like Flickr. You can start an Etsy store. You may not have the energy to truly socialize with others when depression has you in its grips but if you can get access to the Internet and start forming a community there then it can help in many ways, the most obvious of which (beyond pure social connection) is that support and praise for your craft work.

While some people, like Em, use crochet to build their self-esteem, others find that it is the only thing that helps them hang on to the self-esteem that they do have. Aimee O'Neill (see *Meet Aimee!)* found this to be the case when she was stuck in an emotionally abusive marriage. She shared, "I now see that through crochet I took a stand for my independence and individuality. It was the only time my husband was not considered in my decision making process. I chose the yarn I wanted to choose, I chose the project I wanted to choose, I chose who I wanted to share it with. I could escape him in the house through my crochet. I could escape him in the car through my crochet. I could escape him anywhere through my crochet." For twelve years Aimee's self-esteem was eaten away by the negative messages she received from her husband but she held on to a tiny bit of herself in her crochet work. Eventually, with hook in hand, she was able to walk out the door and into a stronger independent life.

Meet Em!

Em is the store owner of Etsy shop nothingbutstring. Em is a 50+ woman who went through an extended period of unemployment after a layoff caused by the economic downturn. She struggled with depression related to self-esteem issues until she got active selling her crochet work on Etsy. The new job, but more specifically being busy with crochet, helped break the cycle of depression.

Em lost her job in December 2008. She had worked for a travel company for several years but the economic downturn caused the company to go south. Although it was tough to be laid off right around the holidays, Em had a positive attitude at first. She had always been able to find work in the past, usually within a couple of weeks of a job ending. Unfortunately this time was different. Two and a half years later, Em hadn't been able to find a job.

It was not for lack of trying. Em just had a lot of strikes against her in the bad economy. Em was over 50. After not too long, she had been unemployed for more than 6 months, which looks bad to most employers. Her credit got ruined because of the unemployment situation and these days there are employers who run credit checks so she would fail those and then not get hired. Despite active efforts to find work, Em couldn't get anything and that's when the depression started to set in. In her own words:

> *"Needless to say there were days where I just didn't want to get out of bed. The depression was terrible. I'd cry all the time, I felt so worthless, and I had no idea what I was going to do if I couldn't get a job."*

Then for some reason she remembered about Etsy. She had actually joined the site a few months before the layoff but hadn't done anything with it. With the encouragement of her boyfriend, she decided to take a fresh look at it, figuring that if she couldn't get someone else to hire her then maybe she could create her own job on the site. Since it's so affordable to get started, she figured that it couldn't hurt. Not only did she start making a little bit of money from her Etsy store but it really helped her to regain her self-esteem. In her own words:

"At first I listed things like doilies that I had learned to make from my grandmother, but as time moved on I developed my own style. I now crochet Irish lace jewelry, and I've recently added some knitted items like fingerless gloves. I've sold some things here and there, not enough to pay all the bills on my own, but enough to be able to make a contribution to the household, and get some of my dignity back.

Prior to Etsy I had not crocheted for a very long time. There just wasn't any time for recreation ... between work, taking care of the house, running errands and everything else who had time to crochet? I found out when I did pick up my crochet hook that my mind was so busy counting stitches and figuring out a pattern that it just didn't have the time to worry. Less worry meant less stress in my life and I began to calm down. I just started to crochet like crazy just to get relief, not to mention I needed the inventory in my shop. Anyway this whole experience has allowed me to really focus on what's important in my life and concentrate on things that make me happy and not just things that I have to do in order to make a living."

What is really great about selling crochet items is that you get the immediate boost of self-esteem from finishing a product and then you get another boost when you see a sale. Em explains that:

"I found one thing that really helped was the feeling of immediate gratification that I got from completing a project. It really felt like I had accomplished something worthwhile, and then to top it off to have someone purchase it gave me a huge ego boost. It really helped with my self worth and self-esteem. That's one of the worst things about being unemployed; your self-esteem just takes a huge hit. You keep wondering: what's wrong with me, why doesn't anyone want me? To actually create something and then have someone else praise it does wonders for the ego."

Em also explained that while she enjoys the whole process of crochet, she especially likes the period when she's just finished creating a finished item that was a challenge for her to come up with.

Like many people who crochet for stress-relief and to get out of depression, Em also found that the craft had some physical benefits as well. High blood pressure is something that runs in her family and the stress of the period after the layoff caused her to experience it. Since she started crocheting, her stress levels have gone down and she's seen her blood pressure go down as well.

Obviously being able to sell some of her items was part of what caused crochet to be healing for Em but that wasn't all that there was to it. The craft might have helped her out of her stress and depression even if she weren't doing it for the purpose of selling it. For one thing, it is a craft that fills her with positive memories. Em's grandmother taught her how to crochet so when she does it she remembers happy memories of spending hours with Grandma at the kitchen table learning crochet stitches and how to read a crochet graph. In fact, she says that she believes crocheting together is what kept the two of them close for so many years. Her grandmother crocheted all the way up until she passed away at the age of 102 despite having arthritis in her hands so Em's positive associations with crochet literally span her own lifetime.

Em likes to work with hand-dyed thread that uses several colors in combination. Her preferred colors are the vibrant colors associated with spring and summer. This is important because she chooses the colors that make her happy. Just making simple choices in crochet to work with the yarn that makes you smile can help increase the positive feelings of the craft.

Em leaves us with these positive words of encouragement that are specific to people dealing with unemployment but may also apply to people dealing with all types of depression and illness:

> *"If anyone else finds themselves in the same kind of predicament: Don't give up. If you can't find a job, go out and create your own job. Maybe it's creating something or providing a service; it doesn't matter ... people are out there that need what you do. Don't let anybody tell you that you aren't good enough because you are. And you can do it!"*

Visit Em on Etsy at www.etsy.com/shop/nothingbutstring.

Meet Aimee!

Aimee O'Neill was a victim of mental abuse in her marriage. Crochet was one tool that helped her on her journey to freedom. It is something that she could do by herself, for herself, independent of anyone else's control.

Aimee went through a heart-wrenching experience with domestic abuse. She shares her story:

> *"I didn't work outside of my home often and I didn't have many friends. The "friendships" my husband orchestrated never lasted long. The friendships I tried to establish were constantly belittled and ridiculed. My maintaining my relationship with my family was accepted but frowned upon and rarely included my husband. To everyone on the outside my husband was a great guy, husband and father. I internalized the notion, verbalized by him and mostly everyone else, that I was lucky to have him.*
>
> *I was led to believe any problems I had with him or the way he treated me or our children were because of something being wrong with me. I was constantly told I was crazy. I internalized and acted upon the notion that things would be better if I thought the way he did, did what he wanted me to do, acted the way he wanted me to and was the "wife" he wanted me to be. Although I felt like I shouldn't take the blame for everything, I focused on my shortcomings and at the same time used all my energy making up for and taking responsibility for his. I spent most of my days in the relationship trying to fix and make happy someone who seemed impossible to satisfy.*
>
> *The environment affected my happiness with me. I always felt disappointed with myself. I would constantly say, "I'm not me." I would always wonder and ask, "How do I find myself?" One of the few things I had with me that tied me to the individual I was before my marriage was crochet."*

Like many victims of emotional abuse, it took Aimee time to realize that what she was going through was a form of victimization. She was separated from her husband after twelve years of marriage. She spoke to a person experienced in domestic violence and that is when she began to realize that nothing was wrong with her and that she had been a victim of mental abuse. Crochet helped her as a coping strategy in her unhealthy marriage and served as a tool to help her gain her independence away from that marriage. She shares:

> *"Crochet was the one thing I possessed that he couldn't (or I didn't allow him to) take away, although he did try. That was the one thing I never shared with him. At the time of my refusal to grant his request and crochet him a hat, crochet him a scarf, or better yet teach him to crochet, I couldn't understand why I was being selfish. I had no problem making things for others and loved showing others how to crochet. I just couldn't bring myself to joyfully make him anything or teach him willingly. I would get angry and disgusted when he asked. Now doesn't that seem odd? I went along with things that I deep down detested to the point that they became my normal, yet in defense of my crochet I took on the characteristics I disliked in him. I guess it was my revenge, my last stand or my fight for survival.*
>
> *I look back now with feelings of wonderment and gratitude. It's just amazing to me, because I always speak of the good of crochet. I just didn't realize the scope of its benefits within my life. I'm amazed because of what crochet silently did for me. Crochet was the true friend by my side. I now see that through crochet I took a stand for my independence and individuality.*
>
> *It was the only time he was not considered in my decision making process. I chose the yarn I wanted to choose, I chose the project I wanted to choose, I chose who I wanted to share it with. I could escape him in the house through my crochet. I could escape him in the car through my crochet. I could escape him anywhere through my crochet.*
>
> *I have just started the conscious healing process. Right now I am in the process of setting and mapping out my short and long term goals for my life independent of my husband. Since we have been separated I am realizing the scope of his control over nearly every aspect of my being and am loving my newfound independence. So right now, most healing for me is the excitement of planning a new project. I get to experience a sense of control and independence. This part of the process is healing because it's like a new beginning. I am*

excitedly approaching this task just as I am excitedly approaching my crochet projects. It's like we are on this journey together. My newfound confidence and renewed love for myself is too my new love for and confidence in my crochet. I look forward to us embarking on this journey together and look forward to seeing the end product, the light at the end of the tunnel so to speak."

Aimee has seen the benefits of crochet in others' lives as well as her own.

"I worked inside of the women's quarters of a local homeless shelter. I think I may have taken my crochet bag to work with me within my first week there and every day thereafter. I taught a few of the clients how to crochet. And now that I look back, the first client that wanted to learn was a client I later learned was a victim of domestic abuse. I noticed a sense of pride in those who learned. I saw feelings of accomplishment. It was great seeing them smiling and excited to show their progress. I just loved seeing them carrying their bags of yarn."

Crochet may also have helped Aimee to be able to cope with the intensity of working in the high-stress environment of the shelter:

"The shelter's environment is a very volatile one and often erupts into violence in one form or another. I have a rather small stature and an even smaller comfort level with confrontation. In that setting, too, crochet was my escape or the peace by my side so to speak. I hadn't seen it that way until one client said to me that it would help her with her anxiety and probably helped me with mine. Up until that point I had merely seen it as a way to stay awake (I was working the graveyard shift), pass the time, and catch up on some projects."

Aimee shared that she felt that the sense of touch is one of the most healing aspects of crochet for her.

"The feeling of the yarn and the rhythmic motions produced by crocheting are very quieting and help me regroup, recharge and become reconnected to my inner self amidst turmoil and confusion."

No matter how dark things got, Aimee had the strength to hold on to that one piece of herself, her craft, that was a significant part of who she is. She has been able to use that to help others learn that crochet can be a healing tool. And she continues to use it as a way to expand her own boundaries because it offers a safe place where she can plan projects, make decisions and branch out into new things.

Developing a New Interest

Crochet was a lifesaver for me in large part because it was the first thing in a very, very long time that I enjoyed doing. All along I knew that I needed to try new things to break myself out of the state that I was in but everything I had tried recently up until then didn't stick. It felt harder than I thought it should feel. It felt like stuff I wanted to want to do but didn't actually want to do. Drawing class intimidated me. Can-can dancing felt more like can't-can't. Meeting up with people to go on public walks was appealing but it required a commitment to a specific time that was too difficult for me to manage in my depression. Sunday dinners sounded lovely but then I had to cook and clean. And it was more than that, really. None of these things really captured my interest. Even reading, the love of my life, had betrayed me. I couldn't focus on sentences long enough to know what was being said. I couldn't get lost in them because I was too lost in myself. My biggest fear was that I was never going to find anything interesting ever again, that no matter what I tried I would end up feeling exactly like I already felt. The future yawned widely in front of me, a gaping hole of never-ending disinterest. And then I found crochet. Crochet clicked for me. And suddenly my life had a little bit of color in it again. I don't know why crochet worked when other things didn't work for me but I am very, very glad that it did.

Margaret Mills is one example of a woman who didn't even really realize she was depressed until she was deep in her crochet work and saw that the crochet was helping her, an experience I've seen re-iterated in the stories that many other crafters shared. Shelli Steadman (see her full story on the page titled *Meet Shelli!)* is another woman who feels that way. Shelli, who suffers from the chronic pain of fibromyalgia and the exhaustion of hypothyroidism shared, "I don't think I consciously thought about it helping me. I just knew I felt good when crocheting and therefore I crocheted more. Of course I realize now how much it has helped me."

One thing that I think sets crochet aside as something worth trying is the fact that it's both a fairly easy craft and one that is affordable. Depression and other illnesses steal from your piggy bank so you need to find ways to pass the time that aren't going to cost you much money. M.K. Carroll shared that when she went through a serious struggle with stress-related depression she was in her college years, a time when she didn't have any health insurance or any money to pay for the mental health help that she probably needed. She relied on two things that she could afford: self-help books from the local library and her grandmother's crochet hooks. She said, "I couldn't pay for therapy, but a few balls of crochet thread cost less than $20 and provided me with many hours of crochet."

Like Margaret and Shelli and M.K. Carroll, crochet just kind of came to me as a thought when I needed it most, but it was not easy for me to find crochet. I can't count the number of interests I pursued before I found something that stuck. In addition to the things I've already told you about there were other things I tried (super slow strength training, hula hoop dancing, cooking), things I thought about trying but didn't (glass blowing, sailing, learning to shoot a gun) and things that I knew before I started that I wouldn't like (running, public speech classes, learning Italian). I just kept aiming my hopes at things and missing and I didn't genuinely believe that an interest would stick anywhere.

But I am standing here today, a fairly happy girl, to tell you that your something is out there. Maybe it's not crochet. Maybe it's going to take more than this craft to capture your interest. But I promise you, that thing is out there, waiting to be found and when you find it again you will feel like it was worth the effort of the search even if you're certain today that you don't have the energy to make that effort. I promise. I'm proof.

I don't have a definitive answer for why crochet clicked for me, instilling fresh passion into my life. But I do know that there are some things about crochet that lend themselves well to enhancing the quality of life for the people who learn it. One of the key things is that this is a craft that stimulates multiple senses without overwhelming them. In particular crochet is a craft that tantalizes your sight and your sense of touch through the color and softness of the yarn as well as the patterns and fabrics that you create from your efforts.

Let's talk a little more about that ...

Color and Mood

> *"Simply looking at vibrantly coloured yarn and stroking different textures can make that first chink in the desensitised armour of depression and demotivation."* Stitchlinks

One of the key images that has stuck with me as I've researched the health benefits of crochet is an image laid out by Margaret Mills in her article titled The Healing Arts and Crafts, in which she said: "As the rhythmic work, the feel of yarn, and the misshapen poncho taking shape under my hands turned the world from black and white to Technicolor, I realized that I was also dealing with a bout of depression. I've since resumed my long-neglected sewing as well, and the world is a brighter place. Making handcrafted items lifts my spirits and boosts my energy."

I think what struck me about this image is the idea that your world is black and white (or merely grey!) and that crochet can bring color back into it. That was certainly the case for me. I saw grey everywhere I turned until I didn't want to bother turning anymore. Crochet reminded me of the simple beauty of color. Not that I started drastically introducing color into my life. In fact, the very first ball of yarn that I picked out when learning how to crochet was a grey ball! Go figure. But I added a beautiful teal color to it that I thought went well with it and thus my exploration of color began. I didn't consciously understand the healing power of color but something inside of me yearned to infuse my life with color to erase the grayness of emotion that pervaded every corner of my days.

And eventually, it wasn't just in the comfort of my crochet corner that color blossomed. I began to notice color in other places again. I noticed the tone of a friend's skin color because I wanted to make her a scarf and wanted to choose colors that would flatter her. I noticed the colors in the skirt of a passerby because I liked the pattern and wanted to create something similar. Before I knew it I was noticing the blue in the sky, the blue in my boyfriend's eyes, in a way that I simply hadn't noticed in a very, very long time. I saw color again because I'd been working with color in my hands for so many months. Depression takes things away without asking your permission. I hadn't realized that my sense of sight had become so limited to a grey world until color returned.

I first read that striking Margaret Mills quote before I'd had the opportunity to interview her so I made sure to bring it up when I did get the chance to speak with her about her crochet experiences. I asked her if she felt that color theory plays a role in how crochet helps to heal depression and she said that she definitely thinks that it does. In fact, she says that it was the color of the yarn and the play of one color against another that really drew her in to the craft. She notes that she often sees yarn described as "luscious" or "yummy" (both words that I tend to use a lot when talking about yarn, actually) and although those are words that we use to describe taste, it is the richness of the color of the yarn that might inspire us to salivate a little. Mills also notes that color is an important consideration in decorating because it affects mood so much so there is definitely something to say for the healing power of the colors in the craft of crochet.

Mills was hardly the only person to make this connection. Em was another person who highlighted it when she mentioned using vibrant spring and summer colors in her crochet because those colors make her happy. And much scientific research has been done into the relationship between color and depression, research that shows that there is a distinct link between the two. Some research even suggests that you can consciously improve your mood through smart focus on color.

Remember when we talked before about mindfulness meditation? A 2009 Psychology Today article by Peter Strong explains how mindfulness can be used with attention to color to overcome depression. He describes a technique where you sit still and become very mindful of your emotions. You use various techniques to do this but the point is that you begin to be able to visualize what the color of your emotion is. Depression is often associated with "gray" but it doesn't have to be, of course. Likewise jealousy is usually green and anger is red. In Strong's exercise, once you've visualized your emotion's color and meditated on it then you can take the next step which is to do a series of things to change the color of your emotion. (So instead of just being mindful of the emotion, like before, you now use meditation and visualization to actually alter the emotion.) For example, you might visualize spray painting your grey emotion with a bright yellow paint. The theory here is that by changing the imagery of your emotion, you can change the actual emotion.

If visualization doesn't work for you, it is possible that exposing yourself to tangible examples of different colors might help alter your mood. Consider for a moment the people who suffer from Seasonal Affective Disorder (SAD), which is a type of depression that occurs during certain times of the year when light levels are low. One of the main treatments for SAD is light therapy, The National Alliance on Mental Health explains that this requires using certain types of light because a full-color light spectrum isn't as beneficial as using light bulbs in a specific color temperature range. They go on to say that when used correctly light therapy can offer total remission from SAD symptoms in 50% - 80% of people. When you consider that color is basically just the way that the eye sees light, there is evidence to suggest that viewing different colors can help to reduce symptoms of depression.

There is a whole body of science, called chromotherapy (or color therapy) that is devoted to using color to treat depression. In describing the history of chromotherapy, researchers Azeemi and Raza (2005) explain that although studies on the topic have been more qualitative than quantitative, the use of color as a possible healing treatment dates back to about 2000 BC and was utilized by people in ancient Egypt, Greece, China and India. If you've ever learned about the chakras of the body then you know that each one is associated with a color, which was historically related to healing techniques that were applied to both mind and body.

The use of color to alter mood has continued in modern times. Maybe you've read about modern marketing techniques where retail stores or advertisers will choose certain colors that lull potential buyers into certain moods. And Azeemi and Raza report that "in 1990, scientists reported to the annual conference of the American Association for the Advancement of Science on the successful use of blue light in the treatment of a wide variety of psychological problems, including addictions, eating disorders and depression" while red light was used to treat more physical symptoms like constipation and flesh wounds.

Maybe you agree with this and maybe you don't. But if you're a crocheter who battles with depression (or even just a crocheter having a bad day) then it might be worth it to play around a little bit with the use of different yarn colors in your projects to see if you can change the way that you feel by changing the colors that you work with. I believe that it's important to listen to your own body when it comes to exploring the healing benefits of color. Nevertheless, many other people have reported on how to use color to improve the way that you feel. The research widely suggests that yellow is a good choice to help lift you out of a bad mood whereas blue and grey are more likely to leave you feeling depressed.

The Paul Goldin Clinic, which offers a free online personality test related to color, agrees that yellow will help cure depression whereas "too much blue could leave you cold, depressed and sorrowful." The site also suggests that red can help with depression although too much red can make you feel agitated and anxious. They say that green is a good color for balancing out your emotions and evoking a feeling of calmness and purple is good for connecting your mind and body to ease mental health issues although you want to drift towards lighter, more lavender hues for optimal feelings of balance. Of course, some crocheters are going to agree and others are not. Take a minute to stop and ask yourself how different colored projects have related to the mood you had while working on them.

Meet M.K. Carroll!

M.K. Carroll is the series editor of a great set of crochet books called Fresh Designs, which are published by Cooperative Press. She is also a woman who has struggled with depression over the years. Crochet isn't just her living; it's her way of life.

M.K. Carroll copes with stress-related depression. Her college years were especially high-stress and she found it difficult to deal with the situations she found herself in. As she says:

> *"I didn't have good skills for assessing situations and for coping with stress. I'd just keep pushing myself, even if all I was really doing was spinning my wheels and going nowhere."*

One of the worst parts of the depression at this time was that she didn't have the money to get the mental health help that she needed. During one of her worst bouts of depression she was uninsured and found it difficult to find help for anyone without health insurance. Even if she had found someone, she would have had to pay out of pocket costs for the care and with her paycheck-to-paycheck situation there was no way that she could do that. So she put all of the energy that depression hadn't sucked out of her into healing herself.

She headed to the public library and checked out a bunch of self-help books. But words can't cure everything so it's a good thing that she also had a handful of her grandmother's crochet hooks on hand. She shares:

> *"I couldn't pay for therapy, but a few balls of crochet thread cost less than $20 and provided me with many hours of crochet. It was also manageable – just pull one loop through another, and if I made a mistake, pull it back. If a crochet project failed, I could start over or just throw it away, and the rest of my life would continue on unaffected.*
>
> *What I didn't know until fairly recently was how meditative crochet can be. Being able to have a small crochet project to work on anywhere – at home, on the bus, while waiting in line – meant I could create a quiet space in my head whenever I had a few minutes to spare. Those small quiet spaces can add up to a lot over time.*

Even if all I'm doing is one long chain, the repetitive movements give me a calm, quiet place where I can work out other problems."

One of the great things that M.K. pointed out is that there is a cycle of calmness that develops with crochet. You have to calm down in order to be able to crochet and then the crochet itself is calming. She offered a story of one experience of this:

"There was one project in particular that I had started for a housemate who had requested a bear hat, based on a hat I had made for someone else. It involved bulky chenille yarn, and if you've crocheted with chenille you know that it can be tricky to work with and almost impossible to undo. My first try at the hat was not successful; I was fighting the yarn and feeling very frustrated with it, so I set it aside and crocheted something else.

When I was calm, I picked up the chenille again and started over, and with what I'd learned from the first time around, I was able to complete the hat quickly and it was fun, not frustrating. Remember, I didn't have good coping skills, so the simple lesson of putting something frustrating aside to deal with later, in a calm state of mind, was pretty big for me. That wasn't the way I'd learned to deal with problems.

By that time, my housemate had moved to a different state, and I mailed the hat to him with a letter in which I apologized for the delay, and added that I thought it was worth the wait, as this hat was infused with joy instead of pain. Making things for other people pulls me out of my own head and gets me to look around, always helpful during depression. Extra points if it's designed to encourage people to smile."

M.K. has learned over the years that she can also use her crochet work to get in touch with her own moods.

A "tell" for me to assess how I'm doing mentally is to see what I'm choosing to work with. I do have a tendency to turn to certain kinds of projects when I'm stressed/depressed. When I'm getting out the fine gauge thread and steel hooks is one tell, and another is setting up a challenge for myself simply for the sake of overcoming a crochet hurdle and not because it will serve a good purpose.

A good recent example of that are the crochet lace rock doilies I started doing recently. Fine thread and seeing how to get lace over an unevenly shaped rock was a big "tell" that I could then use to look at other parts of my life and see what was going on and how I was reacting. This time around, I hit a point where the coping skills I'd developed weren't enough, and I needed to recognize that and deal with that.

Depression is a lying liar that lies, so having a small challenge that I can work through is a nice way to push away the feelings of helplessness and hopelessness. The "a-ha!" moment when I figure it out is a little flash of light in the darkness. "

You can connect with M.K. Carroll via her blog at mkcarroll.com/blog.

Depression and the Sense of Touch

Color (which is related to the sense of sight, of course) plays a big role in the healing aspect of crochet for many people. The other major sense that comes into play is the sense of touch. When you crochet, you feel the cool smoothness of the crochet hook as it plays against the silky warmth of the yarn. Yarns can have different feelings to the fingers (contrast the plush softness of a baby alpaca with a slightly rougher lamb's wool, for example) but in general yarn is soft to the touch.

I have found that touch is a particularly, well… touchy, subject for a lot of people suffering from depression. There is a lot of confusion in the depressed body. It yearns to be touched nicely and softly, yearns for hugs and an arm around the shoulder. And yet, for many complicated reasons, human touch is sometimes too difficult for the depressed person to bear. A touch, even a gentle touch, from someone else can provoke fear, incite tears and cause a whirlwind of negative feelings in the body. And so in order to help yourself enjoy tactile sensation during bouts of depression it can be important to find other sources of joyful touch, sources that don't come from other humans. That's one of many reasons that a fuzzy pet can be a great comfort to the depressed individual. The feel of working with yarn can be one of those healing touch options, as soothing as the calming sensation of petting a cat that is purring in your lap but without the hassle of the litter box!

To this day one of my favorite treats gained from learning to crochet is the joy of touching a particularly soft, plush ball of yarn. I will go to a yarn store or into my own yarn closet and pull out a ball that just begs to be handled. I will marvel at the softness in my hands, sturdy and solid because it is rolled into a ball, and yet lusciously buttery to the fingertips. I will stroke it like it is a pet or a sleeping child or a lover, enjoying the moment completely, bringing me back to the mindfulness I learned from crochet in the first place. I keep basins filled with yarn all over my house and in them I put only the most beautiful, most touchable yarn for constant easy access to that nice feeling.

Many other crocheters have also expressed how the tactile joy of a great skein of yarn can help scare depression away. It can also have touch benefits for others dealing with different conditions. Shelli Steadman explained that with fibromyalgia, "Even a well meant pat on the back can hurt. Feeling a soft yarn glide between my fingers is a luxury. I especially love the 100% alpaca yarn I indulged in buying. I love it so much that I've had a terrible time deciding what to crochet with it!"

Like Shelli, I'm a fan of alpaca yarn (especially baby alpaca), which is a very soft yarn but one that's not fuzzy (like a mohair yarn might be). I also like really soft merino wool and blends of silk and bamboo. Those are among the pricier yarns on the market but you can find soft yarn regardless of your yarn budget because many acrylic yarns are designed to be very soft to the touch. Personally as far as big box brands go I really like Caron's Simply Soft because it is true to its name but I encourage you to get out there and put your hands on as much yarn as possible to find one that feels right to you. Regardless of whether or not you struggle with depression you can certainly benefit from enjoying the pleasant sensation of a yarn that feels good as you crochet.

The act of crochet is the act of turning yarn into fabric. As you do this, the way that the yarn feels will change. If you make tight, small stitches then you may get a fabric that feels firm compared to the velvety feel of a swatch made using a larger hook or a more open stitch. And yet if you work with too large of a hook, making loops that are too large, then some of that softness will begin to dissipate again. If you are crocheting for touch then you will work somewhere in the middle, which is why I frequently find myself returning to the half double crochet, double crochet and treble crochet stitches worked with an F, G or H size hook. The yarn you use matters but with almost any yarn I've used the softest fabric is produced in this range of crochet and working here is where I am happiest because of the pure pleasure of touch as I work. Your own experience may vary, obviously, but that's been my experience.

And of course, the end product that you create becomes something touchable. There is a reason that all of those crocheted fabric pieces wrapped around items are called "cozies." They are cozy to the touch. Wrap yourself in a hand-crocheted scarf or snuggle up in a crochet blanket and you are wrapped in the warm touch of that luscious yarn, made all the better if the yarn itself is a super soft kind like a cashmere / merino blend or that baby alpaca option. On my darkest of days I can still be lifted at least a notch away from depression by languishing in the feel of soft yarn products. I would bathe in yarn if I could.

OCD sufferer Jennifer Crutchfield (whose full story you can find on the page titled *Meet Jennifer C!*) agrees that the tactile sensations of crochet have been quite significant for her. In fact, she considers it one of the most healing aspects of the craft although she's recently started a color-rich afghan that's giving her additional insight into the healing powers of color, too. And Aimee O'Neill noted how focusing on the feel of the yarn, as well as the physical rhythm of working on the yarn, helps her to "regroup, recharge and become reconnected" to her inner self.

Finally, Margaret Mills points out the fact that the tactile sensation of crochet also does wonders for bringing you back into the present moment, returning us back to the idea of mindfulness. She says, "The softness and feel of yarn seems to relax me. I tend to spend too much time inside my head (writing, researching, etc.), and find it helps to do "hands-on" work to balance that – crochet, of course, but also gardening or sewing or cooking." What Mills is saying brings us back to the idea that if you can break the cycle of rumination then you can fight off depression and what she emphasizes here is that mindful attention to the touch of the yarn in your hand can help to do that.

Situational Depression; Postpartum Depression

My own experience of depression was that of having a chronic condition. (My official diagnosis was double depression. This means that at the time of the diagnosis I was in the midst of a major depressive episode on top of having dysthymia, a fancy word that basically refers to being in a state of chronic depression lasting longer than two years.) While some people have ongoing chronic depression like me, there are also many people who go through depression once or twice in their lives. It's not an ongoing thing but it's just as devastating. We've already seen how Margaret Mills experienced situational depression after a series of life difficulties culminated in caring for her convalescing mother. And we've seen how unemployment lead to self-esteem and depression issues for Em. But perhaps the most well known type of situational depression is one that we haven't talked about yet – postpartum depression.

Postpartum depression is a form of clinical depression that begins shortly after giving birth and can last several months or even longer. I emphasize that this is "clinical" depression because it's far more than just the so-called baby blues. Having a newborn in the home can be tough for anyone. The lack of sleep, the constant demands on your attention, the self-doubt you may go through as you learn to parent a new child ... it's tough and it can lead to stress and feeling down some days but this normal set of "blues" is different from postpartum depression. Postpartum depression, like other types of clinical depression, is a pervasive feeling that can include sadness and crying as well as anxiety, irritability, self-esteem problems, sleep issues and more. Women suffering from postpartum depression may have thoughts of suicide or even thoughts of harming their baby, feelings that are more extreme than what would be considered a normal part of the "baby blues".

Crochet can be healing to people dealing with postpartum depression for the same reasons that it is healing for any other type of depression. It can provide meditative, calming benefits. It serves as a focal point to reduce anxiety. It can offer self-esteem boosts. A new parent has a lot on her plate and crochet is a nice crafting option because it is possible to fit small projects in here and there, even if you're a mom on the go, since it's also a portable craft. A ball of yarn and a hook added to a diaper bag can provide much-needed relief in stressful situations as you try to go about normal life while dealing with postpartum depression. And as we talked about before, crochet is an affordable craft, which is important since money is a concern for many parents of newborns.

Rachel Brown of the blog Maybe Matilda (whose full story you can read on the page titled *Meet Rachel!*) explained to me how crochet helped her through postpartum depression. Rachel comes from a family with a history of depression but she hadn't expected that she would experience it. Then her son was born. She explains what happened:

> "I hadn't prepared myself at all for the thought that I might be anything other than blissfully happy when he was born. He was perfect and beautiful and healthy, but he also had awful colic -- and combined with my completely inaccurate ideas about what having a baby would be like and the work it would require, I quickly fell into a terrible depression.
>
> Motherhood wasn't at all what I had expected. I hadn't known I would be so desperately tired all the time, or that it would take weeks for my body to recover from the labor and birth itself,

or that the sweet cherub I had imagined having would scream and cry 23 hours a day, or that it would take months for me to resume a normal lifestyle and schedule and feel ready to tackle even the simplest tasks.

I also found myself struggling with extreme anxiety and insomnia--I simply couldn't relax, and couldn't stop my mind from racing with doubts about my mothering abilities, feelings of worthlessness, and even debilitating fears of unlikely events occurring like SIDS claiming my baby or him being kidnapped or harmed. I started having nervous breakdowns and panic attacks, and was frightened by how helpless I felt in the face of depression.

My husband was as supportive and understanding as he could be, but my PPD was very much my own struggle . . . his reassurances and support did help me to a degree, but could only make a dent in my problems. I remember sitting down with my husband and making a list of things that made me feel happy in the midst of my PPD, and deciding that I would experience at least one or two of the things on my list every day. Some of the things on my list were exercising, leaving the house without the baby, even just getting out of my pajamas every day (which felt like such a huge undertaking) . . . and a big one was crochet. I found that if I crocheted every day, I felt remarkably better.

PPD made me feel terribly anxious, jittery, unable to focus, and worried, but crochet was so comforting and soothing. I could just sit and focus completely on the stitches in my hands and forget about how awful I felt the rest of the time. It was something so simple and ordinary, and I wasn't creating anything huge or impressive, but it helped to reduce my anxiety and allowed me to relax for the first time since my son's birth. Even with him crying in the background, I could sit down with my crochet work and feel a bit of peace and calm. I couldn't obsess over my own thoughts and feelings when I was concentrating on the work in my hands."

Ah, did you notice that last sentence? Rachel said that she couldn't obsess over her thoughts and feelings if she was concentrating on her crochet work, showing yet again how the distraction of crochet can take your mind away from the thoughts that are causing depression whether your depression is chronic or related to something specific like postpartum.

I want to reiterate here that I'm by no means suggesting that crochet alone is going to cure something like depression, including postpartum depression. It's one tool in the toolbox. You may find that it works or that it doesn't. You may find that it works for awhile and then it doesn't. I recently read a related story by 70-year-old Gretchen Houser who shared her experience of postpartum depression with blogger Katherine Stone for the Postpartum Progress website. It was more than 40 years ago that Houser went through postpartum depression but she remembers it clearly. Back then, in the 1960s, there was no postpartum diagnosis so Houser just had to figure out what was happening with her on her own. As she puts it, "There has been no postpartum Brooke Shields on my horizon, offering poster-girl encouragement; only fearful days and nights, falling one after the other in slow succession." She turned to knitting as one way to deal with the surge of depressed feelings that were overpowering her.

For Houser, knitting worked for awhile. She had taught herself to knit because the cast on, knit one, purl one helped heal her in what I think is much the same way that the yarn over helped heal me. She made everything from potholders to Barbie doll ponchos. But eventually even knitting became too hard for Houser. Everything became too hard for Houser. She ended up in the ER, was diagnosed with "neurasthenia" (a sort of catch-all diagnosis of the time for those mental health issues that weren't yet named) and eventually found a self-help group that aided in bringing her out of her postpartum depression.

I share this story because I'm under no illusion that just knitting or just crochet or just trying to keep it all together on your own is going to be enough if you're dealing with true depression. After all, I kept it together for over ten years with various distractions (for awhile, again) but eventually that all crumbled. Crochet and any other crafts or hobbies that may help you in coping with depression are not answers alone and of themselves. But knitting helped Houser for a time and crochet can help other people with their symptoms as they get through the worst parts of depression and let other things (therapy, medication, whatever it may be) take their hold and finish the healing process.

Meet Rachel!

Rachel Brown hadn't anticipated that becoming a mother would leave her in the grips of postpartum depression.

Rachel comes from a family with a history of depression but she hadn't expected that she would deal with any form of it. Then her son was born. She explains what happened:

> *"I hadn't prepared myself at all for the thought that I might be anything other than blissfully happy when he was born. He was perfect and beautiful and healthy, but he also had awful colic -- and combined with my completely inaccurate ideas about what having a baby would be like and the work it would require, I quickly fell into a terrible depression.*
>
> *Motherhood wasn't at all what I had expected. I hadn't known I would be so desperately tired all the time, or that it would take weeks for my body to recover from the labor and birth itself, or that the sweet cherub I had imagined having would scream and cry 23 hours a day, or that it would take months for me to resume a normal lifestyle and schedule and feel ready to tackle even the simplest tasks.*
>
> *I also found myself struggling with extreme anxiety and insomnia--I simply couldn't relax, and couldn't stop my mind from racing with doubts about my mothering abilities, feelings of worthlessness, and even debilitating fears of unlikely events occurring like SIDS claiming my baby or him being kidnapped or harmed. I started having nervous breakdowns and panic attacks, and was frightened by how helpless I felt in the face of depression.*
>
> *My husband was as supportive and understanding as he could be, but my PPD was very much my own struggle . . . his reassurances and support did help me to a degree, but could only make a dent in my problems. I began seeing a therapist and was prescribed an antidepressant, which I felt hesitant to take. I don't have a problem with people using medication to help with mental or emotional problems (many of my family members use them to help cope with depression), but I felt very scared at the thought of becoming reliant on medication. I had been happy before my son was born, and I felt strongly that I could be happy again without medicating if I could just*

manage until my son's colic had passed.

I remember sitting down with my husband and making a list of things that made me feel happy in the midst of my PPD, and deciding that I would experience at least one or two of the things on my list every day. Some of the things on my list were exercising, leaving the house without the baby, even just getting out of my pajamas every day (which felt like such a huge undertaking) . . . and a big one was crochet. I found that if I crocheted every day, I felt remarkably better.

PPD made me feel terribly anxious, jittery, unable to focus, and worried, but crochet was so comforting and soothing. I could just sit and focus completely on the stitches in my hands and forget about how awful I felt the rest of the time. It was something so simple and ordinary, and I wasn't creating anything huge or impressive, but it helped to reduce my anxiety and allowed me to relax for the first time since my son's birth. Even with him crying in the background, I could sit down with my crochet work and feel a bit of peace and calm. I couldn't obsess over my own thoughts and feelings when I was concentrating on the work in my hands.

I can't remember an exact moment when I realized how healing crochet was for me (one of the many downsides of not getting enough sleep as a new mom is having a terrible dearth of memories from those months!), but I just remember thinking one day that crochet had saved me in a very real way. I had been sinking deeper and deeper into depression, but the peace and happiness I felt when I was crocheting were enough to lift me out of it for hours afterward. I remember my husband telling me I ought to go crochet something when he could tell I was getting too stressed or depressed--I viewed it as my antidepressant."

Rachel had learned how to crochet awhile back. She is a crafty woman and when she saw a pattern for a crocheted headband that she wanted but didn't want to pay to have made, she decided to learn to crochet. A little while later she saw her sister-in-law crocheting a blanket and she realized that the idea of "snuggling up under a blanket and working on creating something beautiful" had definite appeal. In fact, it's the process of making something from nothing that she has found to be most healing. She says:

"I love buying a skein of yarn, which is quite literally nothing -- just a lump of fibers -- and turning it into something beautiful to keep or give to someone I love. I also love the repetitive nature of crochet; I think that is what makes it so soothing for me. It doesn't require much thought, but it allows me to just sit and focus on something simple and distract me from any problems outside of the pattern I'm working on."

Rachel also enjoys the true handcrafted aspect of crochet.

"One thing that drew me to crochet was the "homeyness" of it, for lack of a better word. It feels like a lost craft to me -- most people wouldn't dream of crocheting a blanket for their new baby when they could just pick up a blanket at Wal-mart, but I love the old-fashioned notion of spending time to create things for the people you love and big events in life.

I definitely express my love for others through handmade gifts. I feel that crocheting something for someone I love lets them know I love them so much more than simply buying them a present would. I also have felt a sense of connectedness through crochet. I actually don't know very many people in real life who crochet, but I've connected with new friends through the Internet who inspire me with their creativity and passion for crochet."

Rachel has made her way through to the other side of postpartum depression but she continues to use crochet as both a form of self-care and an enjoyable hobby. She says:

"Even now, my husband will send me off to crochet if I'm having a bad day, or am in a bad mood. I love to crochet, even if it's not as "therapy," and it brings me a lot of joy as a hobby, but I also love knowing that I have that activity to turn to when I need to de-stress."

If you're interested in connecting with Rachel, you can find her over at her lovely blog: www.maybematilda.com.

Crocheting through Grief

There is one type of sadness that all of us must go through at one time or another and that is the sadness that is associated with grieving. Life is unfair. We all have to lose someone close to eventually. Death leaves no stone unturned, no heart untouched. We all know that there are many stages of grief and many ways of coping through it and although this isn't necessarily truly a form of depression in the clinical sense it's worth looking at in terms of the potential value for crafting through grief.

In some cases, crafting is literally the only thing that you feel like you can do when you're grieving. You need to be busy but you are too distressed to do much of anything. Crafting can be a touchstone activity for you during this time. Author Ann Hood has described this terrifically in both fiction and non-fiction. She lost a daughter and shared her true story in a memoir called *Comfort*. She had previously shared some of this story in a fictional version called *The Knitting Circle*. In these terrific books she shares how the activity of knitting, and the social support of being part of a knitting group, can help through the grief of such a devastating loss. Actually, *The Knitting Circle* is probably the first book I read that really introduced me to the idea of needlework as such a powerful healing force. I had just started to crochet when I read it, and I already knew somewhere deep inside that it was healing for me, but *The Knitting Circle* put those thoughts into words.

Ann Hood wrote *The Knitting Circle* as a novel in which the main character is largely based on herself. This character has lost a five-year-old daughter to a rapid illness, just like Hood had back in 2002. After reading *The Knitting Circle*, I also read Hood's memoir of this loss, *Comfort: A Journey Through Grief*. I actually liked this book better out of the two. It's a much shorter read (I read it in a night) but it's raw and emotional and really shares the true feelings of grief and the true beauty in the memories that Hood has of her daughter. In *Comfort*, Hood devotes a chapter to explaining how she began knitting as a way to help her through the grief. She starts off her needlework story by saying, "knitting saved my life." Sound familiar? I had actually forgotten all about her saying this until I re-read the book recently, after I'd already named this book. But it doesn't surprise me, because I do believe that needlework can be a lifesaver. I'm not the first person who said it and I doubt Hood was either! I certainly hope neither of us is the last.

In any case, Hood shares an experience that I went through as well, about how words failed her and that's in part why she had to turn to crochet. Hood is a writer by trade and she had always loved books for information and comfort but in her deepest periods of grief, she simply couldn't read or write. Sentences didn't make sense. She couldn't form coherent thoughts. Every single word turned to an image of the daughter that she had lost and that turned to tears. My situation with depression was different from her situation with grief but I, too, had found that the comfort I'd normally found in books just wasn't there for a period of time. I could read for distraction sometimes but mostly I didn't remember what I read even long enough to get to the end of the page. So I found comfort in keeping my hands busy with crochet as Hood did with knitting. (Ironically, I read *The Knitting Circle* first at this time and remembered very little of it so I had to read it again when I started researching for my own book.)

There is something else that Hood says in *Comfort* that really clicked with me because I've heard it so many times - she had never planned to learn to knit. I've told you already that I didn't specifically seek out crochet; it just kind of came to me as an idea when I needed it most. And Hood's experience was similar. She says in *Comfort*, "Learning to knit had never occurred to me before Grace died. Needles, thread, yarn, scissors, all belonged to a world that was not mine. When a button fell off a coat, it stayed off. When pants needed hemming, I paid a tailor to do it." But then randomly in a fit of needing something to do to get her mind off of the loss of her daughter for even a moment, Hood started calling knitting stores and letting people know that she needed to learn how to knit and soon she was learning from a local yarn store owner.

Let me digress here for a moment to say that local yarn stores can be truly wonderful places. Oddly enough, I appreciate this about them immensely even though they aren't actually my personal cup of tea. I usually visit the LYS in any town I'm visiting. (LYS is the term us yarnies use to refer to the local independent yarn store as opposed to the big box yarn stores such as Michael's. I'll add here that there are often classes and groups at those big box stores as well so I wouldn't rule them out but in general the really close knit - so to speak - groups are going to be found at the LYS.) The local yarn store is a haven where you find these magically luscious yarns that have been carefully selected by the store owner, who is usually (but not always) a middle-aged or older-but-always-spry woman who has opened this business not to make money but to stay as closely connected to possible with her craft and the community that surrounds it.

Most, but not all, local yarn stores that I have been in have some place that you can sit down and knit or crochet, either during scheduled classes, drop in nights or at any time that the store is open. The first LYS I ever went to was Greenwich Yarn in San Francisco and the first thing I saw when I entered was a table with some women chatting over their needlework. I would later see this same scenario at nearly all hours of the day in yarn stores across the nation. But even if there is no group inside of your LYS, there's almost always a super helpful woman (or occasionally man) who works there who is more than happy to help you figure out what yarn you might want or how to measure the amount of yardage you're going to need or even how to do a certain stitch or technique.

Now different crocheters have had wildly different experiences with their LYS, which is also something I didn't learn about it until after I'd already been crocheting for awhile. What I found out from other people was that there are crochet-friendly yarn stores and ones that aren't so crochet-friendly. A crochet-friendly yarn store will have books, hooks and other resources for crocheters. It will also offer crochet classes and have someone on staff that can answer crochet-related questions for customers. In the past, most local yarn stores were owned and operated by knitters (many still are, although I don't know if "most" still applies). Although a crocheter uses the same yarn as a knitter, there wasn't always that same experience of being able to go in and ask questions. A new knitter could walk into an LYS and say, "I don't even know how to cast on" and get immediate help from the person behind the counter whereas a crocheter asking how to do a basic crochet stitch might get a befuddled look. In my experience, this isn't really true anymore. Others will argue with me.

Many people tell me that there are still many local yarn stores that are not crochet-friendly. Maybe I've been lucky. I do live in a city with more than half a dozen LYS options. And I actually don't care to ask a lot of questions or get in-person help so I don't even really use my LYS options and therefore don't really have that same experience that true LYS fans have. That said, I believe that there has been at least some growth in the availability of resources, including people with knowledge, at many local yarn stores across the nation. Most yarn stores seem to offer at least basic crochet classes and have someone on staff or at least someone the owner knows who can answer crochet questions. I share all of this because I've heard so many stories from knitters that are like the one Ann Hood shares about learning to knit from the LYS owner inside of a store filled with yarn. While it's not my experience or my desire to have that experience, I can see how it would be a soothing, healing, encouraging and wonderful experience for many people. And I don't want crocheters to be discouraged, thinking that they have to learn to knit instead to have such an experience. If you do go to your LYS and have a negative experience with the (what I believe to be rare) crochet-unfriendly shop owner, rest assured that there are crochet-friendly options out there. Call the shops near you to find out if they have a crocheter on staff or a crochet drop-in night or ask around on social networking sites like Facebook and Ravelry to get recommendations for a crochet-friendly LYS in your area that can offer the comfort that you might be seeking. Ann Hood shares in *Comfort* that she was actually driving about thirty miles each way to go to the yarn store where she learned to knit.

So in *Comfort*, Hood explains that she learned to knit because she needed something that she was capable of doing to get her through the grief period immediately following the loss of her daughter. And she shares something insightful that I loved to read: "A week later, I was struggling through a scarf. I made a mess of it, randomly adding stitches, dropping stitches, then adding even more. When I showed up with this tangle of wool, Jen pulled it off the needle and all my mistakes were miraculously gone. Unlike life, at least this new life of mine – in which I was forced to keep moving forward through the mess it had become – knitting allowed me to start over again and again, until whatever I was making looked exactly like I wanted it to look."

I think that what Hood explains here is so powerful and true about crafting not only through grief but as a means of healing from many other things. You can always start over. In fact, it's even easier to start over with crochet than with knitting because the work rips back so simply to pretty much any point where you'd like to start over. You can't go back and re-do that terrible day when someone died or when a relationship ended or when you lost your job but you can go back to that loop where you accidentally forgot to increase or did a double crochet where you meant to do a single crochet and you can start that over and do it right. It's a little thing, a gesture, but it can be so important at the right time.

I mentioned that I liked *Comfort* more than *The Knitting Circle*, which isn't a surprise because I generally tend to prefer memoirs to fiction. However, I will say that *The Knitting Circle* is the better book for getting insight into how powerful needlework and groups of needleworkers can be for healing from all sorts of things. The experience of knitting is a footnote, although an important one, in Hood's grieving story in Comfort but it is the focal point that carries the thread of the story in *The Knitting Circle*. The main character is based on Hood herself but in this book she meets a group of women that she crafts with and the full length of the novel gives us the opportunity to find out the story of each of these women and the role that knitting plays in helping them heal in those stories. We see how grief and loss can be experienced in so many different ways and how needlework can help no matter what the type of loss is.

I am certain that women have been using needlework to heal for as long as thread has been around. And Hood hints at this history in *Comfort* when she shares a true story that she read in a book called The Art of Fair Isle Knitting, written by Ann Feitelson. The story is about eight Shetland Islands fishermen who lost their lives in a storm back in the late nineteenth century. The women that they left behind needed to find a way to support themselves financially while also dealing with the impact of this massive loss. They turned to knitting. Hood quotes Feitelson as saying, "focusing on the knitting in one's lap keeps death and uncontrollable forces at bay." Of course, knitting can't prevent death but it helps take the mind off of the horror of loss for at least a moment and when you are grieving every moment of reprieve is important.

Hood's story is about knitting but any craft that keeps the hands busy can be healing through a period of grief and crochet is definitely that way as well. Laurinda Reddig (see *Meet Laurinda!*) is a crocheter who has worked through her own grief by combining crafting with community.

Laurinda had a daughter, Rowan, who died on the same day that she was born. Her brief life was spent in the NICU where she was wrapped in a handmade blanket. The touching gesture of that handmade comfort reached a part of Laurinda's heart and immediately lodged in her mind. She immediately knew that she wanted to help crochet blankets for others in the same position as a way to help them while healing herself. She taught a group of women in her life how to crochet so that they could help her with the project. This gave the women a way to be there for Laurinda during her time of grief and it gave Laurinda a focus for helping her get through that time.

Laurinda's project, Remembering Rowan, has grown over the years into a wonderful commemoration of her daughter that provides gifts to many terrific causes but focuses, of course, on handmade crochet blankets for parents who lose newborn children. Laurinda loves the act of crochet and the excitement of new projects but in this case what really helped to heal her was having a focused community crochet project that could help others and give her something to work on. Talking is sometimes the last thing you want to do when you are grieving. Crochet groups provide camaraderie and closeness without requiring you to talk.

Of course not everyone wants to be with others when they are grieving. Some people want to be alone, and crochet works for them, too, because it can be a solitary activity. A woman named Rita shares her experience of that with blogger Melissa McColl on the Close Knit blog. She says that her anguish after her daughter's death was so unbearable that she couldn't stand to be around anyone else, to the point where she didn't leave the house and would just order anything she needed online. Crochet was something that she turned to in this time, sitting there for hours and hours, stitching to pass the time until her grief became more bearable. She shared, "For every stitch I made there was a tear, yet somehow crocheting soothed my soul and my heart."

Laurinda had her daughter for only a day. Rita had her daughter for 31 years. For both, the pain of losing their child was unbearable. And for each, crochet was a way to get through that indescribably awful time.

Not everyone can relate to losing a child but a lot of adults have already lost their parents and know what that grief is like. I am lucky in that I haven't gone through that experience, yet, but I've talked with people who have and they've said that it causes you to almost lose touch with who you are because the root of who you are is now gone. Crochet can be a way to handle that loss. That's especially true if the parent that you lost is the one that taught you how to crochet or is someone who used to crochet with you but it can be healing even when that is not the case.

One of the most touching stories I read about crocheting through the loss of a parent was from a 1975 newspaper article by Judy Werley who shared the story of Mrs. Lena Casilli who learned to crochet after her father died. The journalist writes: "Totally depressed," she said, "following the death of my father, all I did was sit around and cry. I couldn't seem to snap out of it. One of my sons brought me an afghan kit and suggested I try doing that. That kit sat around for so long. I just looked at it and decided I couldn't do it," she commented. "I think my sister-in-law really got me started on this," she continued. "She kept telling me it was relaxing and not hard."

Werley goes on to share that Casilli struggled through the initial steps of learning how to crochet but she received a lot of encouragement and support from the people she had left in her life. Her sister-in-law gave her the instructions to get started. A neighbor taught her how to hold the hook so the yarn wouldn't slide off. Another neighbor showed her "how to keep colors separate so they didn't run into each other." And what was really touching was that everyone in the family wanted to help Casilli stay busy as she grieved the raw loss of her father so they all kept asking for her to crochet afghans for them – and of course, she did. Casilli is quoted as saying it was "the best therapy ever." Within six months, she was skilled enough at crochet work that she created her own pattern to make a full-sized flag all on her own. She had also taught nearly a dozen other people in her life to crochet and found that helping them was also healing. At the end of the article, which was written seven months after she had started to learn to crochet, Casilli said that she still thinks of her father just as much as she did before but that she could relax anyway just by picking up a crochet hook.

Another common loss that I've seen eased in part through crochet is the loss of a spouse. Many older women find themselves living past their husbands and needing to find a way to spend their time as they deal with the loss of someone they've lived with for thirty or forty or fifty years. Crochet is something that many of these women did anyway, having learned it as children, and it is something they can turn to in this time of need. A 2011 newspaper article by Lois Kindle shared the story of Abby Wright, a woman who used crocheting for charity as a means of dealing with the loss of the husband she had been married to for 66 years!

Abby Wright had been married more than six and a half decades when her husband Henry passed away in January 2009. She understandably went through a deep period of depression. She also went through a painful physical fall and she ended up with a doctor who severely overmedicated her. It was a rough time. However, she eventually got a better doctor, entered a grief support course and started to turn her life around despite the loss of the partner she'd been with for nearly her entire life. It was in early 2010 that a friend contacted Wright and asked her if she would like to crochet caps for newborns. That was the start of her crafting for charity and it's something that's been crucial to helping her live a full and fulfilling life since her husband died.

Through her grief group, Wright had seen the value of a support system when grieving. And through crocheting for charity, she had seen the value of using her time to help others. She put the two together and got about ten friends together to crochet caps for charity, something that they continued with over time. They had made hundreds of caps by the time that the article about her was written. The great experience of doing this led Wright into doing many other volunteer acts as well. She bakes for a Sunday school group and raises money for community projects. I can't imagine what it would be like to be married to someone for 66 years and then to lose that person. I can imagine, however, that crochet could be comforting in the time of any loss, even one as great as that.

Yet another newspaper article tells the story of yet another woman who crocheted (and also knitted) through the loss of her loved ones. The 2007 article by Stacey Palevsky tells about 97-year-old Jean Soffa who was part of a needlework group in her residence at the Jewish Home in San Francisco. The group would meet once a week to craft together, talk, and socialize. Crafting as a means of healing was familiar to Soffa who is quoted as saying: "It's my whole life. When my husband died, I took to knitting. When my mother died, I took to knitting. I'm wrapped up in it. In knitting." Later in the article she is quoted as saying, "If I go through any trouble at all, I run right away to the knitting and crocheting." Although she doesn't specifically speak in the article about how the crafting helps her, it's clear that it's something that she turns back to for comfort when she experiences a devastating loss in her life.

Meet Laurinda!

Award-winning crochet designer Laurinda Reddig had crocheted for most of her life and it was something she relied on heavily to help her get through her grief after losing a child. She created a project around this that now helps other woman going through the same thing. And she has taken her work to the next level by also becoming a published crochet designer.

Laurinda has a lifetime of crochet experience. She was in junior high when her campfire leader first taught her how to crochet. In high school a friend taught her the great niche of tapestry crochet. Later she joined the Society for Creative Anachronism, which taught her bead crochet, and she took various trips to Mexico where she developed her skills in lacework. She put these skills to work by teaching crochet classes through Michael's Arts and Crafts for several years after she had graduated from college.

Laurinda's love affair with crochet continued over the years. She sold items through local shops and craft fairs. After the birth of her first child she began to crochet toys and accessories, creating her own patterns. In fact, she ultimately decided that she wanted to focus primarily on crochet design, rather than creating items for sale online or locally, because she finds great joy in the creative process of making new designs rather than repeatedly crocheting the same items. When friends have asked her to make items for them she offers instead to teach them to crochet.

So crochet is an integral part of Laurinda's life but it became critically important for her after she lost her daughter. Rowan was born full-term on August 10, 2008 but she never took a breath due to a problem with her cord at the end of the labor. Laurinda explain this delicate and touching experience and how it came to be linked with crochet:

> *"She spent her one day of life in a Neonatal Intensive Care Unit (NICU) where she was given a crocheted afghan, which she was wrapped in while they examined her. When they rolled me into the storage closet to choose a hand-made quilt for Rowan as well, I was already thinking about making blankets with my local MOMS Club to donate. I had recently become the Administrative Vice President of the Club, which meant it was my job to come up with Service Projects to give back to our community. Our Club had been looking for a project*

that could be personal to members of the Club, and nothing could be more personal than the loss of a child."

Although the creative healing wheels were already turning in Laurinda's mind at that time, for the most part she was numb. She says:

"In the early days, I remember walking through stores, seeing normal, happy people, and wondering if I would ever feel that way again. I am normally someone whose default expression is a smile, unless I have a specific reason not to smile. So it felt very strange to be around other people with a blank expression. I felt like I was carrying this weight I could not share with anyone else."

She found that the new blanket project that she started with the MOMS club gave her something positive to focus on during this time of grief. It also gave her a way to connect to the other women in the group. They were all mothers and felt sympathetic to the terrible thing that Laurinda was going through but they weren't always sure what to say or how to help. The project gave them a tangible way to assist Laurinda through this difficult time.

Laurinda taught the members of the MOMS club how to crochet. She says,

"Some MOMS who learned to crochet in November of 2008 had made 4 blankets by the time we had a Reception and Show at our local library, to show off our blankets before our first donation in March of 2009. I have always derived a lot of pleasure from sharing my passion for crochet with others. I get a giddy feeling helping a new crocheter find that "aha!" moment when they really begin to enjoy my favorite craft. Having a couple dozen members of my MOMS Club (and some dads) so excited to learn to crochet just so they could make blankets for Rowan's Project was an amazing feeling. Teaching them and focusing on our project gave me something positive to focus on as I worked through the grief of losing our baby.

Even those MOMS who were not up to crocheting found ways to help by donating yarn to the project or helping me contact hospitals about donating. We expanded the project to make quilts with the help of our local Quilt Guild, and no-sew fleece blankets for Foster Children, which allowed more members to participate. But the focus has always been on crocheting blankets and hats and teaching moms new creative skills."

Laurinda reiterates that focusing on this project was crucial to helping her get through the experience.

"Rowan's Blanket Project gave me something positive to focus on whenever the grief was too much. Telling people about the project, planning, and teaching gave me a way to talk about our loss without feeling guilty that I was burdening others. I had more than one person thank me because naturally they had no idea what to say when I told them about losing Rowan, but talking about my Project helped ease the difficult conversation.

People say that the loss of a child is the worst thing any parent can face. Yet somehow when it is a newborn, even full-term like Rowan, they seem to expect you to get over it sooner. The anniversary of a loss is naturally the hardest time. Each year around Rowan's birthday, I have come up with a different way to donate in her memory. In 2009 we made our 1st donation of crocheted and knitted blankets in March. We had the local Quilt Guild come teach our MOMS to quilt, and spent every Wednesday working on quilts that summer, as the first anniversary of Rowan's birth and death approached.

By 2010, my 2nd daughter was born in January, and many of my close friends had babies around the same time. With so many little ones I decided to try something smaller, making cat blankets to donate to the Humane Society. My new daughter's favorite animal and first word was cat, and I like to think that Rowan would have loved cats like her sister. In the weeks before Rowan's birthday, I challenged my crochet friends to make 7 cat blankets in 7 days, and collected 139 8"x17" blankets. They are a great learning project for new crocheters because they are quick and cats do not care if the stitches are perfect.

In 2011 I was helping to plan my little town's 1st annual Quilt & Fiber Arts Festival. They offered to collect 9" squares for us to make into blankets to donate. This inspired me to design my first Rowan's Sampler blanket as a Crochet Along on my blog. I wanted to give all those moms who had learned to crochet for our first donation the opportunity to learn something more than double crochet and granny squares. For the next 16 weeks, I posted instructions for a new 9" square every Friday, to be completed in time for the Festival which happened to fall the weekend before Rowan's 3rd birthday.

I encouraged others to make the squares for themselves or to donate anywhere they wanted to, and was pleased to have crocheters from as far as Germany complete the blanket. I even received a surprise package of squares sent from a crocheter I had never even met. This year I plan to self-publish Rowan's Learn To Crochet Sampler, to be sold as a fundraiser for future projects.

Continuing to donate even a few blankets in Rowan's name each year helps us keep her memory alive. Being able to inspire others with my designs to donate locally, or learn a new stitch or technique is one small way in which I feel like I can be a mother to my daughter who never came home. Her brief life has touched hundreds of lives already, mostly through crochet.

Laurinda has clearly done some great work through crochet by teaching others this great skill and donating projects to people and places in need. She personally loves the tactile sensations of working on a project although it's the designing and planning that make her most excited. She loves designing a pattern and then using many different yarns to make it. She's the first to admit that actually finishing a project isn't nearly as easy for her but of course she's motivated by the knowledge that she'll be sharing the finished gift with someone in need. She shared:

"I also attach a label to each blanket we donate, which can still be the difficult, slow part for me. As I hand stitch our Remembering Rowan Project tag onto each blanket I am reminded that the parents who receive these blankets will likely be saying goodbye to their own little baby. I do not believe that will ever get easier. But I attach the tags because I want the recipients to be able to find us. I never was able to find who made Rowan's afghan and quilt."

Recently Laurinda's been channeling her energy into submitting her designs to local magazines and competitions. She shares some good news:

"I submitted two of those designs to the CGOA's annual Design Competition in 2011. They both won awards, including 1st

place in the Afghans category and the People's Choice Award. Motivated by that success, I quickly began submitting my designs to publishers and have had several accepted to be published in various crochet magazines, as well as the Toys and Bags books in the new Fresh Designs Crochet Series being published by Cooperative Press."

A recent update to this story is that Laurinda was the Grand Prize winner of the 2012 CGOA design competition, winning with her Reversible Rowan Tree Vest. Grief is an ongoing process with many stages. How poetic that crochet has been the same thing for Laurinda.

If this story has touched you, make sure that you check out the Remembering Rowan project at RememberingRowan.blogspot.com.

Note: The Fresh Designs Crochet Series mentioned by Laurinda is the same series that is edited by M.K. Carroll who also shared her story in this book.

Cultural Malaise

Before I wrap up this first lengthy chapter on depression, I thought I'd talk about one more type of depression: socio-cultural depression. Like grief, this isn't necessarily strictly a type of clinical depression but it's got many of the same symptoms and can also be treated, in part, possibly, with crochet. In fact, one of the sources we looked at earlier on dealing with depression actually also talked about this type of depression. It was in the Whole Living article, where neuroscientist Kelly Lambert is quoted as saying: "Hands-on work satisfies our primal craving to create solid objects; it could also be an antidote to our cultural malaise."

Cultural malaise is a tough condition to understand but it's basically a widespread social feeling of discomfort whose cause might not quite be clear. It's linked to the philosophical concept of anomie, which basically describes a feeling of disconnectedness between the individual and his or her society. There are plenty of texts out there on this concept but we'll keep it simple here and talk about a common concept that most of us are familiar with to at least some degree: the rat race. Many of us have experienced the feeling that we are racing through our lives trying to keep up – to pay the bills, achieve career success, be on top of the latest technology and keep up with the so-called Joneses. And many of us have felt the nagging feeling that something isn't quite right, that the fast-paced race of our society doesn't jive with our inner needs. This is what is at the root of modern cultural trends like returning to simple living, trying out beekeeping and urban farming and building roots in our communities to strengthen our ties with others. That indescribable nagging feeling of unhappiness is cultural malaise (or socio-cultural depression).

Cultural malaise is difficult to define and even more difficult to solve but there seems to be some answer in returning to a handcrafted way of life that connect us to the generations before us and the people around us today. Many of us have found that crochet can help. I call cultural malaise a form of social depression because it reminds me so much of my own experience of depression. People struggling with cultural malaise often don't recognize it as depression but they know that something isn't "right", just like I didn't know that I was depressed but did know that things were not "right" with me. These people are striving for something "more" and they don't have it and they want it and they feel off kilter because of it. This may lead to frustration or fatigue or anxiety in the same way that depression leads to those things in individuals suffering from the condition.

People of any age group can be afflicted with this feeling of cultural malaise. However, two groups that are particularly susceptible to this are teenagers and the elderly. For teens the problem is a general feeling of anomie or angst as they try to define themselves in relation to their parents and the wider world. For the elderly, it often stems from a feeling of uselessness as they age. They can't do the things that they were once able to do and they may struggle to keep up with technology and the changing times. These groups feel marginalized by society and therefore more at risk of being affected by cultural malaise.

Crochet can help us in dealing with cultural malaise in a variety of ways. It is part of the handmade movement that many people today feel is at the root of combating this social feeling. It provides a tangible way to slow down and to create something with your hands. It provides a sense of connection to the generations before you because almost everyone has a mother or grandmother or aunt who used to crochet. It opens up the opportunity to connect to others around you today through crochet groups. And it gives you a way to feel like you can be useful to society through crocheting for others, something that can help battle feelings of pointlessness that are related to being wrapped up in cultural malaise.

Nessa was someone I interviewed who really benefitted from the feeling that her crochet work had connected her with others in her family. Although her experience was in battling depression related to MS, I think her experience of crafting for connection is relevant to how it may benefit us as a society looking for ways to connect to others. Nessa explained that depression caused her to feel like her body was lying to her and she ultimately decided she had to look to sources around her that had never lied – her family being first and foremost. She wanted to know what they had done to cope through difficult times. Nessa shares:

> "This journey of self-discovery has led me, emotionally if not physically, back to my roots and my family many times. Being

separated by 4,000 miles and by the death of many who were instrumental in influencing me in my childhood has, I believe, strengthened my connection to the skills and crafts that were often the backbone of the identities of so many women, not only in my own family, but of the women who represented the character and feeling of the entire Place that made me "Me." Sewing, quilting, and crochet were an American way of life and surrounded me when I was growing up and had seeped into my own character and make-up. My mother's sewing table was home to me. I had no idea how to use it myself, but I could rely on it being there, along with my mother, and her needles, thread, fabrics and yarn.

When I was young, I didn't like the look of crochet. It stood for tacky toilet paper cozies or old-fashioned doilies. It was something that my mother, my aunt and my grandma did, and I was trying, at that young age, to stand independently separate from my family and make my own identity. So I never learned how to do it. In my mind it would not be a useful tool in the life that I was planning for myself, a life in the workplace, in the city, in fashionable social circles. This is what I imagined for myself. But younger than I could have imagined were these dreams picked apart by illness, by depression, by disability. And when my dreams of career and success were picked apart until there was barely anything left of them, the memory of my mother, my grandmother and the sewing and craft table remained.

After nearly two decades of feeling different to the rest of the world, of having job after job fail, all ideas of an actual career shattered, of having my physical and emotional identity shift on me over and over again, I became drawn to the stitching that never shifted, to the one thing that had never changed in all of my life, despite the losses. The one thing that had never changed was my family. I decided to find my identity in them and in home, despite death and distance. I decided to learn the skills my mother knew, and knew that once I had learned, there would be at least one thing that illness could not take away from me."

Nessa touches on a lot of important things here. She touches on the value of connecting to others, not just in your life today, but also by carrying on traditions that connect you to people of other generations. And she touches on the whole idea of how returning to a handmade way of life, or at least of instilling portions of that in areas of your life, can bring you a sense of identity that helps to eliminate depression whether that is diagnosable individual depression or a vaguer sort of social depression.

I want to end this chapter by mentioning an amazing video project called 7 Billion Others that does a great example of highlighting the value of social connection, both in the immediate sense of being connected to your own loved ones and in the larger sense of being connected to the entire world as a human being. This project, which took more than five years to complete, consisted of interviews of more than 5500 people in nearly eighty countries and over fifty different languages. Each interview consisted of the same forty questions designed to get at the core meaning of life across generations and cultures. For example, people were asked the purpose of life, the definitions of love and happiness and what things in life they would consider unforgiveable. What the videos (some of which you can watch online at http://www.7billionothers.org/) reveal is that there are simple themes in each of our lives that truly connect us all, despite any differences that we might perceive.

I first learned about this project (which at the time was called 6 Billion Others) through a September 2011 newspaper article by Amanda Gonser who had just seen an exhibit of the videos. She shared some of the stories that impressed her and touched her the most. The one that stood out for me was when a girl from Argentina answered that the one day in her life that she could not live without was the day that she sat on the front porch with her grandma and learned how to crochet. It's such a simple thing, in its way, but I think we can all relate to how something simple like that can be profound and its deeper meaning can be translated in any language. I think crochet connects us, and we may not even realize as we do it and share it with others that it's touching them in a way that they will remember and treasure forever, but it does.

Meet Nessa!

Nessa is a woman in her thirties who started dealing with depression in high school. She later learned that the depression was linked to Multiple Sclerosis. Although she's been dealing with the problem for over fifteen years, it can flare up again at any time. For example, she recently tried a new MS treatment that had disastrous mental health consequences. Crochet played an instrumental role in helping her to cope with what was otherwise a very traumatic health experience.

Nessa shares her story here in her own words:

"My journey with depression began in 1992 when I was 16 years old and in high school in the U.S. I believe now, almost 20 years later, that this was my first symptom and sign that in a few years I was to develop Multiple Sclerosis. MS is a neurological condition that causes the body's immune system to attack its own nervous system leaving it scarred and causing progressive disability. Depression in MS is now recognized as not only a reaction to being diagnosed with a chronic condition, but as a direct symptom of the condition, a result of various changes and damage to one's brain and nervous system.

Not knowing the damage that my own body was physically wracking on my brain, no medical advice was sought. I was not diagnosed as having depression by a medical professional until I was 21, so I went unsupported by counselors or medication and knew that I would have to find my own ways to cope with life. My personal interests as a musician were often more a source of feelings of failure to me than a useful tool for combating the depression that was making life so difficult. I moved my University studies from America to the UK in an attempt to change something in my life that might alter the downward spiral I felt I was on. I decided to remain abroad and the UK is still my home today.

In 1996, I was diagnosed with Multiple Sclerosis after several attacks of severe symptoms and the revealing of clear clinical evidence on my MRI brain scan. My medical diagnosis of depression came in 1997 and with these two diagnoses I began on my long and difficult journey of self-discovery, recovery and a continuous rewriting of my life along with the ebb and flow of each condition. Finding the best way to live at every stage of this journey has had to be a proactive process of trial and error and of self-discovery and self-understanding.

My experience of depression has decided and dictated the way that I have lived my life over the past 20 years and in ways I would not have chosen for myself. Depression and MS have been so intertwined at times that it has become difficult to understand whether one is affecting me or the other. Both have created hurdles and setbacks, and the cycle of setback to failure to depression to setback to failure, and so on, has been nearly impossible to break free from. Depression breathes lies to the person who possesses it, holding them back and telling them that they cannot do things and that they are worthless. Learning that these are lies, regardless of the feeling of their truth, and learning how to counter the lies over the years has, in a way, metaphorically led me home. The people who had never lied to me were my family. Of course, they had made mistakes, but they had never lied to me, unlike my own brain and body. What was important to them? What got them through the trials they had known? And there had been many trials.

This journey of self-discovery has led me, emotionally if not physically, back to my roots and my family many times. Being separated by 4,000 miles and by the death of many who were instrumental in influencing me in my childhood has, I believe, strengthened my connection to the skills and crafts that were often the backbone of the identities of so many women, not only in my own family, but of the women who represented the character and feeling of the entire Place that made me "Me." Sewing, quilting, and crochet were an American way of life and surrounded me when I was growing up and had seeped into my own character and make up. My mother's sewing table was home to me. I had no idea how to use it myself, but I could rely on it being there, along with my mother, and her needles, thread, fabrics and yarn.

When I was young, I didn't like the look of crochet. It stood for tacky toilet paper cozies or old-fashioned doilies. It was something that my mother, my aunt and my grandma did, and I was trying, at that young age, to stand independently separate from my family and make my own identity. So I never learned how to do it. In my mind it would not be a useful tool in the life that I was planning for myself, a life in the workplace, in the city, in fashionable social circles. This is what I imagined for myself. But younger than I could have imagined were these dreams picked apart by illness, by depression, by disability. And when my dreams of career and success were picked apart until there was barely anything left of them, the memory of my mother, my grandmother and the sewing and craft table remained.

After nearly two decades of feeling different to the rest of the world, of having job after job fail, all ideas of an actual career shattered, of having my physical and emotional identity shift on me over and over again, I became drawn to the stitching that never shifted, to the one thing that had never changed in all of my life, despite the losses. The one thing that had never changed was my family. I decided to find my identity in them and in home, despite death and distance. I decided to learn the skills my mother knew, and knew that once I had learned, there would be at least one thing that illness could not take away from me. I knew that regardless of the lies of failure and worthlessness that I was hearing, regardless of the loss of mobility and balance and eyesight, I could create. I could create and give and no lie would make me believe that creating and giving was worthless. It was concrete, it was tactile; it was full of meaning and delved right down to the root of my identity. The things that I began to create were more than their physical selves. I could give something that stood for a piece of me to the people who meant the most to me. In the midst of all of this feeling useless and a failure, I could create something good and useful and beautiful and skillful, and it gave me meaning.

So I learned how to crochet and I began to stitch. And I began to create. I could see my physical accomplishments accumulating and I could not deny that they were good. I would learn a pattern and spend hour after hour just playing out my life, one stitch at a time, moving forward. The act of learning how to just complete the stitch I was on, not looking too far ahead and not looking back, felt like it was teaching me a new way to live my life. Just one stitch, one moment, at a time, not allowing the huge overall pattern to overwhelm me, but to just keep going, and it would come to completion. Have faith that I would get there and I would ... but not if I skipped ahead and started thinking about a later stage of the pattern, which would make me forget how to complete the stitches I was making now.

And when I would sit and stitch square after square for a blanket or row after row for a scarf, it was almost as if I was helping my brain to relearn how to use its broken and scattered neurological pathways. The repetition of 3 double crochet, chain 2, 3 double crochet, chain 1... it was soothing, methodical and meditative. The colors and feel of the yarn made me feel like I was home and that I fit once again and the pleasant click of my favorite red, aluminum hook against my wedding ring as I hook the yarn that weaves through my fingers is audible, tactile and grounding. There is no room for worry, for grieving, for regret, for analyzing when I focus on one stitch at a time. The process of healing takes precedence."

Just recently Nessa has gone through another transition in her health. In August 2011 her MS went into relapse. After a rough period, she regained much of her function but she has not been able to resume walking. As a result, she has had to learn to adjust to life in a wheelchair. She reiterates that crochet gives her something to cling to as she deals with this new adjustment.

Nessa blogs at The Last Burnt Sienna Crayon: http://burntsienna.wibsite.com/.

Breathe! Yarn Over! Crocheting to Soothe Anxiety

Anxiety. Ugh.

If I was hesitant to mar my self with the label of depression, I was even less willing to add the problem of anxiety after the name on my mental business cards. Anxiety, when you are not going through it acutely, seems silly. From the outside, it is easy to think, "just suck it up" or "how melodramatic" or "everyone feels anxious about meeting someone new/ public speaking / getting on planes" ... But the reality is that anxiety is a serious problem that can become debilitating, both when suffered seriously on its own and when combined with other types of mental health issues such as depression, Post Traumatic Stress Disorder, etc. Anxiety is anything but silly when you are suffering from it.

In the throes of my depression, I did become anxious. I was anxious about decision-making. I was anxious about trying new things. And I was anxious about socializing with others. Although everyone I knew considered me to be an extrovert who easily made friends, I often found myself terrified at the idea of going to a new place where I would have to engage with new people. I forced myself to do it when I was feeling well but it was too hard to continue forcing myself during my depression. As the depression worsened, I began to really suffer from social anxiety.

What does this mean? Well, for me it meant that I knew that I needed to connect more with people, both those already in my life and new people, but the idea of actually doing it terrified me. I cannot count on my hands and toes the number of meetings that I set up with people and groups only to find myself cowering in my bed, ignoring the phone and trying to figure out if I was even going to bother to make some excuse for why I couldn't make it. Then I would feel bad about the fact that I'd stood someone up, which would naturally make me more anxious about trying to see them and the cycle could perpetuate itself.

I remember one experience acutely, which I hinted at earlier but will share fully now. I had made half-plans with a sort-of friend to get together for dinner. In my mind, the plans had been non-committal and vague so when he sent a text message asking if we were still getting together I didn't respond right away. I wanted to say yes but then I really didn't want to see him. Social anxiety meant for me that I wanted to just stay in my bed and not even have to deal with the pressure of saying "yes" or "no" to meeting up with someone. When he sent a text message saying that he was heading over, I should have responded. But the depression was weighing down on me and I felt like a response was impossible. I turned off the phone. I turned off the lights. I closed the blinds. I hid in my bed alone in my apartment with some crime drama on my computer screen and my mind whirling around with thoughts of feeling bad. By the light of the 13 inch screen I began to hook a line of yarn into a chain and then the chain into a row of double crochet stitches and then the row into many rows.

My friend showed up. He rang the doorbell but the doorbell at that apartment was notoriously problematic so I figured it wasn't a big deal to say later that I just hadn't heard it. Then he started throwing pennies at my window. They hit the window repeatedly for nearly an hour. It irritated and upset me. I got angry with him for "just showing up" (although in fairness we'd had half-plans and he'd text messaged to say he was on his way). I got angry with him for continuing to try to see me for nearly an hour after I clearly wasn't answering. And really, what was I going to do at that point? In my social anxiety was I going to get dressed up and go downstairs and say, "hi, how are you doing?" after he'd been throwing pennies at my window for half an hour? Not likely. What I was going to do was slide deeper down beneath the covers on my bed, turn the brightness of the screen up just a tiny bit to better see the yarn and hook in my hand and keep on making row after row of double crochet. I kept thinking, "go away, go away" but tried to replace that with the repetition of "yarn over, through, yarn over, through, yarn over, through."

My half friend eventually left. And eventually I realized that I wasn't angry at him so much as I was angry at the depression, the anxiety, the fact that I didn't even know what I wanted when it came to friendship. I couldn't do much else that night but I crocheted a scarf to warm myself, creating another layer of crochet between me and the big, mean world "out there." It would be months before I could deal with the emotional stress of getting in touch with that friend again, months during which I made many scarves. When I did, it was fine. It was not a big deal, even though my anxious mind had made it so.

Now for me, this experience was all mostly about depression and the anxiety was just kind of a by-product of that. But the experience did give me some insight into the problems that people have when they are dealing with social anxiety. And social anxiety isn't the only type of anxiety that people may suffer from. There is immediate anxiety in the form of panic attacks. And there is also situational anxiety, where you might not typically be an anxious person but when dealing with a specific situation - such as a pregnancy - you begin to suffer from severe anxiety around the situation. All of these different types of anxiety can be relieved to some degree through crochet. In particular, social anxiety seems to lend itself well to the healing power of this craft.

Crochet and Social Anxiety

When I talk about social anxiety, I'm talking about the fear of interacting with other people and the way in which anticipation of doing so or actually doing so can make you feel extremely worried and stressed. Clinically there are different types or levels of social anxiety but the disorder is generally professionally described as "the extreme fear of being scrutinized and judged by others in social or performance situations" (ADAA). It's worth noting that social anxiety, however mild, is still more extreme that just normal apprehension about being around people. Almost everyone gets nervous when meeting new people or going into new settings but people with social anxiety are suffering from a more intensified version of that natural apprehension and it may limit them. When the social anxiety is persistent and extreme then it may be diagnosed as a true disorder, called either social anxiety disorder or social phobia. Most people who suffer from it obviously aren't at the extreme but even mild social anxiety can make it difficult to complete necessary tasks, meet new people and develop a solid social structure for oneself.

And there are a lot of people who are suffering from social anxiety. The Anxiety and Depression Association of America (ADAA) reports that anxiety disorders are one of the most common mental illnesses in the United States and that social anxiety is one of the most common forms of anxiety. They estimate that nearly 7% of the population, or about 15 million people, suffer from social anxiety. A 2007 ADAA survey found that more than one third of the people suffering from the condition will wait ten or more years before getting help, just struggling along the best that they can. So if you feel like you might tango a little bit with social anxiety then rest assured that you are not alone. And based on my experience and research, I'd wager a guess that if you show up to a crochet group or other type of public crafting group that you will find at least one other person there who grapples with social anxiety too.

San Francisco has a wonderful craft group called Crafting in Public that was started by Alice of the blog Future Girl Crafts (http://www.futuregirl.com). This group of people meets twice a month at a café for a few hours to craft and converse. I learned about it long before I actually went and checked it out. I had been meaning to go for months but had kept putting it off. I had legitimate reasons for putting it off but if I were to honestly look at the real reasons behind those reasons I'd admit that I was still a little bit anxious about starting something new. The anxiety isn't founded in any real, specific fear. I'm not afraid that the people I meet won't like me. I used to be afraid that I wouldn't like the group or event but I've come to accept that I'll like some things and not like other things and I'm okay with that. So the anxiety isn't really about anything; it's just kind of there. And because I did have the experience of more intense debilitating anxiety, I understand a little bit about how that tiny flicker of it that made me put off going to my crafting group can grow bigger and more immobilizing for many people.

Perhaps that's why my ears perked up to notice that more than half of the group members at this meeting mentioned that they liked the meeting specifically because it gave them a focused activity to enjoy with other people who also liked it, providing an immediate topic of conversation in a safe setting that helped to relieve their social anxiety. The group is a mixture of crochet and knitting lovers who also do some other crafts so the benefits of the group aren't limited to crochet but for the purposes of this book we'll focus on the crochet part. More than one of the gals in the group on that first night that I went said that she really didn't consider herself a social person but felt like there was a need in her life to know more people. Going to a group scared them (to different levels, running the gamut from my putting-it-off anxiety to true escalated-panic feelings of terror) but they were able to get themselves to overcome that fear because they were meeting up with a group of other people who crochet. Crochet was safe, it was purposeful and that focus made it possible to go to a group get together with a goal in mind even though going to the group meeting was difficult.

The benefits of this experience are tremendous. First of all, there is a huge benefit to just overcoming your fear and getting out there and having a positive experience. The more positive social experiences that you have, the more confident you are going to feel in dealing with such situations when they arise anew. You may always feel socially anxious but if you have developed a history of skills that led to social success then you will feel safer continuing those skills. The thing about anxiety is that if you are able to push past it and do new things then you are able to increasingly expand your world of experience and each next new thing usually does not seem quite as bad. In contrast, if you are incapacitated by your anxiety and don't find a way to push past it then your world gets ever and ever smaller and even things you used to do comfortably now begin to provoke anxiety and feel impossible.

Another benefit of joining a crochet group is that there is an advantage to your mental health in increasing both the size and quality of your social group. Having a strong support network is crucial to positive mental health. As someone who has worked from home for more than a decade and relocated away from my hometown to a place where I knew almost no one, I know how difficult it can be to create your own support network as an adult ... and also how vital it is to have one. This type of social group seems especially important for people suffering from problems like depression and anxiety due to the fact that when those problems are at their worse the person may not feel any ability to go out and meet new people but they may feel safe enough to show up to the crochet group where they've developed relationships over time.

Putting yourself out there in this way with a new group of people is difficult and those folks suffering from social anxiety find it especially hard. But the very nature of the crochet group relieves a lot of the anxiety-causing pressure. The three key features of such a group that make it easier for people with anxiety are:

1. You can focus on the work in your hand if you are shy.
2. The common interest that you share provides a safe topic of conversation.
3. The crochet community is a loving, kind, generous community.

Let's explore those things further, looking first at the simple fact that meeting up to crochet with someone provides you with a task during the group. Yes, you may end up engaging in a lot of conversation with the group but the nice thing about this type of group is that you don't really have to talk if you aren't comfortable with talking. You can just crochet loop after loop and participate silently in the group in that way. People who are never sure what to say or who feel really anxious when the attention is on them can benefit from this key aspect of a crochet group. The group doesn't mind. They'll turn their heads and listen if you do want to talk or they'll talk around you and let you listen or maybe nobody will talk at all because everyone will be focused on following the patterns for their projects.

In 2011, Natalie of the blog Definatalie.com launched what she called a "Stitch and Twitch" – a weekly pubic crafting group specifically for people who struggle with social anxiety. One of the people who joined the group was her friend Sonya Krzywoszyja who shared her experience in an article for Lip Magazine. She reiterates the value of how crochet and crafting groups help you to become more comfortable with who you are and how you are. She shares, "I'd like to say when I'm at these meetings I completely forget all my social anxiety issues and all of my appearance issues, but I'd be lying. However, they're not as bad as they usually are, because I am in a non-judgmental space. In this space, I feel free to be myself, loud or quiet, lady-like or not. I find that so rare and difficult to do lately that I'm so happy whenever I get the chance."

When you do want to talk, there is the built-in topic of conversation over your shared interest in crochet. This is a nice, safe topic. You aren't forced to delve into your mental health issues, your relationship problems, your lingering childhood traumas, the details of the job that you hate, etc. etc. You can just talk about crochet, a topic that you enjoy and the other person enjoys and you can build a solid friendship based on that shared interest. Remember when I mentioned back in the chapter on depression how I was so happy about finding crochet in part because it gave me something, anything, to talk about other than depression? It was such a relief (to me and probably to the people in my life!) to not be talking about depression, the fact that there's not much point to living, the problems with the man I was dating that were making me depressed ... I can see how having a nice safe topic where you don't have to tell your life story to strangers would be appealing in a setting where you are meeting up with a new group.

In their Guide to Our Theories So Far, Betsan Corkhill of Stitchlinks has something terrific to say about this: "Some of you have cured agoraphobia, panic/anxiety attacks while others use your portable crafts as a way of managing symptoms should they occur. In fact you tell me that the perception of you by others is turned on its head when you take out your knitting or stitching in public – you're no longer seen as someone who's having difficulties, but rather as someone who has a wonderful skill; no longer disabled, but able. Many have also said that this opens up communication channels, so strangers become allies and friends. Simply the reassurance that you have an effective tool at hand can give you enough confidence to face the world without even having to use it."

This makes so much sense to me. When you look at someone on a bus who is sobbing or even just sitting there dejectedly, you see them differently than you would see someone who is productively crocheting away. Knowing this about yourself can make you feel more competent and sane just by virtue of the fact that you've armed yourself with your crochet and know that at least to the outside world you don't look like a lunatic who is about to freak out because there are too many people on the bus and what if the bus doesn't stop where it's supposed to and how are you going to talk to the people at the event that you're taking the bus to in the first place. All of that craziness may still be happening in your mind but to the casual observer you look like someone who is just crocheting something on a bus. This can be a case of "act as if" ... sometimes you have to act as if a trait about you is true until it becomes true. Act as if you are comfortable sitting there crocheting every day on the bus and you just might find one day that the insane anxiety that has prevented you from doing anything at all has actually slipped away for just a minute, maybe just long enough to complete a complicated stitch pattern repeat, and you actually ARE just someone sitting on the bus doing something productive and interesting to the outside world.

And finally, there's point three ... I have found again and again that the crochet community is a really generous and kind community that most crafters feel safe in even when other groups and social situations may make them anxious. People who crochet come from all walks of life and of course there are going to be a few that you meet here and there that just aren't kind but for the most part the nature of the crocheter is a kind and forgiving one. I'll make a scarf and you'll make a hat and we'll live and let live. I'll hold my crochet hook the "pencil way" and you'll hold yours the "knife way" and we'll let each other be. Crocheters celebrate the work that other people are doing with their hooks. They welcome new crafters into their inner circle. They make items to share generously with others. Not all shared-interest groups are this kind and warm and easy to join, in my personal experience, and that can be very comforting to someone who is dealing with the difficulty of social anxiety.

And what is really great in the 21st century is that you don't have to leave the house to be social with people. Sure, it's ideal in many ways to find a local crochet group that you can connect with to feel support in your community. But sometimes that really is too much effort for people suffering from anxiety and the value of a social connection via the Internet shouldn't be discounted. I know many people who have felt their world widen up thanks to blogs, forums and social networks.

In her online article titled "The Healing Arts and Crafts", Margaret Mills makes the point that: "Social connections contribute to our wellbeing, and handcrafters reap an extra benefit by belonging to knitting groups or the guilds associated with many crafts. For those unable to attend meetings due to physical challenges, online groups such as Ravelry provide support and a point of contact with others." Another great website that's relatively new to the scene is Hookey.org, a crochet-specific social networking site launched by Laurie Wheeler (whose story you can read on the page titled *Meet Laurie!*) In addition to various groups that you can join here, there is a text chat room option on this site where you can chat with the main room of people who are online or start private chat conversations with individuals. And yet another twenty-first century option is iYarny, a 24-hour video-optional chat room hosted by Cris of Crochet with Cris (http://crochet-with-cris.blogspot.com/) where you can "meet" with crochet friends to discuss projects or ideas or just to crochet in a room together even though you're not actually in the same physical space. People with severe social anxiety may be able to dip their toe in the water with online groups like these where they can easily flee the scene as needed just by turning off the computer.

Situational Anxiety

As I said, though, social anxiety isn't the only type of anxiety that there is. Another key type of anxiety that crochet can help with is situational anxiety, which can also be called generalized anxiety that gets set off because of a specific situation. For example, there is a program at Alta Bates Summit Medical Center in California that offers crocheting as an activity for pregnant mothers on bed rest who are struggling with anxiety surrounding their difficult pregnancies. These are women who might not normally suffer from anxiety but who are going through extreme anxiety because of the specific high-stress situation in which they find themselves.

When the Alta Bates program first began, founders Gay Rose Soque, RN, and Jeff Sanders, COTA, were really just looking to help their in-bed patients pass the time. However, according to a 2006 *Advance for Occupational Therapy Practitioners* article titled "Crafting Care" written by Candy Goulette and Jessica LaGrossa the group's two founders quickly saw that the patients' symptoms decreased once they picked up their crochet hooks. Sanders specifically reported that he had seen a decrease in anxiety among patients who participated in the institution's craft program, explaining that a key benefit is that it gives them the chance to focus on making something for their babies, helping them to develop a personal relationship with the life growing inside of them and reducing some of their anxiety. He says, "Some come here and because they are high-risk patients who have not committed to having the baby - they have not personalized their relationship with the baby - they are focused on the medical problem ... But when they get into the knitting and crocheting, suddenly they are thinking of the baby." So it seems that what the crochet is doing is helping the mother to get her mind off of her worries (similar to stopping the "cycle of rumination" that we talked about in the chapter on depression). She can focus on what's in her hands and then can focus more calmly about the life that is growing inside of her because the crochet has taken her mind off of its singular focus on all of the things that could go wrong with the pregnancy.

So crochet was beneficial in reducing anxiety for those women in part because it gave them a focused, soothing task. But the social component of joining a crochet group was also something that helped to decrease anxiety among these women. In the past the women on this bed rest ward of the hospital really didn't see one another; they were just doing their own thing in the hospital, surely stirring up that "cycle of rumination." However, in 2007 a support group began to bring the women together once a week to talk to each other. This helped reduce anxiety because the women could clearly see that they weren't the only ones in the situation they were in. They could get outside of themselves and have a more objective perspective on what was going on with their bodies and their babies. The women in the group began bringing their crochet work to the group. Once they did, they began to talk even more openly about what they were going through.

When I muse on this, I think about crochet as a sort of fence from behind which we can talk to our neighbors. If you don't have a fence between you and your neighbor then you may feel awkward about conversing together. You may wave hi from a distance but you are less likely to walk right up close to them and talk intimately. In contrast, a low fence between you gives you a sort of meeting place. Each of you knows that you're going to remain on your own side and so you can feel safe and comfortable enough to engage in chatting. A relationship begins. I think crochet provides a fence of sorts. When you are just sitting in a room talking to other people, you erect your own boundaries to protect yourself. Having yarn and a hook in your lap is sort of like having a fence. You don't need to throw up your own boundaries anymore and so they relax a little and you open up more to the people around you.

Research supports this idea. Stitchlinks' Corkhill shares in her summary of the group's theories that, "Reports from teachers and other group leaders also suggest that communication is improved when knitting in groups. I think this could be down to the automatic nature of knitting. Being occupied at a certain level appears to prevent the brain from applying its normal prejudices and limitations, which helps to lower barriers, making it easier to talk more intimately. Knitting is also one of the few activities that enables eye contact as you talk and knit. This could have implications for developing future therapies for those who find it difficult to talk."

Talking with others in a safe setting about what you're going through, especially when they are going through the same thing, is definitely a key way to reduce anxiety around a situation. If crochet or other needlework facilitates that then it's a tool we should keep in our personal toolboxes to pull out and use as needed.

Pregnancy is just one example of situational anxiety. There can be any number of things that trigger fear in us and set off a bout of anxiety. For example, Donna Rodgers of the blog Comin' Home: Sharing the Art & Heart of Homemaking wrote a post in 2009 titled *Crochet ... The Perfect Solution for Anxiety*, in which she talked about the difficulty of dealing with her father's illness and ailing health. She said that she initially didn't think she could do anything as she dealt with the shock of the changes in her life and the fears they caused but that she found that crocheting caps allowed her to relieve the stress of the situation and reduce the anxiety surrounding what was going on. Next time that you find yourself in a doctor's office or a hospital waiting room, take a moment and look around and I'll bet that you see someone knitting or crocheting. Those are places where people naturally feel stress and anxiety and stitching can be a great way to cope with the waiting period of finding out what is medically wrong with you or your loved one.

In my research I met a wonderful woman named Liza who shared her story of using crochet to help deal with the terrific anxiety she experiences when she goes through temporary bouts of blindness due to a currently undiagnosed medical condition. Here is some of what Liza shared. (Learn about her on the page titled *Meet Liza*!)

> "The first time I lost my eyesight I thought I was also going to lose my mind. As a mother of two, a wife, a gardener, a professional, a crafter and a volunteer, my eyes are everything. I sat in my living room thinking of all the plans I had for the day and how nothing was going to get done, that day or perhaps ever. As I sat there, my foot hit the basket at the side of my sofa and there I found a purse I had been working on for a piece of sanity. I started to work on it. Very slowly I began to feel the stitches in my hands, the rounds, and the growth of the project.
>
> I felt the need of the yarn to form each stitch, very slowly at first and soon with ease, which worried me. It became easier and easier and I was certain that someone was going to ask me what was the mess I was making. The purse was a simple messenger

style bag made with half double crochets. My vision began to return slowly, first in gray colors and then sepia tones. I didn't dare look at the project I was working on for the mess that I thought I would see, so I continued with my eyes closed. Day 3 since that first episode I finally peered in the basket ... not bad. My bag was almost complete! I was impressed. Not so much with the fact that I had been able to crochet while blind, but with the fact that those first forty-eight hours just flew by.

Crocheting kept me busy counting, feeling the stitches back and forth to make certain that I had not skipped or doubled, and keeping the yarn from knotting. I had no time to feel pity and worry about what was to come. I had no time to make lists of everything I had to do. I just needed to concentrate for those two days on my project; I needed to know that I was still useful. Once I realized that I could crochet simple projects without my eyes, I knew I could do other things too."

Liza may not have had anxiety before her illness but it's understandable that it set in when she found herself going blind. She didn't know if the blindness would pass. She didn't know what it would mean for her life if it didn't. Anyone would get anxious about that. Liza found that crochet helped her and she has been able to use that to help her ever since.

Illness like Liza's can definitely cause the onset of anxiety. My dad went through an experience with temporary blindness as well and he gave me some insight into the thought process behind the anxiety. My dad was a diabetic. (I say "was" because he eventually had a pancreas transplant that effectively eliminated the diabetes he'd lived with for more than twenty years.) Because of complications with the diabetes, the small blood vessels in his eyes would burst and the blood would cover his vision, leaving him partially or entirely blind.

So my dad might be going about his day, running a machine down in his woodshop or driving his truck, and the blood vessels could burst and leave him unable to see. The word he used to describe what he felt during this period was "despair" but it is clear that he also felt anxiety. Without his sight, he couldn't do the things that he would normally do. He couldn't build furniture or drive. What would happen in his brain was something along the lines of, "I can't work. I can't drive. I can't function. I can't start over my life as a blind person at this age. I can't have the same life I've always had. What if the blindness is permanent ..." The blindness wasn't permanent but when it would go away, the anxiety would remain. "What if it comes back again? What if I'm driving and I go blind behind the wheel?"

The situation for my dad wasn't the same as Liza's, since he knew the source of the problem (officially called diabetic retinopathy), but it had its own complications. The biggest one was that the more that the doctors tried to do to fix the problem, the worse the problem became. For example, at one point the doctors tried to go into his eyes and cauterize the vessels with a laser to stop the bleeding but the surgery had the opposite effect, causing his eyes to actually bleed more. And so the anxiety doubled, because now the thoughts included, "should I try to get this taken care of? What if the doctors can't fix it? What if they make it worse? What if surgery does permanent damage?" And around and around it went.

My dad doesn't crochet. He is a woodworker and tried to work as much as he could but of course it's risky to operate that type of equipment when you can't see. So one of the things that he turned to at this time was music. Much of my childhood is characterized by the seemingly constant memory of my dad sitting outside, cigar puffing away, strumming at a guitar or a banjo or maybe a dulcimer. I consciously know that he didn't do this every single night of my life but sometimes I remember it that way. And I do know that during the time when his eyes were bleeding he would often be out there with his guitar, focused in that moment of just keeping the hands and mind busy as a means of coping with the stress and anxiety of health conditions he couldn't control. In the end, dad got his eyesight back. He had a vitrectomy and the problem went away, the anxiety becoming a distant memory over the years.

But it shows how a trauma related to illness can cause anxiety. So can other traumas. In doing my research I also met a special woman named Fran who endured the trauma of a brutal sexual attack. Since the attack she has been dealing with symptoms of Post Traumatic Stress Disorder including anxiety, panic attacks and flashbacks. I'll talk a little bit more about crochet for PTSD in a later chapter but for now I'll say that Fran has been able to use crochet to help her through her struggles, specifically in her experience with anxiety. Fran's anxiety is worsened by the fact that (at the time of this writing) she is dealing with the ongoing high-stress criminal case to bring her attacker to justice. Having to relive what she went through and dealing with the question of whether or not he will have to pay for his crime creates undeniable and understandable anxiety for Fran. Fran focuses her mind by purposefully crocheting small items for others in need. Easy, small projects give her a manageable thing to do to bring herself into the current moment and remind herself that there's nothing to be anxious about right now since she is just sitting there, pulling one stitch after another up onto her hook and making an item that will be ready to send off to someone else soon. While some crocheters may not be able to relate to what Fran went through, we can all relate to the soothing relaxation that occurs when we crochet and can see how that might help Fran and other women like her.

Meet Liza!

Liza has an undiagnosed condition that causes her to periodically experience temporary blindness. Crochet has helped her cope with the anxiety and stress she experiences during those times because she knows that if she can crochet blind then she can do other things blind as well. It gives her a sense of competence and calm that battles the anxiety of the situation.

Here is the story that Liza shared with me:

> *"I wanted to let you know the role crochet has played in my life just recently. I am a new crocheter. Despite having a mother who is a professional seamstress, an avid crocheter and knitter, and all around crafter, I didn't take up crochet until after I was married and had my first child, 7 years ago. Because I work and now have two children, I do not consider myself even an intermediate crocheter. In my opinion, I am a newbie. I usually crochet late at night when everyone else is asleep and its mommy time, which means I am usually tired too. As a result, projects go uncompleted or take months to complete.*
>
> *On Valentines Day 2011 I temporarily lost my eyesight. My doctors expressed concerns over MS but as of July 2011, I do not have a strong diagnosis as to why I lose my eyesight on both eyes from time to time. I also become light sensitive (it could be a mild form of MS and a type of migraine, but they just aren't sure yet.).*
>
> *Luckily, I can still crochet with my eyes closed.*
>
> *The first time I lost my eyesight I thought I was also going to lose my mind. As a mother of two, a wife, a gardener, a professional, a crafter and a volunteer, my eyes are everything. I sat in my living room thinking of all the plans I had for the day and how nothing was going to get done, that day or perhaps ever. As I sat there, my foot hit the basket at the side of my sofa and there I found a purse I had been working on for a piece of sanity. I started to work on it. Very slowly I began to feel the stitches in my hand, the rounds, and the growth of the project.*
>
> *I felt the need of the yarn to form each stitch, very slowly at first and soon with ease, which worried me. It became easier and*

easier and I was certain that someone was going to ask me what was the mess I was making. The purse was a simple messenger style bag made with half double crochets. My vision began to return slowly, first in gray colors and then sepia tones. I didn't dare look at the project I was working on for the mess that I thought I would see, so I continued with my eyes closed. Day 3 since that first episode I finally peered in the basket ... not bad. My bag was almost complete! I was impressed. Not so much with the fact that I had been able to crochet while blind, but with the fact that those first forty-eight hours just flew by. Crocheting kept me busy counting, feeling the stitches back and forth to make certain that I had not skipped or doubled, and keeping the yarn from knotting. I had no time to feel pity and worry about what was to come. I had no time to make lists of everything I had to do. I just needed to concentrate for those two days on my project; I needed to know that I was still useful. Once I realized that I could crochet simple projects without my eyes, I knew I could do other things too. I have had two more episodes since that Valentines Day; but now I know better. I have slowed down during those other episodes and used the time to crochet ... to count stitches and let the time roll around my yarn. I know that this too will pass and in the end I will have a great little project actually finished on time."

Meet Fran!

There is no easy way to describe what happened to Fran. She was brutally raped and it left her with both physical and emotional pain that she is still healing from. She always loved to crochet but since the rape it has become a crucial part of her healing process, allowing her to help others as a way of regaining her own personal power and healing herself.

Fran went through one of the worst experiences that a human being can go through. She was heartlessly raped by a salesman at a well-known company. The attack was vicious. Her virginity was stolen from her in a violent invasion that left her bedridden, with a wound VAC on her spine for the next several months. (A wound VAC, also known as negative-pressure wound therapy, is a sealed dressing with a drainage tube that uses vacuum suction to help heal difficult wounds.)

But we all know that the emotional damage of a traumatic situation can be as devastating as the physical wounds and Fran has had a lot of that to deal with. She developed PTSD and suffers from panic attacks and flashbacks. She has to cope with anxiety as well as depression. These emotional conditions are worsened by the fact that she can't just pause her life to heal but is also dealing with an ongoing high-stress criminal case to bring her attacker to justice.

Fran had always enjoyed crochet as well as other crafts. She used to do very intricate work. She embroidered The Last Supper. She did praying hands out of needlepoint. And with crochet she would work on dainty cross bookmarks, detailed doilies and intricate scarves and large afghans. But things changed after the rape. She could no longer work on such detailed projects. Part of this was physical; she had lower energy, for one thing. But a lot of it was emotional. She says that after the rape she really lost sight of what beauty is and what beautiful things there are in life. It was too hard to find the beauty in those detailed projects anymore. She knew somewhere deep inside that crochet was healing for her and she wanted to use it therapeutically but she had to change the way she crocheted to adapt to her new mind.

She has found a way to do that. She has focused on crocheting small items with a specific purpose in mind, crafting special things to give to others in need. This gives her immediate help with healing because it provides a focus for her hands and mind. And it does long-term psychological good by reminding her that she has the power to help others and no one can take that away from her.

Fran works with Sandie of Crochet Cabana (http://crochetcabana.blogspot.com/) to do ongoing charity crochet work. She tries to crochet one square per month to send to Sandie and then Sandie joins the squares together to make blankets and scarves for donation. A recent project that she did was to crochet teal squares because teal is the color for rape victims. Fran says:

> *"I remember when Sandie had crocheted me a beautiful prayer shawl after I was raped. I cannot put into words the comfort that that shawl has brought and brings to me to this very day. I hope that the teal scarf will do that for some other victim as the prayer shawl has done for me."*

Fran has worked hard to heal herself. She is going to physical therapy and counseling. She is doing the work that she needs to do to get well. She is relying on the help and support of people like Sandie and her former pastor to help her trust people again. And she is using crochet to heal herself and others one stitch, one square, at a time. Eventually Fran hopes to get back to doing her more intricate crochet work. She has her sights set someday on opening an online store to sell her crochet work. Hopefully she will achieve that goal but even if it's a long time in coming she is helping people right now, today, with her crochet donations.

Generalized Anxiety Disorder

I have to be honest in saying that I wasn't sure when laying out this book about whether or not to create different sections for different types of anxiety. Ultimately, the reason that crochet works for any type of anxiety is the same across the board. And yet, the conditions are all a little bit unique from each other. (And actually later on I'll include an entire section on OCD, which is actually a form of extreme anxiety). Since the conditions are unique, I think it's worth looking at how people with each of the different types of anxiety can utilize crochet. So now I'll talk about Generalized Anxiety Disorder (GAD).

In contrast to social anxiety, generalized anxiety disorder doesn't mean that you're necessarily worried about interaction with others (although your ability to do so can be hindered). Instead, according to the Anxiety and Depression Association of America, GAD means that you are excessively worried about everyday things. You may be worried about money or your health or problems at work. Of course, everyone worries about those things but people suffering from GAD worry about them to the point where it overtakes their minds, making it difficult to function. The ADAA explains that, "Sometimes just the thought of getting through the day produces anxiety. They don't know how to stop the worry cycle and feel it is beyond their control, even though they usually realize that their anxiety is more intense than the situation warrants." And GAD is diagnosed if those feelings persist for six months or more.

In many ways, GAD is the same as the anxiety that I've called situational anxiety in the previous section. The worry is the same but in the case of situational anxiety the fear is about a single specific thing (like a difficult pregnancy) or it has been triggered by a specific situation (such as a rape). With GAD, there may be no obvious cause of the problem and yet the excessive worry is there.

One of the women that shared her story with me for this book was Martha Stone (see *Meet Martha!* for her full story). She was first diagnosed with Generalized Anxiety Disorder in 2003 and used medication to help get her through that tough time. GAD is something that can be controlled with medication and eventually you can get better and not need the medication anymore. That's what happened for Martha.

However, she had a relapse of her condition in 2011. She immediately went and got medication but the medication takes a couple of days or even a couple of weeks to kick in and Martha had to deal with her anxiety until then. In fact, when the anxiety struck this second time, Martha's husband was out of town and she had two young children to take care of so she needed to get her mind under control quickly, much more quickly than the meds alone can do. So she turned to crochet.

Recalling that time, Martha says that she knew she needed to do something that would keep her mind busy to reduce her anxiety. Almost everything felt too difficult. She couldn't choose a book to read. She didn't want to do a craft like rubber stamping because her desk was cluttered and the idea of having to clean it just stressed her out more. She didn't want to occupy her mind with laundry because it was a dull task that didn't sufficiently keep her mind busy. But crochet worked. She could stitch something for someone else, so she did. She noticed that with each stitch her heart rate would slow down from its anxiety-racing pace and her body would become calm. Anytime that Martha feels anxiety like that coming on again, she now immediately reaches for her hook.

Another story I read that talks about crafting through anxiety is the memoir by Kathy Gleason called Obsessed: A Tale of OCD, Knitting and Inappropriate Men. Gleason shares her experience with a combination of obsessive-compulsive disorder and generalized anxiety disorder, characterized by panic attacks. She tells the details of her panic and obsessive thoughts but the majority of the book is really about the many poor choices that she made in romantic love affairs throughout her life. Perhaps the reason that I enjoyed the book was because she did the same thing that I did in some ways – surrounding herself with crazy, dramatic situations and people who were "sicker" than she was as a self-medicating distraction for the mind. Gleason doesn't write extensively about her knitting but she does mention more than once that now instead of indulging in dramatic behavior she picks up the needles and yarn.

She says, "Knitting has been such a wonderful soother to my troubled mind that it's amazing to me that more people haven't discovered its therapeutic benefits. I think that in many cases, rather than a prescription for the latest designer anti-anxiety medications, doctors should write out prescriptions for several skeins of soft wool, and for the really desperate, cashmere." Now let me say that anti-anxiety medication can be a wonderful, important, useful thing for many people in many situations. (I would probably still have a mouth full of rotting teeth if I hadn't had anxiety medication to get me through going to the dentist!) After many years of being anti-medication, I'm now 100% for appropriate medication as needed. But I also believe that people who are taking medication for their mental health conditions should also do all that they can to change their behavior and lifestyle to supplement, enhance and possibly eventually replace the medication. So I get what Gleason is saying here.

I wish that experiences with doctors could be different than they usually are for most of us. I wish that we had doctors who knew us so well that they could prescribe the right medication along with a side of therapy and a recommendation to try crochet or some other craft in order to ease the symptoms of our conditions. That's not the way that it works, unfortunately, so the next best thing is for communities of crafters and communities of people struggling with various illnesses to come together in spreading the word about the different options, choices, hobbies and behaviors that help heal them. For me, it's been crochet, so that's what I share.

This makes me think of a Martha Graham quote that I have always loved, which reads: "There is a vitality, a life force, an energy, a quickening that is translated through you into action, and because there is only one of you in all of time, this expression is unique. And if you block it, it will never exist through any other medium and it will be lost. The world will not have it. It is not your business to determine how good it is nor how valuable nor how it compares with other expressions. It is your business to keep it yours clearly and directly, to keep the channel open. You do not even have to believe in yourself or your work. You have to keep yourself open and aware to the urges that motivate you."

I first discovered that quote when I was about nineteen and I promptly copied it onto a pretty photographic background and hung it on my colorful living room. I've been reminded of it again and again since, primarily because I do live a creative life and with that comes much self-doubt about the artistic things I'm putting out there into the world. But I am reminded of it again here for a different reason ... I believe that there is value in sharing your specific story with all of its details (gory, glorious or mundane). Each of us has our own specific story and by telling it honestly, we let other people see the ways in which they can relate to us. By telling others what worked for us and what didn't, we provide suggestions and ideas that may help another person in some small way, whether it's a tangible way (like encouraging them to pick up a crochet hook and craft through anxiety) or a less tangible way (like helping them feel, even for a moment, like someone else understands the crazy way that they experience the world). I liked Gleason's book (and I like memoirs in general) because of this belief that sharing our stories is powerful and important and probably the most human thing that we can do. That's also the reason that I wanted to share not only my own story in this book, but also the stories of many other women who have dealt with a variety of health issues through crafting.

I digress, a bit, but as I write this I'm still thinking about Gleason's story because one of the things that she writes about is how she was terrified to tell anyone about the thoughts that were in her head. She eventually figured out on her own that she had anxiety, panic attacks and OCD. Interestingly, she was willing to tell people about the anxiety and panic attacks because she felt like that was a socially acceptable form of mental illness and something that most people could relate to in at least a small way. She was unwilling, however, to share her OCD and the thoughts that accompanied it, to the point that even when she desperately tried therapy she refused to share those thoughts with her therapist (and subsequently didn't get much out of therapy as a result). She felt like the OCD was shameful and embarrassing and would stigmatize her or make people hate her or get her committed to a horrifying mental institution out of some bad memoir from the 1970s. (I'm adlibbing here but I think that's the gist of what she was feeling.) So she didn't tell her crazy OCD thoughts for a long time and then eventually she did, including through this memoir. And I think that is not only brave but very powerful. My point here is that sharing our stories is healing and that your story matters, no matter how anxious you may be about sharing it!

Meet Martha!

Martha Stone was first diagnosed with Generalized Anxiety Disorder in 2003 and used medication to help her get through it. However, when the condition came on again eight years later, it took time for the meds to kick in. She needed to do something while waiting and crochet was what helped her to get through.

Like many of us with mental health conditions, Martha didn't realize that she had Generalized Anxiety Disorder until things got really bad. She believes now that she probably suffered from it for her entire life but it was in the summer of 2003 that the condition reared its ugly head and forced her to do something about it. She was twenty seven years old and in her third year of marriage when her husband had to move from their shared home in Oklahoma City to work in Seattle for four months. Martha thought that she would be okay, but she wasn't.

After only about a week of being alone in her home, her anxiety started to kick into high gear. She became afraid of being in the house alone. She worried that she would die alone in the home and that nobody would know that something bad had happened to her. She couldn't eat because she didn't like to eat alone. She knew that it was better to be around people and therefore that going to work was good for her mental state but she couldn't always bring herself to get into the car and drive to work. Martha would have panic attacks that included hyperventilating and that would cause her to become dizzy and tingly all over, symptoms that only made her more afraid.

Luckily, Martha had the support of others even though they were not in town with her. She would call her long-distance husband, her sister and her parents at odd hours just to hear someone else's voice and to not feel so alone. Her parents are pharmacists in Texas and they made the smart suggestion that Martha go see a doctor about her symptoms. She took their advice. That is when she was finally diagnosed with Generalized Anxiety Disorder. She was put on medication and it helped solve her physical symptoms. She was able to go off the medication after about six months.

Unfortunately, conditions like anxiety often come back when you least expect them. In February 2011 Martha was stuck inside the house for a week because of a major snowstorm in her area. She wasn't alone this time; she had two young children to take care of now. The same panicked feelings returned. However, she knew what was wrong this time and immediately put a call in to her doctor to get back on medication. The problem with the medication, though, is that it takes about two weeks to kick in. With young children to care for, Martha had to do something else to get her panic under control until the meds began to work. And this is where crochet came into play.

Once again, Martha's smart parents made a wise suggestion that changed her life. They told her that she needed to "do something." Martha needed to stop sitting around at home ruminating on her worries. In her own words, Martha shares:

> *"My dad suggested that whenever I felt a panic attack coming on, I should go read a book, fold the laundry (isn't there always laundry to fold?), stamp some cards (my other crafting love is stamping/card making) or crochet. My mom suggested going outside and getting some sun. Everything sounded just way too difficult to go do, except crochet.*
>
> *To read a book, I'd have to decide which one to start (too many choices); laundry meant just laundry (ugh); rubberstamping meant I'd have to clean off my stamping desk; it was cold and snowy outside so that left crochet. I needed to make some wrist warmers for my sister anyway, so I pulled up a simple pattern (love Ravelry!) got some of my sock yarn from my stash, grabbed a hook and got to work. I realized that as I counted the stitches my heart rate had dropped (racing heartbeat is part of my attacks) and I was feeling much better. I think for me, this was really the best craft to have served as my distraction. It took a minimum of supplies that were readily available to me, I could do it in my living room on my comfy couch, and I was making something for someone I loved.*
>
> *I have always loved crochet, ever since my grandmother taught my sister and me many years ago. I don't know how many feet of foundation chains and single crochets we made! I really enjoy making crochet items for people. In fact, I very rarely crochet anything for myself. I did keep 2 pair of the 10 or so pairs of wrist warmers I made that winter! I think in some way I have always known that making something for someone makes me happy; it was just nice to realize it during my high anxiety moments. It was almost like a physical form of biofeedback. I have since learned how to get myself to a relaxed state,*

but crochet with its repetitiveness and thinking about the intended recipient had the same effect!"

Martha explained that the repetitiveness of crochet is really a key part of why it's so relaxing for her. That same stitch, again and again, that same motion of the hand moving to bring the yarn up and over the hook ... it's easy and healing. And it's also healing to be able to focus on where the project will go when it is done.

> *"Part of it is creating the project and watching it grow and part is thinking about who will receive the end product. It's difficult to be worried when you're thinking about how someone else is going to enjoy your handmade item. You know how people say that food cooked with love tastes much better? I think that's absolutely true ... and I think it applies to handmade crafts, too. When I make something, I don't necessarily consciously "infuse" love or good wishes into the project, but I do think about the receiver often and imagine how they will enjoy it."*

You can connect with Martha on Twitter @martha_stone.

Panic Attacks

One of the things that I got really curious about when doing the research about the role of crochet in treating anxiety is whether or not it could be beneficial even for people suffering from panic attacks, an intense and immediate form of anxiety that is characterized by shortness of breath, feeling faint, sweating, dizziness, hyperventilation and other such physical symptoms of fear. Fran suffers from panic attacks as part of her PTSD-related anxiety and she crochets as a comfort so that suggested that it could be useful. Additionally, a small bit of research has been done in this area, which concludes that crochet may indeed be able to help reduce panic attacks.

A 2009 press release article by FaveCrafts titled "Knitting and Crochet Offer Long-Term Health Benefits" cites related research completed by Dr. Herbert Bendon, the Director of the Institute for Mind, Body Medicine at Massachusetts General Hospital as well as an Associate Professor of Medicine at Harvard Medical School. Bendon specifically studied knitting, looking at how it can be used to create a "relaxation response" in the body. This response lowers blood pressure and heart rate. The press release draws the conclusion that, "Knitting and crochet have a calming effect overall which can help manage anxiety and may even help conditions such as asthma or panic attacks."

As someone who has asthma and who has been hospitalized for it a few times, I'll admit that I'm not one hundred percent convinced about that note in the research that crochet can help with asthma attacks. Then again, I do think that my asthma was exacerbated by panic and maybe if there were some possibility that I could have slowed down enough to focus on crochet then my breathing would have regulated itself. I am thinking of one time in particular when I experienced the physical symptoms of asthma but it was definitely correlated with anxiety that I was experiencing at the time. Because I have asthma, it presented as an asthma attack, but looking back I can see that it was probably really a panic attack.

During the time that I am referring to, I was undergoing a significant amount of stress in my life. I wasn't properly taking care of myself in a way that would allow me to even acknowledge that stress, let alone be able to deal with it. I had just become a foster parent to a troubled teenager, was returning to college to get a degree in youth social service and was beginning to work in the sex abuse unit of Child Protective Services. This was the classic case of doing what I described earlier in this book – subconsciously surrounding myself with people whose problems were so much larger than mine that I could feel functional in comparison to them and therefore deny, sublimate and ignore my own depression. But by now the depression was getting worse and worse and it would manifest itself in physical symptoms (although I wouldn't realize until much later that this is what had happened.)

So, everything was coming to a head. I'd had a particularly bad night with the teenager that I was caring for. The night was over and I was in bed when I started to have that familiar feeling of gasping for air that comes upon anyone who has had an asthma attack. It starts with a little twinge in the chest, a feeling as though someone has tightened a corset too tight at the top of your body and you can still breathe but the breath is shallow. It continues with a wheeze, an audible sound that reflects a feeling that your throat has been coated with dust and you are trying to breathe through it. In normal cases, you reach for your inhaler, take a deep breath and it as if the inhalation blows the dust back out of your lungs so that you can breathe without the wheeze again. The corset strings relax, your chest loosens and everything is fine.

But this was not a normal case. I used my inhaler. It didn't help. I used it again. The layer of dust felt like it thickened in my throat, making it even harder to breathe. I tried the inhaler again. I gasped. I started wondering if I should call 911. I took another puff off of the inhaler. Now anyone reading this who has asthma will immediately realize that I was now overdosing on my inhaler. I was taking in more and more medication, which speeds up the heart rate, increasing the potential for anxiety, which exacerbated the panic associated with not being able to breathe. The situation worsened. I called 911. I called my parents to come stay with my foster teen.

On both occasions that I've ever called an ambulance to my home, including this one, five or six large men have shown up to help. I personally find this experience overwhelming. But on this night, my mom took over care of the teenager and I relaxed into the mental embrace of having these big men take care of my problem. I got on a nebulizer, went to the hospital, was given some temporary steroids and I was fine. On the one hand, I do believe that the physical things that they did to treat my asthma were what fixed the problem. I physically couldn't breathe.

However, I also believe that a major part of the problem was that I was panicked. The inhaler medication and the feeling of not being able to breathe caused a peak in a feeling of anxiety that had been growing for months as my depression burgeoned in the background of my busy life. Stepping back and getting taken care of for a little bit was just as healing as the actual medication that they gave to me. How I wish I understood all of this at the time.

Looking back, I wonder if crochet could have possibly helped me with this combination asthma / panic attack. I don't really feel like it could have because I was not in touch with myself enough to realize that the panic was making up most of the problem. I would not have been capable of slowing my mind down enough to focus on crochet and resolve the physical problem. But I won't deny that someone else in the same situation might have been able to alleviate her own symptoms with a focused craft like crochet.

And I will say that I think crochet is one of the tools that I have that helps prevent problems like this from occurring now. Crochet gives me downtime in my life to reflect on what is happening with me, to take time for myself to reduce the stress and anxiety in my life. While I remain unconvinced that it could solve panic attacks for me, I'm certain that it plays a key role in prevention (which is a better form of treatment anyway, right?)

And I'll also say that if I'm ever in a situation where I am having a panic attack or asthma attack and I can't reach medication but can reach crochet I'll certainly try to focus on it to get me through the situation. The idea of that makes me think of one of the most amazing crochet stories I've ever read – the story of 98-year-old Maria D'Antuono who was trapped in the rubble of an earthquake for more than thirty hours and crocheted to pass the time until help reached her.

D'Antuono was one of the victims of the big earthquake that shook Italy in 2009. This earthquake, a 5.8 on the Richter scale, hit near L'Aquila in the Abruzzo region of central Italy on April 6, 2009. More than 300 people died, which was shocking because earthquakes in Italy are rarely strong enough to be deadly. But it was the damage to the buildings that really caused problems in the area. Thousands upon thousands of old buildings in L'Aquila were damaged, many of which actually collapsed. This left more than 60,000 people homeless. And it meant that there were people trapped in the rubble for more than a full day before help could be received.

The Telegraph explained that, "The stone house where the 98-year-old was buried under her bed in the village of Tempera, was a scene of devastation having completely collapsed on one side." It went on to explain that D'Antuono had actually experienced an earthquake-related trauma when she was a child. At the age of four, she had survived an earthquake but three years later her childhood home collapsed due to the earthquake damage and her two sisters were killed in the collapse. Given D'Antuono's situation being stuck inside ancient debris without a way out, as well as her personal past with a related trauma, I know that I would have felt in a panic if I were her.

Try to picture that with me for a minute. You're nearly one hundred years old. You are trapped under a bed in the rubble of your now-destroyed home. You remember your sisters dying in a similar situation. You have no idea when help is going to reach you and you cannot get out. A full day and a full night pass and you remain stuck. Even if you aren't prone to panic attacks, don't you think that at some point your mind would get the better of you and put you at risk of one ... worsened by the fact that you absolutely can't get out of the situation? And there's your crochet, by your bedside, within reach. I'd certainly try to use it to calm down, regardless of whether or not I believe it can stop a panic attack in its tracks. You'd have to try. And this woman is an example of it succeeding. Her story made headlines and a lot of attention was given specifically to the fact that she was just down there crocheting as she waited for help. It sounded crazy to some people. It makes perfect sense to me.

Jonesing for the Hook: Crochet for OCD and Addiction

While researching the role that crochet can play in resolving symptoms of anxiety, I came across the topic of how crochet can help with Obsessive Compulsive Disorder (OCD), a form of anxiety disorder that is towards the far end of the spectrum in terms of anxiety. I also came across the topic of addiction and although OCD is very different from addiction, the two problems have some things in common. Many of those things can be grouped together in terms of treating the conditions' symptoms and improving them through the use of crochet. We'll look first at OCD and then look more closely at addiction. By no means am I suggesting that these two conditions are the same thing or that they should be treated the same way. But as you'll see, they have some similarities when it comes to how crochet can be used in dealing with them.

Obsessive Compulsive Disorder

What is OCD? The Mayo Clinic describes it in part as: "an anxiety disorder characterized by unreasonable thoughts and fears (obsessions) that lead you to do repetitive behaviors (compulsions). With obsessive-compulsive disorder, you may realize that your obsessions aren't reasonable, and you may try to ignore them or stop them. But that only increases your distress and anxiety. Ultimately, you feel driven to perform compulsive acts in an effort to ease your stressful feelings."

What OCD looks like varies from person to person and may be characterized by such things as repeating an action over and over, hoarding, cleaning excessively or doing things by the numbers (such as opening all doors five times). Notably, many people who are diagnosed with OCD don't have a single-focus compulsive behavior like this that stays the same over time. Instead, they have a version of OCD referred to as a spectrum disorder, meaning that they have compulsions in many areas and may have some that come and go with time.

I want to reiterate that OCD and addiction aren't the same thing. A major difference between an addiction (such as an addiction to food, gambling or sex) and OCD is that the addict tends to feel at least some pleasure from their tasks whereas the OCD patient typically does them compulsively without pleasure. Although it's not related to crochet, a great book to read to get a sense of what OCD is all about from the inside is the memoir *Passing for Normal: A Memoir of Compulsion* by Amy S. Wilensky. Wilensky has both OCD and Tourette's (a sort of sister condition to OCD) and shares great insight into what it's like to live with these conditions.

Crochet can help manage some of the symptoms of OCD. One of the best ways is that it provides a healthy replacement for the negative habits that have become a way of life for the person suffering from the condition. Instead of picking at your skin until it bleeds, you can crochet. Instead of opening and closing a door thirty times, you can crochet. Instead of washing your hands until they are chapped and cracked, you can coat them in the soothing feel of yarn. I want to emphasize again that I'm not in any way discounting the true difficulty of living with any mental illness or health condition, including OCD. It's not as though I think someone who goes to a doctor for intense OCD symptoms should be told, "oh, just crochet and you'll stop being compulsive." Of course not. In the same way, it wouldn't have sufficed if my psychologist had looked at my intense depression and said, "oh, just keep your mind busy, just crochet." Clearly I needed more than just that, but it was one tool in the tool belt of behavioral changes and meditative healing options for me. And I've encountered people who feel that it can be that for them with OCD as well.

In a comment on a 2009 Lion Brand blog post titled "Can You Crochet Away Depression?", Yarn Over Mama blogger Alissa shared: "I have been using crochet for several years now to help me control my OCD - otherwise I tend to scratch in one place until I break the skin. I think the calming motions of crocheting, plus the joy from finishing something useful or beautiful, help my mental health tremendously!" And a Crochet World reader named Paula said: "I have obsessive-compulsive disorder and suffered for years from all sorts of obsessive counting behavior. As part of my therapy, I began to crochet. The repetitious counting helps me manage my illness by replacing my unhealthy counting compulsions with something that is productive." (Talking Crochet, 2011).

If you aren't familiar with OCD then you may not realize that it is actually an anxiety disorder. The key difference between OCD and many other forms of anxiety is the compulsive behavior itself. Another notable difference is that many forms of anxiety, such as generalized anxiety disorder, involve being excessively worried about many different things whereas with OCD the worry is typically centered on just one or a few things to the point of, as the name says, obsession. Jennifer Crutchfield (*see Meet Jennifer C!*) shared how she used crochet to deal with the anxiety of having people working on her home:

> "I was concerned that something would go wrong with the construction and I wouldn't know how to handle it. I was concerned that I would have to leave the house while the workers needed to be here and I didn't want to leave them at my house alone. While they seemed trustworthy to me I still would have been uncomfortable with this situation.
>
> The work took two days. On the first day they cut out the window and wall and placed the door in the space they created. It was also during the autumn of the year so it was rather chilly in the house over these days. The second day was finishing work.
>
> I started a pattern for a round afghan, which was very easy except for keeping the increases consistently located. I did horribly at that part. I don't think I'll ever finish this project (but) it served me so well in helping me to be calm during that stress."

The need for a productive, helpful distraction is a shared therapeutic need for people suffering from OCD as well as for people who are trying to break an addiction. (Like I said, OCD and addiction are very different things with different roots but what they have in common is a persistent need to focus on one thing, whether that's getting a cigarette or closing and opening a door.) A focused activity that is do-able and keeps your hands busy assists you in pushing through some of the OCD thoughts that may come into your mind. It also keeps your hands occupied to prevent you from picking up that next cigarette or drink. As with depression (perhaps even more so) crochet alone isn't going to get rid of the problems of OCD and addiction but it can be a help in managing the symptoms. That is often half the battle with mental health problems.

Crochet as a form of distraction can play a role in the third step of the four-step model of OCD treatment outlined by Jeffrey Schwartz. Schwartz is an author and Associate Research Professor of Psychiatry at UCLA School of Medicine who has made major breakthroughs in the understanding and treatment of OCD including the development of this oft-used four-step model of treatment. The four steps are to re-label, re-attribute, re-focus and re-value to improve OCD.

In step one the patient learns to recognize when thoughts are obsessive or compulsive and then to label them as such. In step two the patient learns to re-attribute these thoughts to the OCD and not to the value of the repetitive thought itself, learning for example to say "I need to wash my hands because my OCD says so, not because my hands are actually dirty." It is in step three where crochet can come into play because in this step the goal is to re-focus, mindfully choosing to ignore the obsessive compulsive thought and instead to engage in some other behavior. Crochet can be that behavior. This refocusing on constructive behavior is considered by some to be the most important step in self-treatment of OCD. This helps you get to step four in which you can re-value the thought as not having the value it felt like it did before and therefore avoid the OCD behaviors entirely.

For obvious reasons, crochet can be particularly useful as a re-focusing tool for people who typically engage in compulsive behaviors that require the use of their hands. Compulsive hand washing, nail biting, dermatillomania (skin-picking) and trichotillomania (the pulling out of one's own hair) are examples of behaviors that can be successfully reduced if the person is able to keep their hands busy with crochet. These behaviors may be annoying, irritating, frustrating and embarrassing to the person with OCD but more importantly also cause physical damage to the individual's body so finding a functional distraction is of great importance. If your hands are busy with yarn in one hand and a hook in the other then it's difficult to bite your nails or pull out your own hair.

One question that came to mind for me was whether the very symptoms of OCD would make it difficult for someone to complete crochet projects. After all, if you are obsessively counting or checking for errors, etc., then maybe it would be unlikely that crochet could benefit you in this particular way. However, I found an answer to this in an article about the health benefits of knitting that I think would also apply to crochet. Gail of the blog Straight Jacket Knitting shared in an interview on the Compassioknitter blog: "As a self-taught knitter, I found that my OCD often worked to my advantage because my obsessive tendencies made me keep working through a project, when others would have thrown the knitting down in frustration. Despite having ADHD and Tourettes, both of which make it extremely difficult to focus, knitting helped calm the tics and allowed me some peace." Gail also added, " If you were to ask me for the best way to treat any illness, I would answer without hesitation, "Yarn." That is the basis on which my website was founded and continues to operate: yarn is the basis of everything I do. Yarn is not only the medium in which I choose to create, but it is also the medicine I prescribe for whatever ails me." So Gail seems to confirm that although her conditions can make it difficult to focus, her OCD itself helps her to be able to focus on knitting.

I got some insight into all of this from my interview with Marinke (see *Meet Marinke!)* who has Asperger's Syndrome but also was diagnosed with OCD when she was younger. She shared, "I used to count EVERYTHING. At the office (when I still had a job) I could be doing the same thing for a while, such as cutting images and saving them. I would go into a trance and just cut, save, cut, save, cut, save until it was finished. 'Regular' people might find this boring to do but for me it was relaxing! Crocheting works the same. Crochet is basically repeating the same thing over and over again, and for me that flow really helps me get through the day. But at the same time, you have to keep thinking about what you're doing, so it never gets boring. And you get to be creative while you're at it – what more can you want?"

Meet Jennifer C.!

Jennifer Crutchfield uses crochet to help her deal with the symptoms of OCD. She enjoys the challenge and excitement of taking on a new project. However, she also appreciates how the meditative process of repetitive crochet can reduce symptoms of anxiety.

Jennifer Crutchfield had Obsessive Compulsive Disorder (OCD) for a long time but she only started to realize about two years ago that this was a "condition" and not just a part of her personality or "who she is." Adjusting to this new way of seeing OCD has been a transition and she has only recently started realizing just how beneficial crochet may be for her condition although she had been using it for awhile to cope with various symptoms. Some people self-medicate with drugs, not realizing that they're taking them because they ease the pain of an as-of-yet undefined problem. Jennifer self-medicated with crochet.

Jennifer specifically notes that crochet has served as an aid to her when she knows she's going to have to go into situations that are stressful, uncomfortable or produce higher levels of anxiety. Those types of conditions can trigger the symptoms of OCD so it's important to manage them. She says:

> *"I can carry a granny square with me to work or just about anywhere. The repetitive motion is very calming for me, especially when I'm working on a pattern that is memorized."*

For example, Jennifer recalls one specific time when crochet helped her deal with anxiety. Her family was having a sliding glass door installed in their home. Her husband had to go away on business and she was home alone with three kids, dealing with having workers around cutting a huge hole into the side of her house. She shares how she dealt with the situation:

> *"I was concerned that something would go wrong with the construction and I wouldn't know how to handle it. I was concerned that I would have to leave the house while the workers needed to be here and I didn't want to leave them at my house alone. While they seemed trustworthy to me I still would have been uncomfortable with this situation.*

The work took two days. On the first day they cut out the window and wall and placed the door in the space they created. It was also during the autumn of the year so it was rather chilly in the house over these days. The second day was finishing work.

I started a pattern for a round afghan, which was very easy except for keeping the increases consistently located. I did horribly at that part. I don't think I'll ever finish this project because it served me so well in helping me to be calm during that stress. I've thought about picking it up again several times but I almost think I associate it with that stress and don't want to revisit it."

This shows how for many people it is the process of crochet, rather than an end product, that is so healing. However she doesn't necessarily think that's always the case. In fact, it's not her favorite part. She shares:

"I absolutely love the planning and excitement of starting projects. The middle, the creating, can get quite boring for me if there are not challenges along the way, and the end product is really more of a letdown than anything - except that I get to move on to planning something new! Of course, I do that all the time anyway. Like I said before, the rhythm of the crochet activity is very soothing for me on an immediate level. But the planning and starting a new project, the challenge of learning a new pattern, are what grab my attention the most."

If you're interested in learning more about Jennifer, she blogs at http://jencrutchfield.blogspot.com.

Meet Marinke!

Marinke has Asperger's, which causes her social awkwardness. She has found a community in the online world of crocheters thanks to her blog. And crochet has helped to reduce the depression and stress of her condition.

Marinke always knew that she felt different. She wasn't sure how to explain what exactly made her different. Like many people struggling to understand themselves, she began trying to apply labels to herself as a way of defining what was "wrong." She was just being an adolescent, or she was just being bisexual, or maybe she was quirky and weird. But after failing for the third time at keeping a job, she started thinking that maybe there was something actually not right with her and she started digging deeper. She eventually stumbled upon a description of Asperger's Syndrome, and in 2009 she was professionally diagnosed with being on the autism spectrum.

Marinke's failure to keep her job was due to a burnout related to the social awkwardness of her condition. She felt misunderstood by her co-workers and often just couldn't bring herself to get out of bed and get to work in the morning. She shares some of what it has been like dealing with Asperger's:

> *"The biggest "thing" for me is my social awkwardness. I can behave perfectly normally when I'm with someone else, or even with just two other people, but any group larger than that and you can really notice a change in my behavior. I just get literally awkward, not knowing what to say or when to laugh, or when to make a joke or what's funny, and often in big groups of people I just shut down and move to the background.*
>
> *When I go out in public, such as a visit to the city or being in public transport, I make sure I always have my big headphones with me. When I listen to music it drives out the sound of the crowds and I really need that. I'm very sensitive to (sudden or unexpected) sounds and light. For that reason I kind of dislike summer, because it is just too bright!*
>
> *When I receive too much stimulus (from anything really; noises, people, conversations, impressions, the news, touch) I shut down. I might make it until the end of the day, but after that I crash*

hard, meaning I stay in bed the day after with the blinds and windows closed."

Having Asperger's isn't all bad. Marinke points out that she has an above average intellect and that she's a very creative person. And she has found that crocheting allows her a creative outlet that also assists her in managing her Asperger's symptoms. She shares:

> *"A lot of people with Autism find repetitive activities or actions soothing. When I was little I'd rock myself when I was in a chair, to calm down. I also had OCD when I was younger; I used to count EVERYTHING. At the office (when I still had a job) I could be doing the same thing for a while, such as cutting images and saving them. I would go into a trance and just cut, save, cut, save, cut, save until it was finished. 'Regular' people might find this boring to do but for me it was relaxing!*
>
> *Crocheting works the same. Crochet is basically repeating the same thing over and over again, and for me that flow really helps me get through the day. But at the same time, you have to keep thinking about what you're doing, so it never gets boring. And you get to be creative while you're at it – what more can you want?"*

It was in 2010, a year after her diagnosis, that Marinke figured out that crochet could be healing for her. She was really depressed after the diagnosis, to the point where she had to be hospitalized for three months. She knew that she needed something to do to keep her busy while she was in the hospital. She thought that crochet looked cool, so she decided to teach herself.

> *"When I was released from the hospital, I was home alone a lot, and without a job. I quickly realized that crocheting was the perfect thing to do to get me through the day! I just love picking out yarn and thinking of new things to make, and the process of crocheting it is just so-o-o soothing. It calms my thoughts and keeps my hands busy."*

And although Marinke may be socially awkward in large groups in person, crochet has helped her feel like part of a great community ever since she started her crochet blog in May 2011. She shares:

"I get a lot of responses to things I post and that makes me feel so so blessed, I'm really part of a community that before last year I never knew existed! Also, since I started crocheting, a lot of people in my family have started as well, because I told them how much it helps you when there's something troubling you. I have a lot of aunts that have made countless bags, potholders and stuffed animals because of what I told them!"

You can connect with Marinke on her website at www.acreativebeing.com.

Addiction

OCD is an extreme form of anxiety, not an addiction, but the same tools of distraction that can help with OCD can also be very helpful to people trying to beat an addiction. I'll reiterate that they're different, though. A basic difference is that OCD involves compulsive behaviors that often give little or no pleasure to the individual performing them. The person with OCD usually knows that the behaviors don't benefit them and may be harmful but cannot stop themselves from performing the behaviors. In contrast, addiction generally provides pleasure to the individual, who often doesn't realize that the behaviors they're engaging in are dangerous or self-harming and do them because it feels good. In some cases, a person with OCD may have a dual diagnosis with addiction.

In the same way that crochet can serve as a replacement task in Schwartz's step three of OCD treatment, it can be a distraction that aids in the treatment of all different types of addiction. Or we could look at another model … In his book *7 Tools to Beat Addiction*, Stanton Peele, Ph.D., J.D. identifies a person's individual resources as one of the seven tools required to overcome an addiction. There are many different types of resources that a person may rely on including relationships with others, work skills and accomplishments and more. One key resource he cites is "leisure activities" meaning both "hobbies and interests" and "ways of relaxing." Crochet certainly falls into this category and therefore can be construed as a valuable resource for some people combating addiction. In this chapter he also cites the importance of recognizing and valuing your own strengths as an internal resource. If you know that you are good at certain things then you can at least imagine that you can be good at ceasing your addiction. If you feel like you are good at crochet then it can benefit you in this sense as well.

Considering this in a more concrete way, Peele goes on to reference the work of psychologist Saul Shiffman who looked at the techniques that cigarette addicts could successfully use to resist the urge to start smoking again. Three of the five behavioral techniques that he named are relaxation, selecting a distracting activity and selecting a delaying activity. All three of these things are things that crochet can be used for. Crochet may relax you so that you don't feel the need to smoke or it may distract you entirely from the urge to smoke (or engage in other addictive behavior). Alternatively you may tell yourself that you are going to finish this many rows or that project before you go smoke, delaying the addictive behavior as a means of cutting back and eventually ceasing the behavior.

Identifying and using your resources is only one of the seven tools that Peele cites to beat addiction. A second important tool that relates to crochet is tool number seven, which is to pursue and accomplish goals. The idea here is that you set goals that are important to you so that you can have a bigger reason for quitting your addiction than just "it's bad for me" or "everyone says I need to quit." Having a bigger goal will help you to be able to actually quit the addiction instead of falling back into it after just a short period of time.

One of the types of goals that Peele names is "personal goals", which he defines as goals "you pursue to make yourself a better person, to improve and advance your life." One huge goal that comes to mind for me in relation to crochet is the goal to use the craft to express yourself in positive and creative ways. If you are struggling with an addiction, you can ask yourself if taking an action to feed that addiction (such as going to the bar) will help you to express yourself in positive and creative ways. It will not, whereas your crochet work can, and therefore perhaps you can convince yourself to skip the bar and stay home to crochet (or go to a craft group instead of the bar!)

Finally Peele points out that it is valuable to include goals that contribute to the community around you. He explains that when you contribute to your community, it therapeutically strengthens you as an individual because you need to be more responsible thanks to your interactions with others. Crochet can clearly be a community activity, whether you want to set a goal of teaching crochet to local schoolchildren or simply volunteer your time to crochet squares for charity. The more your goals connect you to the community, the more likely it is that you will beat your addiction.

OCD is a serious mental health condition. Addiction is a serious problem. People dealing with these issues should clearly work with professionals, support groups and loved ones to deal with the underlying issues through medication and / or psychology. But in both cases, a key part of healing is physical distraction for the destructive behavior associated with the condition. Crochet can distract.

There may also be a more scientific benefit to using crochet to beat some addictions. Mary Shoman shared her story about quitting a cigarette addiction in a 2011 About.com article and started off by explaining that she had tried almost everything there is to quit cigarettes from acupuncture to nicotine gum. Finally, she started working with a therapist who focused on the way that smoking affects the brain waves. Basically the theory is that smokers often smoke because their brain waves are in a busy "theta" pattern and the cigarettes relax them by stimulating their "alpha" waves. The therapist's idea was that finding other ways to stimulate those relaxing alpha waves would help Mary end her cigarette addiction. They tried many alpha-wave-stimulating activities (such as listening to relaxing sounds) but in the end only one thing worked – needlework.

Mary and her therapist found that both sewing and crocheting immediately shifted her waves into an alpha pattern so that she could relax. In her article, Mary reports that she "embarked on a program of crocheting." Every time she wanted a cigarette, she crocheted. In four months, she crocheted half a dozen queen-sized blankets. Maybe it was the distraction of the craft or maybe it was the way that crochet released her alpha waves, but that was in 1996 and she hasn't smoked since!

Mary isn't the only person out there who has used needlework to help break a cigarette addiction. In fact, a group called the UK Hand Knitting Association has an entire page on their website dedicated to "knitting for quitting" where people can share their stories about how they used needlework to stop smoking. Although the emphasis there is on knitting, people have shared their "crocheting to quit" stories as well.

And of course crochet could be used to quit addictions to other things, such as drinking. A 1979 Boca Raton News article reported briefly on a man named Wayne Dalby who was using crochet to help him "lick a problem with alcohol." He is described as a "burly block mason" who needed something to keep his hands busy so he couldn't hold a beer and so he took up crochet. It worked for him.

Just how serious of an addiction could crochet be helpful in treating? In 1989, Gazette reporter Mary Pinkans Burt shared the story of Fran Adams who had been smoking daily for thirty-seven years when she decided to quit. She had never tried to quit before and it wasn't easy but she was successful in her efforts. She had gone without a cigarette for two years by the time that Burt interviewed her. One of the key reasons that she was successful in treating her cigarette habit was that she replaced her smoking time with other activities that would keep her busy. Crochet was one of the most important replacement activities. Interestingly enough, Burt had tried to learn to crochet several times before this and hadn't succeeded but she channeled her frustration over wanting a cigarette into doing more productive things and was successful this time around in learning crochet.

Burt also reported on the fact that The Cancer Society was holding an annual Smoke Out Day, which is a day dedicated to encouraging smokers to quit cigarettes for twenty four hours. At the time they reported that there were about 50 million smokers in America and more than one third of them participated in the smoke out although only about ten percent succeeded in quitting for at least twenty-four hours. The Cancer Society offered tips for participants to help them succeed in the Smoke Out, including simple things like hiding all of the ashtrays in the home. One of their tips was to "change your routine to avoid the habit of smoking." Adding crochet to her routine is what Fran Adams had done. Her previous routine included drinking coffee and talking on the phone a lot and those were things that she associated with smoking (since she always had a cigarette in her hand when doing them) so she had to switch it up and do activities she'd never done while smoking, like crochet. Adams reported at the time of the article that she no longer felt any cigarette cravings.

A 2008 article by Licensed Clinical Social Worker Kathryn Duffy indicates that needlework can be used in therapeutic settings that help treat substance abuse. The article is about a women's-only drug and alcohol rehabilitation center called Interim House. Interim House was founded in 1971 as one of the country's first specialized treatment centers for women and has become widely known as a place that's on the leading edge of using innovative treatment options, such as art therapy, to help heal their patients. Duffy founded a group knitting program at Interim House in 2004. It meets once a week for two hours at a time and has approximately two dozen participants.

Duffy's article explains that the knitting group is a multi-purpose aspect of treatment in this center. It is designed to:

- Engage the client in the therapeutic process, decrease isolation and encourage group participation. Knitting is a safe way to participate in a group. Regular group talk therapy can feel threatening to many people whereas knitting does not. It has been found that there are fewer arguments and more participation in the group when it includes knitting.
- Practice affect management. Here knitting serves to keep the patient grounded so that they can think before reacting and alter their affect appropriately.
- Build self-esteem. Low self-esteem and its assorted problems is common among women with a history of substance abuse. By sharing their work, finishing their projects and being praised by the rest of the group they can help grow their self-esteem.
- Nurture creativity. Studies indicate that self-expression is important in healing from substance abuse. Learning to knit, choose colors and projects and practice a craft all help nurture creativity that has been lost to addiction.

Duffy says of the group's goals that they are "both tangible and intangible in that it results in an object that is creative and useful, such as a piece of clothing or handbag, while providing a skill that has the ability to self soothe, increase self-esteem by mastery of a task, and foster creativity by allowing one to choose, touch, and blend colors and textures. Finally, once learned, the benefits can be called upon throughout a lifetime."

As you can see, the ways that needlework can help in a therapeutic setting are designed not just for the craft to serve as a distraction from drugs and alcohol but also to treat other underlying issues that often plague people who fall into substance abuse. Duffy reports that more than eighty percent of the women at Interim House have PTSD or a mood disorder that must be treated in order for them to beat their addictions. Knitting is used as a group activity, a means of self-expression and a path to relaxation, all geared towards treating those problems in a creative manner. Crochet could certainly be used in the same way in a therapeutic setting to help people trying to overcome heavy addictions.

PTSD: Reduce the Impact of Flashbacks with Crochet

"Sufferers of post traumatic stress (PTS) have told me that knitting and stitching enable them to sort and process their thoughts." – Stitchlinks, Guide to Our Theories So Far

Post Traumatic Stress Disorder (PTSD) refers to a combination of thoughts, feelings, attitudes and behaviors that occur in someone who has experienced a trauma. For example, earlier in this book you met Fran, who suffered from PTSD following a violent sexual attack. Other types of trauma that commonly cause PTSD are war combat, car accidents and childhood abuse. The causes may differ but there are patterns of behavior and stages of recovery that tend to be similar for all people that are suffering from PTSD.

The National Center for PTSD explains that there are four major symptoms that sufferers commonly experience. The most common is a flashback to the event, also known as re-experiencing the symptoms. For example, a car backfiring might cause a soldier to feel like he's back in the middle of a war. The other three symptoms are avoiding situations that may remind you of the event, feeling numb, and feeling like you're in a state of hyperarousal. The specific manifestation of those symptoms can vary from person to person. For example, hyperarousal in one person might mean insomnia whereas for another it can mean constantly feeling angry.

All of these four symptoms can lead to a feeling of constant stress. Many say that crochet has the potential to assist the person suffering from PTSD in distracting the mind to deal with the stress. It may even help in coping with the first symptom, the flashbacks, which is a symptom that can significantly hinder the life of someone who has dealt with trauma. Crochet can help in several ways; it can be a way that you treat yourself with kindness, a tool for calming both the mind and body and possibly even a way to prevent your PTSD symptoms from flaring up in the first place.

First let's talk about the simple fact that crochet can be a hobby that you choose because it is something you enjoy. Doing this is a means of treating yourself with the gentle kindness you not only deserve but also truly need when recovering from a trauma. In her book *Healing from Post Traumatic Stress: A Workbook for Recovery*, Monique Lang, LCSW emphasizes that one of the most important things that you can do for yourself if you are suffering from PTSD is to devote adequate time and attention to self-care. She explains that "trauma truncates our homeostasis, our normal way of being in the world" and that an environment of self-care is necessary for emotional repair after trauma. It's simple, really ... when life has done something that treats you horribly, you need to go overboard in treating yourself well to make up for that while you are healing. If you enjoy crochet, you should give yourself plenty of time to just sit and crochet while you heal, allowing yourself to relax with your craft rather than pressuring yourself to do other things that you may feel like you need to do such as take care of household chores or attend work functions.

Taking time to crochet is a great way to be kind to yourself. First of all, you are giving yourself the luxury of time to just sit and do something that is special for you. Second, you can make choices that enhance how special it is for you by spoiling yourself with the yarns that you love. Third you can make things for yourself that will continue to spoil you and to remind you of the value in taking care of yourself. You can be kind to yourself in the moment and again and again just through the act of crocheting.

Being kind to yourself as you deal with PTSD is important but it's not going to do what's necessary to resolve the symptoms of PTSD. These symptoms include not only the flashbacks that we have all heard about but also feelings and even physical symptoms associated with fear, stress and anxiety. PTSD can manifest physically in many ways including sweating, shaking and even pain. One key way to reduce all of these symptoms is to take actions that calm the mind and the body, because remember, the physical symptoms in the body are a manifestation of the mind with this condition. Crochet, with its meditative features and its slow physical activity, can be one great tool for bringing calmness to your life when you are feeling the effects of PTSD.

The most prevalent symptom for many people is anxiety. When you experience a traumatic event, your body goes into "fight or flight" mode. Adrenaline pumps, your heart races and your entire body goes into a state of hyperarousal. What often happens for sufferers of PTSD is that the body ceases to realize that it is now safe. This can cause periodic or even persistent feelings of stress that keep the mind anxious. As we already looked at in the previous chapter on anxiety, crochet can be a terrific tool for helping to calm yourself down.

Author Monique Lang offers numerous suggestions for quelling this anxiety, one of which is to "engage in an attention-demanding or engrossing project" (such as crochet!) Basically if an activity is taking up all of your focus then your mind can't continue to focus on stress and the anxiety in the body decreases. Another valuable tip she offers is to become acutely aware of the times when you do not feel anxious so if your crochet time is one of those times then you can boost its benefit by realizing that and relishing it. We've already looked extensively at how crochet can help with anxiety, including perhaps even panic attacks, and that information applies as much to people dealing with PTSD as it does for people dealing with other forms of anxiety.

If you find that your anxiety doesn't decrease when you crochet then you might want to ask yourself where your mind is going as you work. The meditative nature of crochet is a benefit but not if it allows rumination on things that cause anxiety. You may need to try a new technique that requires more focus if you're going through this issue. One great tip is to bring yourself back to the present moment and ask yourself, "what danger am I in right now?" If you can realize that the greatest danger is that your crochet project won't turn out right then you can get a little bit of perspective and reduce your anxiety levels. These are tools that need to be learned, of course, and are often best dealt with in therapy.

This kind of "coming back to the moment" can also be a great tool for dealing with flashbacks. Flashbacks refer to when the PTSD person actually feels as if they are back in the exact same situation that caused them trauma in the first place. They really feel like they are there. So the war veteran doesn't actually know that he's in a suburban area of Middle America in 2012 but instead hears that car backfiring and actually believes that he's back in a war zone. However, with practice, the PTSD patient can learn to bring themselves back to the present, to say to themselves, "this is just a flashback and I am in a safe place." It may be a benefit to have a go-to thing like crochet that you always reach for when you know you're experiencing a flashback, something that can ground you as you bring yourself back to the present moment. Being able to grab a soft ball of yarn and a smooth hook as you say, "look, I am here in the moment and things are soft and smooth" can be another tool for the sufferer of PTSD.

Basically, what I'm describing here is another version of using crochet as a tool for mindfulness. About.com Guide Matthew Tull explains that this type of mindfulness is called "grounding" and that you can use it to "retain your connection with the present moment and reduce the likelihood that you slip into a flashback or dissociation." Some examples that he gives of how to ground yourself are to turn on loud, jarring music or to bite into a lemon. These are things that immediately titillate your senses and bring you back into the present moment. Crochet, or simply grabbing up your hook and a particularly plush ball of yarn, could be used in the same way (although it may not provide an intense enough sensation for all people dealing with flashbacks).

Of course, all of this sounds nice in theory but is anyone out there actually using crochet to heal from PTSD? Well, we already looked at how Fran uses crochet to help cope with her symptoms. And I know another woman, Laurie Wheeler, who is now free from PTSD symptoms and used crochet to help her get there. Laurie's PTSD had two traumatic sources. She was psychologically, emotionally and sexually abused for thirteen years beginning at age two. Then when she went to get help, her first therapist treated her horrifically and that caused a second trauma. It was many years before she got the right kind of help and in that time she used crochet to cope with the symptoms caused by trauma.

She shared: "(Crochet) made it easier; it kept me calm, it stopped me from having too many adrenaline and cortisol spikes. I had more than just myself to think about; I had a 5 and 2 year old to raise and no one I trusted enough with their care if something should happen to me. So, if I was sitting, I crocheted." Laurie had a particularly difficult situation to heal from because in addition to PTSD she was dealing with multiple personality disorder (MPD). She didn't want to take any type of medication to help her through her PTSD because she was afraid that doing so would cause her to split personalities again. Laurie says, "So I crocheted and spun yarn and baked. ... I also created the Crochet Liberation Front. Yes crochet liberated me from the bondage of disorders that kept me in invisible chains made of fear. Did crochet heal me? Not by itself, but it was one of many tools that helped get me where I am today."

Meet Laurie!

Laurie Wheeler is known as the Fearless Leader of the Crochet Liberation Front and the founder of Hookey.org, sites that help to bring together crocheters of all skill levels to connect to one another and learn from one another. However, one does not become a Fearless Leader without facing down some struggles. Laurie has suffered from Post Traumatic Stress Disorder and Multiple Personality Disorder caused by childhood trauma and she has overcome those conditions through strength, perseverance and yes, crochet.

Laurie was only two-and-a-half when a family member began to psychologically, emotionally and sexually abuse her. The abuse went on for thirteen years. In order to cope, she had to separate herself from the world she was living in and escape to a safer place. She shares:

> *"To survive the abuse, my coping mechanism was to mentally put myself somewhere safe. It required a good imagination, intelligence, and a strong will. I was often accused as a young girl of being a "daydreamer" and frankly, I really did prefer living in my head in worlds I created. They were by far more interesting than the world we live in. My world had creatures from fairy tales and nothing was scary or bigger than me, or if it was then it was a gentle creature. I liked living in my own world as a small child because it meant nothing hurt, and nothing there made me sad. Being in the present moment was something I did not like to deal with and I learned to fake it pretty well."*

The abuse went on until Laurie was fifteen, and even the way it ended was traumatic. Laurie shares:

> *"When I was 15 the abuse ended, also in a traumatic way, and I was sent to therapists who are still nationally renowned. I thought I would finally be receiving help. I didn't want to be afraid of life; I wanted to be as normal as I looked.*
>
> *I came from a middle class family. I had nice clothes. I was smart and I was pretty. I wanted a boyfriend like every other girl my age. I had believed Oprah on TV when she said therapists could help.*

And wanting to be helped, I went to my first therapy session willingly. Help wasn't what I got.

The male therapist, let's just call him Bob, sat me in a metal folding chair in the middle of a room, shined a bright light in my face and screamed at me, "What did you do?!!!" I was in shock. I had done nothing, I was the victim and I was being screamed at. I looked at him and said calmly, "I didn't do anything, why are you screaming at me?" He didn't answer me, he accused me of being uncooperative, he threatened to have me taken from my mother, and I was done. "You can yell all day long, I will leave now."

"Bob" smiled the cruelest smile and told me if I left then that would seal me going into foster care and never seeing my mother again. I smiled back; I'd spent my entire life being in my head and not my body so I knew what to do. I waved at him, said goodbye, and I was gone. I have no recollection of what he said past that point. I wasn't "home."

I tell this because it's important that one therapist did as much damage to me as anything my molester/rapist did. I was unable to trust any kind of help for the next 15 years, and of course that meant my dissociative orders became more acute."

Laurie didn't receive help from professionals at that time but she was determined to help herself. She studied abnormal psychology on her own to try to self-heal, and it did help a little bit. She tried running to get into her body but she found that the rhythmic pounding of the pavement made it too easy for her to remain inside of her own head. She learned to manage some of her PTSD and MPD symptoms through meditation, although it was something that didn't come naturally to her. But mostly she was looking for something that would allow her to sit still and yet force her to stay physically present in her own body. Crochet was the answer.

"In my late teens with nowhere to turn (so I thought), I turned to crochet and baking almost exclusively as my healing arts. I put the hooks down in college, and didn't pick them up for about five years. When I was pregnant with my first child I needed something to do with my hands in that last and very long month. That marriage was doomed before it started, two young passionate people with a truckload of issues, and crochet helped me stay as centered as possible as I

replayed my issues and he replayed his.

I left the marriage, two kids in tow and started life over; PTSD further aggravated and MPD diagnosed through a discreet and trusted therapist specializing in NLP (Neuro-linguistic programming). As I worked on integrating the many splits of myself, I crocheted a lot. It made it easier, it kept me calm, it stopped me from having too many adrenaline and cortisol spikes. I had more than just myself to think about; I had a 5 and 2 year old to raise and no one I trusted enough with their care if something should happen to me.

So, if I was sitting, I crocheted. I made things for my friends, my kids, the pets, I made rugs for the floors and doilies and even jam jar cozies. I did this to stay sane; it was a constant, it was predictable, it was a way to be in the here and now."

Crochet gave Laurie as an adult what her fantasy world gave to her as a child: a home base, a place to be safe where nothing hurt. It was a creative outlet that she could turn to for relief so that she could remain in her body and get comfortable staying there. Laurie shares her progress:

"In the first year after I left my marriage, I integrated. I spent the next decade healing from PTSD. I never used drug therapy. I was too afraid it would cause me to split again. So I crocheted and spun yarn and baked. I found a good therapist four years ago, one who was quiet and gentle and kind. We worked on things together, dealing with the diagnosis of severe PTSD with anxiety and depression for two years.

In that time I also created the Crochet Liberation Front. Yes crochet liberated me from the bondage of disorders that kept me in invisible chains made of fear. Did crochet heal me? Not by itself, but it was one of many tools that helped get me where I am today.

Diagnosis? Clear of MPD, clear of PTSD, clear of depression and mild anxiety. It was a long road to get here, a hard road, one that is paved in thousands of yards of yarn and thread. I can't wait to see how that road looks by the end."

You can connect with Laurie at http://www.crochetliberationfront.com.

PTSD Prevention

We don't often talk about the possibility of preventing PTSD. After all, we certainly don't plan for traumatic events and would obviously do all that we could to prevent them if it were possible to do so. But I do believe, based on my research, that there is some potential for adults in the midst of certain stressful situations to identify that they could be at risk of PTSD after the event and to work towards preventing that stress in the way that they cope with the trauma as it is occurring. The idea is that if you can bring yourself to a greater place of calmness during a trauma, without actually dissociating from the traumatic event, then you may be able to move forward after the trauma with less distress and therefore avoid the potential impact of PTSD episodes.

This isn't going to work for all types of events, of course, and certainly wouldn't work for immediate short-term traumas (such as an attack on the street, for example). It probably won't work for all types of people either. And being able to get through a situation doesn't inherently mean that you will prevent PTSD without therapy after the fact. But could it help? Two things indicate that it could: the story of Maria D'Antuono and the research done by Dr. Emily Holmes at University College Hospital in London in 2002.

We already learned about Maria D'Antuono in the chapter on anxiety and panic attacks as I mused about how this near-centenarian might have used her crochet to help stave off panic as she waited 30 hours to be rescued from the rubble of an earthquake. I mention it again now because it is possible that this would have helped her to deal with the trauma as it was happening in a way that would prevent future PTSD. Now, let me say here that these are just my own thoughts on the situation. I didn't interview D'Antuono and I'm no expert in PTSD. But if research shows that finding a way to remain calm during a trauma has the potential to prevent PTSD and if D'Antuono used her crochet work to stay calm during the earthquake rescue then one can hypothesize that it may have prevented her from getting PTSD (which by all accounts she did not develop after the event).

And I am not the only person to have this thought. An article on the Stitchlinks website about D'Antuono's situation drew a link to research that was done in 2002 by Dr. Emily Holmes that also suggests that it's possible that the 98-year-old Italian woman actually prevented her own possible PTSD flashbacks by keeping her mind busy with crochet during the trauma.

Holmes' paper, which references knitting but can be related to crochet, explores how engaging in a visuospatial task during the time that a traumatic experience is happening can result in significantly reduced PTSD flashbacks after the event. It is based on three research experiments completed at University College London, in which participants were exposed to videos of traumatic scenes both with and without the aid of a visuospatial task. They were then asked to record their experiences of flashbacks for a time period following the experiment. The results were published in the March 2004 issue of *Journal of Experimental Psychology: General,* which is published by the American Psychological Association (APA).

This research indicates that if you don't perform any activity during a trauma then your mind is much more likely to produce flashbacks to the event. If you do a repetitive task like crochet then you can prevent flashbacks. In her paper, Holmes' suggested that additional research be done into the potential benefit of needlework during a trauma and even went on to hypothesize that the women who spent their time during the French Revolution knitting by the guillotine may not have suffered flashbacks in comparison with their non-knitting peers. We can't say that for sure, of course, but it's a theory based on what the research that has been done indicates.

A more recent study that Oxford researchers Lalitha Iyadurai and Ella James reported on at the 2012 British Psychology Society Annual Conference similarly found that engaging in visual-spatial tasks can help prevent PTSD flashbacks but their research differs in that the tasks were completed immediately following the trauma rather than during the trauma. In this case, they had their test subjects watch a traumatic film and then within six hours after the viewing they had them either play Tetris, answer trivia questions or do nothing. The visual-spatial task in this instance was the Tetris video game and the research found that the people who did that were least likely to experience flashbacks of the film.

Is it possible to prevent PTSD by crocheting in the midst of a trauma or in the hours immediately following the trauma? Is it possible that crochet can minimize the symptoms for people who do have PTSD? The research is limited and even the available anecdotal evidence is minimal but what is available suggests that the answer just might be yes. It's certainly worth a try!

Crochet for Continuity in Dealing with Schizophrenia

A desperate person who feels crazy wants to know what is wrong with him or her. And yet, sometimes hearing the diagnosis makes them wish they didn't know. That's because some diagnoses are still really scary. A diagnosis of schizophrenia is perhaps one of the most frightening diagnoses to get, for both the individual and those who love him or her. This is a terrifying, confusing disease with a lot of stigma still attached to it and I don't mean to suggest that something as simple as crochet can solve a problem as complex as schizophrenia. In fact it is generally agreed that a diagnosis of schizophrenia requires psychiatric medication. But perhaps crochet can help with managing the symptoms even for a condition this difficult to bear including the fear (and the related anxiety) that just knowing you have this condition can illicit.

There are a lot of reasons that schizophrenia is frightening. One of them is that doctors still don't know what causes schizophrenia. Another is that the symptoms can come on slowly and are often misdiagnosed early on so that the prescribed treatment doesn't help. Symptoms include memory problems, difficulty paying attention, irritability and social withdrawal. The person may find it difficult to think or respond logically or experience "normal" emotional states and therefore will often have trouble relating to others in common social situations and relationships.

When in its full state, schizophrenia often causes the individual suffering from it to have serious difficulty telling the difference between what is real and what isn't, experiencing hallucinations and delusions that feel like reality. The layperson often thinks of schizophrenics as people who "hear voices." Hallucinations may indeed get that intense but may also be subtler than that. Merrell Dow of Schizophrenia.com explains, "Hallucinations are false perceptions, inaccuracies that affect our senses & cause us to hear, see, taste, touch or smell what others do not. In the acute phases of schizophrenia, patients are likely to insist they are hearing voices that no one else can hear. Sometimes they hear noises, clicks or non-word sounds. On occasion they are disturbed by seeing, smelling or feeling things that others do not."

The experience of these symptoms is further complicated by the fact that there are different types of schizophrenia. According to the A.D.A.M. Medical Encyclopedia, there are three different types of this condition:

1. Paranoid schizophrenia, which is characterized by anger, anxiety and the certainty that the people you love are harming you.
2. Disorganized schizophrenia, which is characterized by childlike behavior, difficulty thinking clearly and trouble expressing emotions.
3. Catatonic schizophrenic, which is characterized by physical symptoms including rigid muscles and lack of affect as well as emotional disconnectedness.

Clearly, any type of schizophrenia is going to be a seriously difficult illness to deal with. Can crochet really play a role in helping someone with a mental disorder this complex? One of the most touching stories that was shared with me as I did my research for this book indicates that for at least one person, Aurore, crochet can help manage the difficult symptoms of being a schizophrenic.

I should note before I share Aurore's story (which you can read in full on the page titled *Meet Aurore!* but will learn all of in this chapter) that there was a bit of a language barrier in our communication but I found her story so powerful that I wanted to work to share it with you anyway. Her native language is French, which I don't speak. Her actual diagnosis translates in English to something called chronic hallucinatory psychosis but by her account and our combined research it seems that this is similar to what we call schizophrenia. What is certain is that she experiences hallucinations similar to those of a schizophrenic and that she uses crochet to maintain a connection to reality in spite of those hallucinations.

Schizophrenia is a complicated disease in part because the symptoms come on so slowly. They can be mistaken for other illnesses like depression and anxiety. Additionally, schizophrenia can present as a dual diagnosis with these other conditions (so you can be both schizophrenic and depressed, for example), meaning that some of the symptoms could be from the schizophrenia whereas others are from a different mental health condition. It means that schizophrenia is not only difficult to diagnose but can also be extremely confusing and frustrating for the patient, especially in those early days. That was the case for Aurore, a case that was complicated by the fact that her diagnosis was hidden from her.

Although Aurore didn't know exactly what was going on with her, she began to experience the full effects of her mental illness in 2002. She went through what she describes as a "burnout", a low period during which her symptoms worsened and she had increasing difficulty functioning. It's what some of us might call a breakdown. She began to see a psychiatrist. He treated her for her condition but did not tell her what her diagnosis was, subscribing to a method of psychiatry that holds the belief that patients who know the label of the disease are likely to conform to that label and therefore shouldn't be told what their illness is. That's a controversial approach to medicine these days, particularly for those of us in America, but Aurore experienced it as common in France. She was told only that she was "psychotic" and her doctor treated her accordingly.

The treatment worked for awhile and Aurore's symptoms subsided to some degree. However, in 2008 she went through another "burnout." This one was worse than the first one and she continues to feel the effects of it to this day (at least in 2012, as of the writing of this book). In 2010, Aurore accidently saw her specific diagnosis on some legal papers that her doctor had to fill out when she applied to gain status as a handicapped worker (allowing her to have a legally protected job and a pension despite her mental illness). So, after eight years of being treated for an array of debilitating symptoms, Aurore learned that she was diagnosed with "chronic hallucinatory psychosis, generalized anxiety and acute depression." She notes that those words are translated specifically from the French and aren't necessarily the same terms as used in English but it is her understanding, and mine, that essentially she has a form of schizophrenia with related anxiety and depression. Crochet has played a key role in helping her to feel stable and sane despite the disassociation, time loss and hallucinations associated with her condition.

There are four key ways that Aurore has found that crochet can help her in coping with the symptoms of her condition, which I'll outline and then we can look more closely at the specifics of how those things help her and how they might have the potential to help other people struggling with a similar diagnosis. Crochet helps Aurore in the following ways:

1. She knows that crochet is real which helps her manage her hallucinations and the anxiety that accompanies them.
2. Crochet is a productive outlet for channeling some of her magical thinking.
3. She is able to get a better grasp on the passage of time and to experience a sense of continuity that she doesn't get elsewhere and desperately needs because of her schizophrenia.
4. The act of crochet assists Aurore in dealing with the anxiety that surrounds her condition.

Handling Hallucinations

Let's look first at how crochet helps Aurore deal with her hallucinations, since this is often the most frightening aspect of schizophrenia and the one most individuals desperately desire to get under control. Aurore explained in her interview that she not only experiences hallucinations but also has massive anxiety around the hallucinations because she knows that she hallucinates and is therefore terrified that she is one day not going to be able to tell the difference at all between what is real and what is just a fantasy played out in her head. Basically, even when she's not in the midst of a hallucination, she may wonder if what is happening around her is real since she's experienced hallucinations in the past.

In their book *Coping with Schizophrenia*, authors Steven Jones and Peter Hayward ask the seemingly odd question, "what is reality anyway?" The question is designed to help someone without schizophrenia understand the reason that hallucinations are so scary. They explain that the terror of experiencing hallucinations is two-fold, first in the hallucination itself and then in being told that what they experience as real is not real and that it is this second part ("what is reality?") that is often worse.

The authors pose this scenario to the reader and so I will pose it to you: you are reading this book sitting in a chair in a room when someone walks into the room and insists that you are not actually in a chair in a room with this book but are really floating on an iceberg in the middle of the Arctic Ocean. You're certain that this isn't true, of course. You know that you are reading this book on a chair in a room. But if enough people tell you that it isn't true, that you're on an iceberg, that you're wrong, then you begin to doubt yourself and then you begin doubting everything that you think is real and then there is a level of terror that you can't understand unless you've been there. If indeed you are on an iceberg, the iceberg is scary but the true terror comes from not actually knowing that you're there, from your reality not being "real", from wondering what is real and what reality is.

I recall another version of this scenario that David Edgar wrote, and Elizabeth Wurtzel excerpted in Prozac Nation: "Imagine, if you will, a worldwide conspiracy to deny the existence of the colour yellow. And whenever you saw yellow, they told you, no, that isn't yellow, what the fuck's yellow? Eventually, whenever you saw yellow, you would say: that isn't yellow, course it isn't, blue or green or purple, or ... You'd say it, yes it is, it's yellow, and become increasingly hysterical, and then go quite berserk." With schizophrenia, you sometimes have no way of knowing if your reality, your perception that this color is yellow, is accurate or if you are stubbornly insisting that it is accurate when really it is just a hallucination.

Since most of us haven't experienced hallucinations, I think it's worth looking specifically at the kind of thing Aurore was dealing with. Hallucinations can obviously vary from one schizophrenic to the next and from one situation to the next that any individual might be experiencing. One example from Aurore's life comes from 2008 when she was working in a highly stressful environment during the Christmas holidays. She began to hallucinate that she was hearing the store's Christmas music playing over and over even when she wasn't at work. She would also hear angry voices berating her and experience the phone ringing when those things were not actually happening. So if you can picture that, she's going about her day and she hears the Christmas music playing but she realizes that she's at home and there is no Christmas music so she knows that she must be hallucinating it. Then she hears angry co-workers saying mean things to her but she's not at work so they can't really be there saying those things. While Christmas music and even angry co-workers aren't inherently terrifying, being certain that you hear them when you are equally certain that you can't possibly be hearing them is unnerving indeed.

In his book *Schizophrenia Revealed* Michael Foster Green explains that auditory hallucinations like the ones that Aurore was experiencing are the most common type of hallucinations that people with schizophrenia experience. That's why the layperson often thinks of this as the disease of "voices in your head." Green explains that these voices are hallucinations that sound like real external voices and yet are distinct from the individual thoughts the person has. People suffering from schizophrenia may also have visual hallucinations or they may hallucinate smells or tactile sensations that aren't real, but auditory hallucinations are the most common type of schizophrenic hallucinations.

Aurore explains that crochet is something that has helped to ground her to reality as she has experienced her auditory hallucinations. She says that she knows that her crochet is real, that it is something concrete and tangible that she has really actually made, and that therefore she can feel in touch with reality when she works on her crochet. Moreover, the physical feeling of tangibly working with the texture of the yarn combined with the experience of actually seeing the stitches grow into fabric as she works are things that aid her in knowing that right here, right now, while she's sitting and working on a crochet piece, she's doing something real that is actually happening in the physical world.

I don't know for sure how this works or why it works for Aurore. But here's one guess ... Schizophrenia.com explains that in addition to responding well to anti-psychotic stimuli, hallucinations can be reduced by decreasing stress and replacing it with a positive distraction. The site says, "Keeping busy is important as it provides helpful distraction. Competing stimuli can sometimes 'drown out' the voices." We have already seen how crochet can be a stress-reduction tool and a positive distraction for many people. So maybe that has something to do with why Aurore is able to focus on her crochet as a means of fighting back against her hallucinations and grounding herself in reality.

Magical Thinking

In addition to the types of hallucinations Aurore experiences that include auditory hallucinations, she frequently experiences another symptom of her condition that she called "magical thinking." What happens is that she thinks that if she does something (or doesn't do something) then another thing (seemingly unrelated to an outside observer) will occur. For example, you know the old saying that if you step on a crack you'll break your mother's back? Someone dealing with the magical thinking aspect of a condition like Aurore's may actually believe that if she steps on a crack in the sidewalk her mother's back is literally going to be broken. You and I know that this isn't true but it feels so true to her that she must act on it. Because of her condition, she will go out of her way to not step on any cracks and if she accidentally does so then she may feel extreme fear that she's caused her mother's back to break.

I believe that what Aurore refers to as magical thinking is the same thing or similar to what professionals would call delusions. The two major symptoms of acute schizophrenia are hallucinations and delusions. Hallucinations refer to experiencing sensations that are not actually there (voices are auditory hallucinations, for example, or you may smell something that's not there and that's an olfactory hallucination). In contrast, delusions are thoughts or ideas that are not true. If you won't eat your food because you believe (for no objective valid reason) that your sister is poisoning it, you're dealing with a delusion. When a television message seems to be specifically intended only for you, that's a delusion. Although I can't say with certainty that magical thinking ("if I do this, that will happen") is a delusion in the psychological sense, it seems like it falls into this same general category of schizophrenia.

Aurore has found that she can channel her magical thinking into crochet. She admits that she doesn't know if this is a positive thing or a negative thing. She would ideally like to be able to get rid of the magical thinking issue altogether. But while it's got her in its grips, the best that she can do is to manage the symptoms, and she does this with crochet. So, for example, she may believe that if she finishes a crochet project by a certain date then she will be protected from having a terrible thing happen to her. As a result, she may work actively on her crochet to achieve the completion of the project and therefore avoid the bad thing. While she's afraid sometimes that this reinforces the magical thinking, she also knows that it can be a safe way to channel those feelings. She says, "crochet creates a safe place where I can imagine something and make it real without anxiety or harm attached to it".

I want to share a quote from a 2009 study called Craft as Context in Therapeutic Change here because I think it's relevant to what Aurore does in replacing dysfunctional magical thinking with more positive forms of thinking using her craft: "It can be concluded that craft can be an empowering way to functional mental health as it minimizes the exposing stressors and holds positive illusions, while it can strengthen the sense of coherence and self-confidence and self-acceptance. Craft may act as a cognitive filter and distraction by maintaining positive mood in cases where a cognitive filter is needed to distort negative information or thoughts in a positive direction, or where it is needed to isolate or represent them in as unthreatening a manner as possible." So crochet may serve as a distraction to help move negative thoughts into a positive distraction or present them as unthreateningly as possible – say, for example, using magical thinking in crochet work instead of in taking actions outside the home.

Other research also seems to bear out what Aurore is saying. A 2009 Everyday Health article on schizophrenia reported on research showing that schizophrenic delusions could be moderated through intentional distraction. "Focusing on a task, reciting numbers, taking a nap, or watching television can help distract the person from delusional, often paranoid, thoughts. A recent study showed that the choice of distraction is important. Researchers found that choosing favorite music or a news program was a more effective distraction tool than white noise." It goes on to say that meditative activities (which crochet arguably is) have also been found to help reduce the impact of schizophrenic delusions.

I know of at least one other blogger dealing with hallucinations and delusions who uses crochet and knitting as a healing tool for coping with them. Lil of the blog Idiocratic Mind Soup (http://wireddifferently.wordpress.com) has had almost daily auditory (and sometimes visual) hallucinations for more than one dozen years. In an August 2011 post she noted that she was "indulging in knitting and crochet to keep myself occupied and hopefully calm. I think it's working, it seems to triumph over the hallucinations and stops me from getting too distressed or involved in my paranoid fantasies." Lil has chosen to keep her real identity a secret because, as mentioned before, there is a stigma attached to the diagnosis of schizophrenia. Nevertheless, she shares her story on the blog and it indicates that crochet has helped her from time to time.

So, the evidence from these two women along with some of the research seems to indicate that it's possible to use crochet to resolve or cope with the two main symptoms of schizophrenia: hallucinations and delusions. The evidence is minimal, I admit, but it hints at the possibility of using needlework to calm the worst aspects of this alarming condition. I would love to see more research done in this area!

A Sense of Continuity

Although the hallucinations and delusions are the two key features of schizophrenia that present themselves, there is another aspect of Aurore's condition that is particularly frightening for her. That is the feeling that life lacks continuity. Schizophrenia causes her to have extreme difficulty placing events in time. So, she might know that something happened in the past but she couldn't tell you if it happened in 2002 or 2005 and she couldn't place the event in time in relation to other events that had occurred.

Having an accurate perception of the passage of time is more important than it seems at first glance. Time is how we orient ourselves in this world, helping to keep us attached to reality. You may not know if you went on a trip in 1999 or 2000 but you know loosely that it was about that time and can say that you graduated high school before that and started such and such job after that. Your sense of time passing and events anchored in time creates a storyline for your life so that you can understand it and therefore relate to others. Gungsadawn Katatikarn writes in *The Importance of Perception to Schizophrenics*, that with this disease "various sensory input mechanisms are altered causing external time constancy to differ from internal time constancy. This perpetuates the schizophrenic's feelings of isolation and distress. To the schizophrenic, time becomes irrelevant. To lose constancy of time is to lose the basis of reality because time represents social order in daily life."

Aurore shared that from 1995 to 2008, most of her life was a big haze of events that had no relationship to one another. That's thirteen years of random events that didn't have a place in any sequential story in her mind. Aurore further shared that she believes that crochet has helped significantly with her ability to develop a better sense of continuity over time. She says, "seeing the stitches actually forming under my fingers helped me restore my sense of continuity." She not only gets a sense of time passing during the crochet process itself but also feels that it's assisting her in skill development to better mark the passage of time in all areas of her life. She is teaching her brain to understand how to see time passing and how to cement events into sequential stories in her mind and crochet is helping her with that.

Just imagine how frightening that would be, to vaguely know that some things happened at some point in your life but to have absolutely zero connections between different events. Although I have found no medical evidence suggesting that crochet builds skill-development for helping the schizophrenic to better place events in time, I do believe Aurore when she says that this is exactly the personal experience that she has had from this craft.

Anxiety and Related Conditions

Finally, Aurore mentioned that she experiences significant anxiety as a symptom of her condition. This anxiety is sometimes specifically about the condition itself (such as the terrified fear that she will lose touch with reality) but can also manifest in a variety of other ways. In the same way that crochet helps with generalized anxiety disorder, it can help with the anxiety associated with other mental health conditions such as schizophrenia. It can provide a calming, meditative release that offers a focus for that anxious energy and provides a reprieve from the anxiety.

Aurore notes that when she gets anxious, she feels "a hollow hull" inside and says that "crochet helps fill the void." She also described some instances to me in which her anxiety significantly impacted her self-esteem and she came to crochet as a means of helping regain some feeling of self-worth. For example, it helped in 2008 when she was working in retail during the holidays and she was having difficulty getting along with her co-workers. They didn't understand her condition and wanted her fired and this created a highly stressful working environment in which Aurore felt like everyone was against her. It was at this time that she started really getting into crochet. She started showing her work on her blog and she would receive praise for it, which helped to boost her self-esteem during a time when all feelings of self worth were being completely eroded in other areas of her life. We saw earlier in this book how Aimee used crochet as one area to maintain independence and self-esteem within the confines of an abusive marriage that otherwise ate at her ability to value herself. And Aurore describes a similar thing in relation to how a mental illness can eat at your sense of self-value but being able to be proud of crochet work can help you hang on to at least a shred of self-worth.

On a related note, it seems that mindfulness is a tool that is being used by at least some therapists to help manage both the delusions and hallucinations of schizophrenics by, in part, reducing anxiety and refocusing attention. We looked at mindfulness earlier in this book and saw how it can relate to crochet, providing a focused activity for assisting the individual in remaining in the moment and letting go of the distracting thoughts trying to filter through. If mindfulness techniques can help with the symptoms of schizophrenia and crochet can be a path to mindfulness then crochet has the potential to help ease the symptoms of schizophrenia.

I think it's worth noting that for Aurore, it is the process of crochet (as opposed to the project planning or the finished product) that is truly healing. All aspects of crochet can offer benefits to the crafter, as we have seen again and again throughout this book. For Aurore, it is the physical process of crocheting that offers the most rewards. In fact, there have been many times in the throes of her condition that she does not complete a project at all, but rather stitches, unravels the work, and stitches it again. It is the creation of the stitches that helps to keep her grounded in reality, aiding the most in her specific condition.

What really touches me about Aurore's story is how crochet has been able to help her with such an intense condition and how it has helped her not in just a single way, but in many ways. It has helped her deal with hallucinations. It has helped to soothe her during periods of stress and anxiety. It has helped to restore her sense of self-esteem.

We've seen through Aurore's story that crochet can provide a variety of benefits to someone dealing with a diagnosis like schizophrenia. But even if it does nothing else, it can be a positive use of time for people who are going through therapy for conditions like this. In fact, I'm aware of at least one therapeutic program for schizophrenics that incorporates knitting and crochet into a regular recreational routine for patients: the Anne Sippi Clinic. This clinic opened its first location in 1978 and so has more than thirty years of experience in treating psychotic and affective disorders like schizophrenia.

A 1999 newsletter by Jack Rosberg explains that the Anne Sippi Clinic believes strongly that positive recreation is crucial to healthy treatment because, "Individuals with schizophrenia commonly do not know how to use time productively when not in therapeutic sessions, and are frequently restless, bored, and listless. They spend a great deal of time in bed, and focus their waking activities on eating, and smoking." As such, a core part of their evening and weekend program at this clinic is, "residents work with a case manager learning how to make jewelry, decorate ceramics, make seasonal crafts, and how to knit and crochet. They learn how to select a project, plan use of materials, maintain focused attention, and follow a task to completion. In addition, these activities increase their fine motor skills, concentration and creativity." In other words, it helps to stay busy with focused, creative activities ... just like with depression it helps to stay busy to stop that "cycle of rumination".

Is crochet a cure for schizophrenic hallucinations? Of course not. But can it be a useful device for people who are dealing with such a diagnosis? Clearly it can. People diagnosed with schizophrenia live on a continuum with some people having a very poor prognosis for a "normal" life but others living normal lives quite well and productively. This depends on a diverse range of things but for each individual there is potential for a healthy experience of every day life. Crochet just might help with that for some of those people as Aurore has shown us.

And perhaps there is some scientific basis for this as well. In a 2007 article published on Knit on the Net, Stitchlinks founder Betsan Corkhill posited the theory that the back and forth motion of the eyes that you do when working one row and then another in knitting (and sort of with crochet) is similar to a treatment called Eye Movement Desensitisation and Reprocessing (EMDR) that is sometimes used to treat serious mental illness including schizophrenia. EMDR is an integrative therapeutic technique that differs from other techniques because it includes an emphasis on bilateral stimulation primarily through eye movements. It is a relatively new type of therapy, developed in the late 1980s, and it has been quite controversial with many studies suggesting that it doesn't work even though there is anecdotal evidence showing that some people believe that it does. In any case, it is a type of therapy that utilizes a back and forth motion of the eyes as part of the treatment process and Corkhill suggests that perhaps that could be extrapolated to the use of back-and-forth needlework as a treatment. It's just a theory, but it's an interesting one, isn't it?

EMDR may be a controversial treatment for schizophrenia but there's a much more accepted treatment that also relates to crochet: occupational therapy. Occupational therapy (which we will look at in more depth later in a chapter specific to the topic) simply refers to treatment that helps individuals develop daily life and work skills. For example, a treatment center might use occupational therapy to teach its patients how to establish and keep a daily routine, how to manage their money, how to engage in leisure activities and how to develop social skills. Crochet isn't necessarily a "life skill" but it can be used as one aspect of an occupational therapy program. As mentioned before, the Anne Sippi Clinic uses recreation as part of its therapeutic program.

A 1958 book called *Chronic Schizphorenia* reports that typical occupational therapy tasks in treatment centers of the time included crafts like knitting, sewing and rug-making. Interestingly, the authors noted that a lot of the participants in the crafts would do what Aurore found herself doing – start a project, work on the process and then unravel it and start over. They found, however, that the craft was more likely to be finished if there was a specific purpose for the project – to make a rug that would be displayed in the treatment center or given to a nurse the patient was fond of, for example. In all cases, the crafting of this occupational therapy was part of an "ego-building treatment", reiterating the possibility that having a craft that you can successfully complete can help restore your sense of self-worth even when you're suffering so badly from a mental illness that you find yourself in an inpatient treatment center.

More recent research continues to indicate that there are benefits of occupational therapy for schizophrenic patients. A 2009 article by Mark Cowen reports on research done by Dr. Sarah Cook of Sheffield Hallam University that concluded that "engagement in meaningful and satisfying occupations contributes towards health and well-being, social inclusion, improved functioning and self respect." Today's occupational therapy programs tend to focus more on life skills, like money management, than the domestic arts that women would have been doing in treatment centers in the 1950s. Nevertheless, knitting and crochet can play an important role in those programs. They offer the opportunity to develop skills related to designing and completing a project, to boost the self-esteem as we've already seen explored and also to connect with others in a social setting which is a crucial part of the skill development goals in occupational therapy.

There are many schools of thought on how to best treat patients with schizophrenia. My personal philosophy is that the best treatment for all mental illness is a holistic approach that incorporates different ideas and therapies, drawing on everything from art therapy to psychopharmacology. I believe that treatment should be individualized because each of us is different and unique and what works for one person does not necessarily work for another person. And I believe, because of this, that crochet and other crafts may be able to play a small role in the full and complete treatment of individuals with serious mental illnesses like schizophrenia even though it isn't something that will work for everyone. In short, I believe that what works works ... and for some people, that's going to include crochet.

Meet Aurore!

Aurore is a French woman with a diagnosis of chronic hallucinatory psychosis, a condition that is comparable to schizophrenia and is characterized by difficulty maintaining a sense of what is real and what is not. This strong woman uses crochet as one tool to help her maintain a connection to reality as she deals with this condition.

Aurore has had a really tough experience with mental illness. Aurore's illness first began to really reveal itself to her in 2002 at the end of a two-year mental health decline that ended in her first "burnout." Like many people with mental illness, she didn't really know what was going on with her at the time. To complicate matters, she did begin seeing a psychiatrist but the psychiatrist did not give her a specific diagnosis. Aurore explained to me that a common belief among many French psychiatrists, and one that her psychiatrist subscribes to, is that that it is better for patients not to know the label of their diagnosis lest they begin to conform to that label. Aurore was told only that she is considered psychotic.

In 2008, Aurore had what she describes as a serious burnout, and the ramifications of that burnout continue to this day. In 2010, Aurore accidently saw her specific diagnosis on some legal papers that her doctor had to fill out when she applied to gain status as a handicapped worker (allowing her to have a legally protected job and a pension despite her mental illness). It was in 2010 then that she learned that she was diagnosed with "chronic hallucinatory, psychosis, generalized anxiety and acute depression." She essentially has a form of schizophrenia with related anxiety and depression. Crochet has played a key role in helping her to feel stable and sane despite the disassociation, time loss and hallucinations associated with her condition. Aurore explains:

> *"Crochet helped me cope with this because it's something that's tangible. I wasn't sure of anything but what I made with my hooks. Because of my hallucinations, I'm also terrified I eventually could not differentiate between what's real and what's not, so crochet helps me because <u>I know it's real</u>. It's like an anchor into reality, and*

*it's all the more important to me because <u>it's something real **I've made**</u>."*

Aurore explained that touching the yarn and feeling the actual physical process of stitching helps to ground her. It also helps her to deal with the anxiety related to her condition; she says, "when I'm anxious, the concrete feeling of the yarn against my fingers is something to focus on." In addition to being something tangible, crochet has helped Aurore maintain a sense of continuity over time in spite of her condition. She explains:

> *"Another thing I'm getting better at is placing an event in time. But from 1995 (last date I remember because I passed my Baccalauréat exam that marks the end of high school in this year and I remember seeing the date on my exam papers) until about 2008, I could tell if an event happened in the past, but I couldn't date it and couldn't tell if another event was before or after it. It's as if the past was a big haze. So seeing the stitches actually forming under my fingers helped me restore my sense of continuity.*

Crochet also helps Aurore in another way, although she's not one hundred percent certain that it's a benefit – more like a useful adaptation for her given her condition. She explains:

> *"I often have magic thoughts of all kinds. One I often have is: if I finish such crochet project by such date, I will be protected from XXXX. I know it's not particularly good for me to reinforce this kind of behavior, but I don't have yet the state of mind where I could cope without thinking like this."*

It can certainly be argued that using crochet to reinforce magical thinking isn't a good thing. Then again, it could be argued that crochet itself is a harmless, and even healing, craft and that if Aurore is going to experience magical thinking then this could be a relatively safe way of coping with it. Aurore explains that her magical thinking and daydreaming do frighten her, because she's afraid that she's going to lose touch with reality altogether, but that "crochet creates a safe place where I can imagine something and make it real without anxiety or harm attached to it".

Hearing about how beneficial crochet is to Aurore's health and wellbeing, I was really curious about how she came to crochet in the first place. I wondered if it was something that she had always done. Like many of us, she didn't do so much crochet until she really reached a crisis point in her life and then she came to rely on it heavily. Here's her story in her own words:

> *"It was after my second burnout, in 2008. I was working as a sales assistant in a shop, which initially helped me coping with being confronted with other people but, as time went by, I felt more and more anxious when there were crowds. I coped because my coworkers were like a family to me, very strong women who helped me a lot. But the direction changed and they were all fired or they resigned.*
>
> *The new team was more neutral at first, but then became more and more hostile when faced with my difficulties, saying things like "Aurore only weeps when there's too much work" and belittling me because I'm slow and need to check several times what I'm doing to be sure I'm actually doing it and not imagining it. I was trying to do my best and was belittled for it. That's when I really began to rely on crochet, initially because it was something I'm good at, and I got praise for it when I showed what I made on my blog, so it helped restore somewhat my confidence.*
>
> *During the first six months of 2008 (I didn't work from January of 2008 till September of 2009, if I recall well), I was so obsessed with work that I almost constantly hallucinated the music that was played in the shop during the holidays (very specific music I couldn't have heard anywhere else, so I'm sure it was job-related; I heard and heard it again during my anxious moments, along with phantom phones ringing and angry voices berating me). I couldn't concentrate on anything but obsessively crocheting.*
>
> *When I'm anxious, I feel like a hollow hull. Crocheting helps fill up the void.*
>
> *Then I got back to work in September of 2009. Things went well during the holiday season because they needed all the people they could hire. But in the beginning of 2010 they downsized the shop. I couldn't be fired because I had a very protective, unlimited contract, so they used my health as a pretext, requesting an appointment with the doctor who was legally in charge with the health of the employees*

of the company and sending him a letter with a big list of my behavioral problems, some true (like pacing obsessively the floor), others untrue (it said in particular that I looked funny at pregnant women, which is not true and really shocked me). The doctor then pronounced me unfit for working with the public. As a result my depression got worse and I had to go in a nursing home to recover. While there, I didn't finish anything but I obsessively kept on crocheting and unraveling. You see, I was too confused to have a goal and have a definite crochet project but the process of forming the stitches and working with yarn soothed me so I kept crocheting und unraveling my work."

Since that time, Aurore has been crocheting consistently, because she knows that it is such a healing craft for her. Aurore has a French blog where she writes about all types of different things. I mention this because although she doesn't write specifically about the health benefits of crafting in her blog, she notes that the style and subject of the posts suggests a lot about her experience with the ups and downs of her mental illness. Aurore explains:

"Most of my entries are either posts I made during moments of crisis or more serene posts about crafts and most importantly, crochet. I didn't link healing and crafts per se, but the juxtaposition of these two types of posts suggests it enough, in my opinion."

You can check out Aurore's blog at http://cynalune.blogspot.com/.

Bipolar: Managing Mood Swings with the Repetition of Crochet

Bipolar disorder is a condition that is characterized most specifically by wild mood swings (although there are variations in bipolar types). Periods of intense depression are followed by periods of intense euphoria or mania. We've already looked closely at how crochet can help people in dealing with depression. But what about the manic periods? Betsan Corkhill's research for Stitchlinks turned up stories of people who use knitting and other stitching to help balance out their moods, using it to feel better during periods of depression but also "to induce calm and slow down their thought processes" at the onset of a manic episode.

People who don't have personal experience with bipolar disorder sometimes think that the manic part of the condition isn't really so bad. Who wouldn't want to have greater energy levels and more productivity? You might even think, "this is terrific, now I can get tons of crochet work done!" But the truth is that the manic episodes of bipolar disorder are just as difficult and distressing for the individual as are the depressed periods. Manic phases are characterized by hyperactivity, irritability and anger, racing thoughts, insomnia, poor judgment and reckless behavior. This can lead to taking actions that become regrettable and plague the person when they enter a depressed period.

Crochet to Help Moderate Moods

Like schizophrenia, bipolar is a tough diagnosis to receive because it isn't one that's easily "fixed." Bipolar disorder typically requires both therapy and medication to be brought under control. But even those things can't always solve the problem. In fact, according to the National Institute of Mental Health, periods of depression and mania will typically continue to return for a majority of bipolar sufferers, even those who are getting treatment. This website cites the goals of bipolar treatment as:

- Avoid moving from one phase to another
- Avoid the need for a hospital stay

- Help the patient function as well as possible between episodes
- Prevent self-injury and suicide
- Make the episodes less frequent and severe

Now let's talk about where crochet has the potential to come into play in meeting these treatment goals. The creative but repetitive task of crochet can aid some people in avoiding the huge swings from one phase to the other, which is a primary goal of bipolar treatment. Crochet can be used during the early stages of a manic period to help make the mania less severe, calming the individual and bringing them back to the task at hand. Bipolar isn't "fixable" but by focusing on moderating moods, much of the problems associated with it can be adequately handled.

There are people in the real world who are using crochet this way, either for themselves as they struggle with bipolar disorder, or as part of a community program to aid people with this destructive mental disorder. One individual posting on the Life, Love and Bipolar forum board shared, "On nights when I am manic, I knit or crochet and the repetitiveness sometimes numbs my brain or slows it down and I can go to bed and not stay up all night!"

The New York Times has shared several stories about the benefits of crochet for people with bipolar disorder in their reports on their Neediest Cases fund. The fund, first established nearly 100 years ago, currently provides aid to seven different New York social welfare agencies. The stories share information about where some of that money is going and show how sometimes crochet can really help bipolar people in need through those programs.

For example, in 2009, author Jennifer Mascia reported on a Neediest Cases project called Project Moving On, which was a day treatment program for adults with severe mental illness operated by the Brooklyn Bureau of Community Service. This important Brooklyn organization provides numerous services for people with a variety of mental illnesses, many of whom have been court ordered to receive treatment. This is often the case for people who are suffering from bipolar disorder because the reckless actions they take in a manic phase result in criminal repercussions. Project Moving On was based on the idea that art of all kinds can be therapeutic for people with severe mental illness. Mascia reports about one woman, Vanessa Rogers, who was crocheting when Mascia visited the program. Rogers was a 52-year-old woman with bipolar disorder who had spent time in jail because of actions that she took when she went off of her medication (also a common problem for people with bipolar disorder, related to the recklessness associated with the manic phase of the condition). Although Rogers didn't want to come to the treatment program at first, she ended up finding her place in the art program and was doing well as of the time that the article was written. Crochet was a key contributor to her healing; her personal specialty was crocheting sock puppets.

The NY Times published another Neediest Cases story in 2010 (authored by Amanda M. Fairbanks) about a bipolar woman who was moving into the Brooklyn Bureau of Community Service's Transitional Living Community. 56-year-old Janet Dennard is a highly creative woman whose illness has caused great devastation in her life and family. She chose to go off of her medication in 2006 and wreaked havoc around her that resulted in her having to be forcibly removed from her daughter's home by New York Adult Protective Services. Dennard received help for her mental illness. She also received a $240 grant from the Neediest Cases Fund to get a vending license so that she can use her creativity to make and sell her handmade items throughout the city in order to help support herself while channeling her energy in a positive direction. Although she is primarily someone who sews, she does also crochet, and takes pleasure in both crafts. This bipolar woman uses crafting to keep her self-esteem up, moderate her moods and hopefully even eke out a small living for herself.

Why are programs like these interested in using the arts to help people with bipolar disorder? One key reason is because creative actions like crochet can help reduce stress and stress is one of the leading triggers of bipolar mood swings. And it may be even better if you do it in a group. A 2011 Yahoo! Health News report by Laurie Herr cites: "According to research published in the *Australian and New Zealand Journal of Psychiatry,* people with bipolar disorder who cultivated hobbies through local community groups found sharing such mutual interests to be as beneficial, if not more so, than what they gained from traditional mental health groups." So not only is crochet potentially helpful, joining a crochet group could be even better! This relates to the point we discussed earlier about schizophrenia and crochet … that crocheting in groups can be a way to help build important social skills that are sometimes difficult for people with severe mental illnesses.

Productivity in Hypomania

As you may have noticed from the stories shared here, or from your own knowledge about bipolar disorder, there is a strong link between the disease and great creativity. Kay Jamison, Ph.D., has written extensively about this from her own personal experience as someone with bipolar disorder. In fact, she has put a positive spin on bipolar, recognizing the advantages that the condition offers rather than the disadvantages of having it. She writes in *Night Falls Fast*, "Extremes of emotions are a gift – the capacity to be passionately involved in life, to care deeply about things, to feel hurt; a lot of people don't have that. It's the transition in and out of the highs and lows, the constant contrast, that fosters creativity."

Part of the period of transition is a state of being called hypomania. It occurs in the period when transitioning into mania but before full-blown mania develops. Whereas mania itself is characterized by restlessness, recklessness and disordered thinking hypomania is an excited state in which a lot of energy, optimism, self-confidence and productivity can occur. If channeled properly, hypomanic states can be a terrific time for intense creativity. If you are someone who crochets, this can be the time when you begin truly creating your own innovative designs, for example. Successes achieved during this time period can be something to look at when self-esteem wanes during depressed periods.

It is important to note, however, that hypomania is not a fully positive state. This point was made in most of the books that I used to research bipolar disorder, with the terrific point being made that if it were "normal" then it wouldn't need a name or any attention. The major risk of the hypomanic state is decreased self-awareness. The individual gets so lost in the intense pleasure of their creative pursuits that they lose track of time and lose touch with themselves. For example, they may forget that they need to stick to a regular sleep schedule because they are so immersed in their creative work. This is the dangerous part of hypomania that can lead into full manic episodes. About.com guide and bipolar sufferer Marcia Purse shared a story on her site in 2008 about when crochet went from being a positive distraction to an obsession for her.

Purse actually started crocheting as a means to break some addictions that she had – to both food and cigarettes. As we saw in the chapter on addiction, crochet can busy the hands and mind and be a positive replacement for negative habits. At first, this seemed true for Purse. However, she eventually found herself in a period where she was obsessively crocheting to the exclusion of doing anything else. She would crochet and watch television all day every day to the point that her therapist finally actually asked her to bring all of her crochet supplies to him to leave in his office to end this obsession. Purse refused to do that. She committed to a program of doing two hours of work for every one hour of crochet but she failed at keeping that commitment. She was obsessed with her crochet. This isn't a common response to using crochet to treat addiction but it makes sense as a condition of her bipolar disorder (as well as possible OCD, which she's also been diagnosed with in the past.)

Some people with bipolar might find it useful to keep a blog or journal about their crochet work, tracking their projects and the amount of time they are investing in their projects. This can be a simple way to help notice if extreme amounts of time are being lost to projects, a tool to make the individual aware of the potential hypomanic state. Goal-setting for crochet projects can also assist with this. In their book *New Hope for People with Bipolar Disorder,* authors Fawcett, Golden and Rosenfeld suggest that two key components of realistic goal setting are to set specific limits for each project and to watch carefully for signs of obsession. Taking a proactive approach to goal setting with your projects can help crochet be the beneficial source of creativity that you need without allowing it to become obsessive and therefore detrimental.

A related thing to remember is that there are different forms of bipolar, some of which are more extreme than others. For example, there is a mild form of the disorder called cyclothymia, in which both the mania and depression are prevalent but in a much more subdued form than in other types of bipolar disorder. For people with cyclothymia, the manic periods may be more likely to resemble hypomania than true mania and therefore may be modulated in part by the creative benefits of art, craft and crochet.

Mindfulness

As we've already seen in several spots throughout this book, mindfulness training can be useful to people who are struggling to stay in the present moment without getting lost in the ups and downs of their own minds. The authors of *New Hope for People with Bipolar Disorder* note that Mindfulness-Based Cognitive Therapy (MBCT) is commonly used in modern psychotherapy to assist people in dealing with bipolar disorder. They explain that mindfulness training provides patients with the ability to identify their current thoughts and emotions and then to alter them rather than replaying the same scenarios again and again in their minds.

The authors go on to say later in their book that mindfulness meditation in general can be a highly positive method of attaining a level of non-self-judgment that is critical to the health and wellbeing of people struggling with bipolar disorder. It has proven to be an effective form of mood management. A bipolar patient who has studied mindfulness may find it beneficial to keep the hands busy with the calming repetition of crochet while working through the mental aspect of mindfulness training.

There is another important issue here related to mindfulness and non-judgment. It has to do with the fact that many bipolar people feel like medications stifle their creativity. This is something that Kay Redfield addresses in her work and something that is highly common among people with bipolar disorder. Moderating moods is the goal of most treatment and yet this can leave the bipolar individual feeling like the benefits of the "highs" or hypomanic states are gone. I mention this because I saw one crocheter, named Edyn, who had taken a really positive viewpoint on the topic, which she shared on the MDJunction Bipolar Support Group forum in January 2012:

Edyn says: "Too often here I see ourselves commenting about how our creativity has been stifled by our bipolar meds. I too thought of myself as stifled; not able to complete any 'creative' things at all. I've recently come to a conclusion. My creative outlet, I mostly crochet, isn't done to create something absolutely original. I crochet for the love of crochet. The simple rhythm of crochet is comforting to me. I find myself not thinking of my issues and problems and becoming one with the item I'm creating. And when it's finished I marvel at how my creation differs from the pattern I'm 'following' and how it has become uniquely mine. I also find that the more I crochet and meditate, the more creative and calm I am in other aspects of my life. Is crochet the answer to all my problems? No. But it has taught me to do things for the simple pleasure of doing them. Not for the end result."

People with bipolar disorder contend with many different difficulties. There are the symptoms themselves, of course, and the various ramifications of those symptoms. There is the social isolation and fear surrounding a difficult diagnosis such as this one. And then there's the battle with the self about how to best utilize and enjoy the positive aspects of the condition (such as the potential for creativity in a hypomanic state) without allowing the intense highs and lows to take over. People like Kay Redfield have shown that it's possible to have a positive viewpoint about the condition and people like Edyn show us how crochet can play a part in realizing that positive approach.

Remember! Crochet for Alzheimer's and Age-Related Memory Loss

Author's note: I am going to use the terms Alzheimer's and dementia interchangeably throughout this chapter to refer to the general concept of age-related memory loss. I should note, however, that this is not medically correct. Alzheimer's is one type of dementia. There are many types of dementia, and there are also many other reasons for age-related memory loss. I don't pretend to always understand the difference as a layperson. What I do know is that many of the symptoms are similar across the different diagnoses and that's what I'll be talking about in this chapter so bear that in mind as the various terms get bandied about here.

Let me share a memory ... It is four o'clock in the morning, already beginning to get warm in my parents' Arizona home. I awake from across the house to hear my grandmother calling out from her bedroom. "Help me, help me," she wails. The harsh truth is that none of us really wants to get up and go to her because there is no way to help her. She doesn't know what she needs. Sometimes she doesn't know who we are. All that she knows is that she's losing her mind and she wants it to stop. She wants everything to be normal again, and she's begging for help.

My mother goes to help her. My grandmother, frail, has wet the bed again. Sometimes she realizes that she is not supposed to be wet so she will try to change herself, but she doesn't usually get the order of the clothing right or get all of the right pieces onto her increasingly slim body. On this day, she hasn't even bothered to try. From outside of her mind, there is no way of knowing if this is because she doesn't know anymore that she's not supposed to be wet or if she's not sure what steps to take to make the wetness go away. My mother helps wash her and change her and gets the sheets and blankets into the laundry machine. My grandmother continues to beg audibly, although quieter now, "help me." We all want to put the pillows over our ears but this is it, the day has begun. For my grandma, the hours only make the condition worse. There is little to look forward to.

Alzheimer's or some other form of dementia has affected the lives of the loved ones of just about everyone that I know. I mention to someone that my grandmother has Alzheimer's and they inevitably respond with the story of someone they know who has it as well. In the best possible of scenarios, it is always terrifying. It is terrifying to witness and I have seen the look in my grandmother's eyes that says that it's even more terrifying to have it happen to you. In my case, both of my maternal grandparents were afflicted with some type of age-related memory loss in their later years.

My grandfather lived into his late nineties and still had a lot of his mind left when he passed away but definitely suffered from some uncomfortable memory loss. Towards the end he was miserable, certainly due in no small part to the fact that he knew that he was forgetting things and hated losing his capacities. He, like many older people, suffered from what they called "sundowning" where he would be much more alert and aware during the morning hours and much worse off at night. We weren't close and I never talked to him about his condition but I can only imagine that waking up every day and knowing that the day is only going to get worse as the hours drag on must be a terrible way to live out the end of your life.

My grandpa, in typical male fashion, acted out his frustration. He ranted. He demanded. He expressed big ideas. He was occasionally aggressive. And towards the end when all he wanted was to no longer be alive there were hints that he may turn that anger and frustration on himself in attempted suicide although he died before it ever came to that. As a bystander, it was awful to see and hear about all of this. At the same time, you could kind of respect his verve and vigor. And these days, we (my family and I) can laugh at many of his antics from this time. In the face of ailment, he held on to much of his personality. So while it is sad that my grandfather passed away, and that he had some memory loss as it happened, it also happened quickly enough and with enough of his mind left towards the end that it was bearable.

(I should note that I say this cautiously, from a distance. I don't live in my parents' hometown anymore and only go home once or twice a year. By the time that my grandparents moved in with my parents and then moved on to nursing homes I was no longer living in the same city as them. I wasn't close with either of my grandparents. I say this because I don't want to downplay the difficulty of watching what my grandfather went through for those who were actually there – specifically my mother and sister – and am only saying what my experience of it was to highlight how it differs from the experience of seeing my grandmother deteriorating from afar).

So, on to grandma … I think that there are three key reasons why watching her memory loss has been more difficult for me than it was to see what happened to my grandfather. First, although I wouldn't say I was close to either of my grandparents as an adult, I was much closer to Gram than Grandpa due certainly to the bond I'd established with her as a child. Second, my grandmother has slowly been losing her mind over the course of the last decade. Although she's younger than my grandfather was when he passed away, the actual process of memory loss has been much more extended.

And finally, Gram's reaction to the situation differed a lot from my grandpa's. Where he had a typically male reaction of outwards frustration, she had a typically female reaction of internalizing most of the frustration and pain until it would come out in terror and helplessness. For me as a "child" of these people, it's much easier to see Grandpa angry and fighting it than to see Gram with her pajamas wet, crying, "help me" in the early hours of the morning.

I was 26 during that visit that I've described. I was visiting home for a vacation. My grandparents had both moved in with my parents but then grandpa had ended up moving on to a nursing home so grandma was the only one who was still living there. My mother was her primary caregiver and I can honestly say that I have no idea how she did that for as long as she did before my grandmother ultimately ended up needing the kind of medical care that is more suited to a nursing home staffed by professionals. What I can say is this; when we were children my little brother had boundless energy and my mother would be out in the yard with him throwing the ball for him to bat again and again and again. And every single time, she would enthusiastically respond to his attempt to hit the ball with what seemed like a very genuine, "good job" or "great hit" or "awesome." I swear that she could do this for hours on end, long past the point where I would have set up the ball on a t-ball stand and told my brother to figure it out himself. This same mothering instinct came out when my mother was caring for my grandmother, telling her again and again how to do something when the rest of us just wanted to snatch whatever it was from her hands and do it for her despite knowing that this was more than rude.

My grandmother was an interesting woman back in her heyday. When my mom cleaned out her house she found an old photo album that showed these gorgeous pictures of Gram surrounded by lots of good-looking friends. She was with a different man in every picture and seemed to have lots of girlfriends. She was perched cheekily on a motorcycle in one image. She was wearing what looked to be a daring swimsuit for the day in another. She was standing in front of the White House in another, which makes sense since she had a job for awhile in Washington, D.C. She looks out from all of these photos with mischievous eyes that suggest that she's just about to go on a wild adventure. I bet she learned something new every single day back then.

Unfortunately, we don't know a lot about her from that time because after she had kids her life became all about her family. The grandma that I know was a woman who spent a lot of time alone in the company of my grandfather. Grandpa was a good man but one who had been seriously affected by the many negative things that he had seen throughout his life and had therefore retained a rather negative view of the world. I remember visits over there primarily as Grandpa ranting about something that was in the newspaper that day and Grandma preparing food or washing dishes or putting her feet up while she drowned out the noise with a soap opera on their small television screen, one of her few regular indulgences.

Due to complicated family dynamics there was a period of about five years during which we didn't see my grandparents. It started when I was about nineteen and so absorbed in my own dramatic life issues and battles with depression that I scarcely noticed it happening although I heard about the drama from the sidelines. By the time that we saw them again, I was a little bit more interested in getting to know these characters from my life than I had been before, but by this time it was really too late with my grandma. In that time her brain had declined considerably. She didn't make a lot of sense and I'm not sure if she quite knew who I was. She did know that I was related to her and she seemed to know my siblings, probably because they were around a lot more than I was.

The forgetting is scary. I can't even hazard a guess at what it feels like to my mother when my grandmother looks at her and doesn't know who she is. And I don't even want to try to get into the mind of my grandmother as she tries to understand who all of these people are taking care of her. Although it's been years of this, she still usually tries to fake that she knows what is going on. I can only guess that this is because she still knows somewhere deep inside that she's supposed to have a clue and she is terrified by the fact that she does not.

Yes, the forgetting is scary, but it's not actually the scariest part of Alzheimer's. The scary part is all of the feelings that come along with the helpless terror in someone's eyes as they slowly lose their faculties. Gram would start at three or four in the morning with her, "help me" and it would only worsen throughout the day. For hours on end, she would ask again and again, "what can I do? What can I do?" She was sad and lost and frustrated and confused and no answer to her repetitive question would suffice. We would try to give her tasks and she wouldn't do them. We'd try to explain that she didn't have to do anything; that we'd take care of her now. She would just repeat again and again, "what can I do?" Explaining things to her didn't make her feel any better. I am only guessing because she wasn't able to articulate what was going on with her but I imagine that she still had a vague sense that she was losing her mind and what she wanted help with was keeping it. Nobody knew how to help her with that.

My mom tried valiantly to find a way to connect with Gram and to keep her happy. She would sit there at the kitchen table trying to play cards with her. Gram used to play cards with us when we were kids but the more complex games now had rules that she couldn't remember for the duration of a game. Crazy 8's, for example, just didn't make sense to her anymore. Eventually, trying to play cards with her just didn't work. Nothing worked. And so my grandma would sit there at the kitchen table as the day went on. She would tap her hand over and over again on the wood, counting "one, two, three, four ... one, two, three four" for hours and hours and hours, interspersed only with "what can I do?" and "help me".

We tried various things for her to do. Sometimes she could fold clothes or wipe down a table. However, five minutes later the task would be complete and she would be confused and the "what can I do?" would begin again. Somewhere along the line I had heard that tasks like knitting that keep the hands busy can be helpful in situations like this. If I had known how to crochet by then I think I would have tried to teach her, to see if this was something that she could do to pass the time and feel useful. You don't have to remember much to be able to make a scarf. You can make a scarf just by repeating a single crochet stitch over and over. The body can learn that and I think the mind isn't so necessary to keep it up once the body learns it. But it was another two years before I discovered crochet myself and by then Gram's mind was gone and her coordination was waning with it.

What has always stood out in my mind was the fact that my grandma didn't really do anything during her days once her kids had left the home. She went from that exciting woman in Washington D.C. to a mom and housewife and then she seemed to have little left when her kids became adults. My siblings and I were the only grandkids living in the city so she would watch and care for us when we were little but once we got older even that task was gone. That side of the family is Jewish and she had gone to synagogue for years, which was where all her friends were. However, as my grandpa got older, he became more and more opposed to the religion. Grandpa lost family to the Holocaust and had to escape from Europe because of what happened there and it was then that he lost his faith although he raised his kids in the Jewish faith because of my grandmother. In his older age, he became intolerant of it. He stopped going to synagogue and seeing their Jewish friends and because of the nature of their relationship this meant that my grandmother stopped seeing her friends as well. She never worked outside of the home and she didn't have any hobbies so this meant that she sat around most of the day doing nothing. I have always been certain that this was the major contributing factor as to why the Alzheimer's hit her so bad, so quickly. There was just nothing in her brain to stave it off.

My grandpa had some weapons in his arsenal. He was an avid walker who walked five miles per day into at least his late eighties. Gram walked with him for many years but as she aged she wasn't as physically capable of doing this. Grandpa also had a driver's license and would go out to run his errands. He was a tailor by trade and although he closed his shop years before he still continued to do some tailoring work for clients in his home into his later years. He wasn't social and there definitely could have been more activity for his brain but he did more in his daily life that required engagement than my Grandma did and I have little doubt that this is a contributing factor as to why his Alzheimer's never got as bad as hers.

Watching what my grandparents went through makes me terrified of Alzheimer's. I'm terrified by the thought of ever having to go through it myself. I'm terrified that whoever my life partner ends up being will go through it. I'm terrified that my parents will get lost to it. And I am not alone in this fear. In her book *100 Simple Things You Can Do To Prevent Alzheimer's and Age-Related Memory Loss,* author Jean Carper cites surveys that show that Americans over age 55 are more afraid of Alzheimer's than any other disease including such common conditions as cancer and heart disease.

There is no cure for Alzheimer's at this point. However there is a lot of scientific evidence out there that shows that there are many different things that you can do to prevent Alzheimer's. Basically the goal of treatment right now is to delay the onset of Alzheimer's so far into your individual future that you pass away of something else before it can set in. For example, you may delay it until you are 100 years old and since most people don't live to be 100 they wouldn't end up suffering from the condition. The thing is that it is ideal to start young to take actions to ward off Alzheimer's. And crochet has the potential to be one of those tools in your toolbox.

Jean Carper explains in her book that there is no way to know for sure right now what type of actions are going to assist in preventing or delaying Alzheimer's. The research is just too young and there isn't enough known about this disease yet to be certain. However, there are many steps that you can take as you get older that are believed to have some effect on preventing age-related memory loss. Carper presents one hundred of these things in her book but she notes that they basically fall into four important categories:

1. Keeping your brain active and engaged. It is imperative that you keep your brain thinking and one of the key ways to do this is to introduce new things into your life on a regular basis, filling your leisure time with brain-stimulating activities.

2. Regularly engage in the right amount of physical activity. It seems to be very important for older people to get steady amounts of aerobic exercise. They must also engage in muscle-building, stretching and balance-maintaining exercises.

3. Proper diet. There is always a lot of controversy around what the proper diet is for anyone and there is no exception when it comes to Alzheimer's prevention but eating properly (whatever that is determined to be) seems to be a key part of the deal.

4. Proper emotional self-care. It has been found to be critical to Alzheimer's prevention that the individual takes steps to be social, feel engaged with others, reduce depression and stress and feel like an active part of the community.

Keeping your brain stimulated with crochet

So first let's take a look at category number one in Carper's four basic categories to prevent age-related memory loss. It's something that you've probably heard before: keep your brain active and engaged as much and for as long as possible in order to prevent Alzheimer's. Let's take a look at a Mayo Clinic study that "found that engaging in cognitive activities like reading books, playing games or crafting in middle age or later life are associated with a decreased risk of mild cognitive impairment. Mild cognitive impairment (MCI) is a transitional state between normal aging and the earliest features of Alzheimer's disease." (Rice, 2009). It says right there that there is a decreased risk of moving from normal aging into Alzheimer's when a middle aged or older person engages in crafting, which obviously includes crochet.

The Mayo study clinic cited above was completed by neuropsychiatrist Dr. Yonas Geda. Geda was excited by the results because the implication of the study is that aging doesn't have to be a passive thing that we just give ourselves over to, that we just let happen to us, but rather it can be something that we take steps to control to some degree. By choosing to engage in brain-stimulating activities throughout life, and especially as we start to get older, we can create some protection for the brain to avoid age-related memory loss. Margaret Mills (*see Meet Margaret!)* explains that Geda's research "indicates crochet and knitting are 'neuroprotective.' Those elderly who engage in knitting/crochet and who have for many years just do better cognitively. A lot of crocheters and knitters have said that, but it is nice to see some serious research backing it up."

Crochet can come into play on both the first and fourth criteria for Alzheimer's prevention laid out by Carper. Reiterating the first criteria, crochet can be a mentally engaging activity especially for people who are new to it. The great thing about crochet is that there is always something new that you can learn. I know people who have been crocheting for decades and there are still things that they haven't tried. First of all, there are all of the different stitch types to learn. Beyond the basic stitches there are many other stitches that aren't always used like the bullion stitch and the cluster stitch and the crab stitch.

Even if you've been successful in mastering every crochet stitch there is, there are different techniques that you can learn such as how to create different types of garment shapes or how to change colors in different ways or how to block your finished projects out on blocking boards using pins or wires. And even beyond that there are actually many different types of crochet beyond basic crochet that can be learned including overlay crochet, Tunisian crochet, freeform crochet, mosaic crochet and interlocking crochet. If crochet is something that engages you then it can be a great leisure activity that allows you to regularly introduce your brain to something new and stimulating in a way that is non-stressful and non-threatening. If it does indeed help to continue learning new things and keeping your brain engaged then crochet is a great craft to take up because it will always offer something new to learn if you want to.

There is science behind the belief that continuing to engage your brain can help to prevent Alzheimer's. Carper explains in her book that your brain begins to shrink sometime in your thirties and the more it shrinks as you age the more likely it is that you'll develop Alzheimer's. However, this shrinkage can be prevented through active learning. Learning that takes a little bit of non-stressful effort helps you to actually grow new brain cells and to increase the size and ability of existing brain cells. In other words, choosing to actively keep learning as you age is something that can make your brain grow bigger. The bigger your brain, the more likely it is that you will retain memory despite other Alzheimer's factors. Of course, this only works with crochet if you challenge yourself to learn new areas of it … and of course you shouldn't limit yourself to learning crochet alone ... but it's one more thing that you can do to help your brain stay big.

Notably, meditation also assists in growing or retaining brain volume. As we've seen, many people say that they achieve effects similar to those of meditation when they are immersed in their crochet stitching. This suggests that crochet may be valuable to brain growth not only because it offers the opportunity to engage the brain with new learning but also because it offers the option to engage in the repetitive, meditative type of crochet that many of us enjoy even when not learning a new stitch technique. Betsan Corkhill of Stitchlinks explains that, "The automatic nature of knitting in particular means that often those suffering from dementia remember the process of knitting. They may not be able to follow or process a pattern but they'll often remember how to knit." Stitchlinks' research has also found that people who have suffered strokes but who are physically still able to knit report an improvement in memory and concentration attributed to their knitting. The conclusion can be drawn that similar memory-protective benefits may apply to crochet.

Furthermore, while it is great to learn new things with crochet in your older age, there may even be a benefit to learning new crochet techniques now, regardless of how young you are. That's because all of the learning that you do in your thirties, forties and fifties helps to build up what Carper calls "Cognitive Reserve." She explains that this theory, studied by neuroscientists from respected institutions like New York's Columbia University, shows that the reserves collected in your brain over the years can actually prevent the manifestation of Alzheimer's symptoms despite the physical changes going on in the brain that suggest that Alzheimer's is present.

You see, the Alzheimer's brain is sometimes referred to as the Swiss Cheese brain because it is riddled with actual holes. More accurately, in addition to holes, there are "plaques and tangles" that run all over the brain. In her book *How to Live Well with Early Alzheimer's*, Deborah Mitchell explains these two terms:

- Plaques occur when the beta-amyloid that is normally excreted from the body bundles up around the nerve cells. This causes death and damage to not only the nerve cells but also other types of cells in the body, like the mitochondria, which then leads to Alzheimer's.

- Tangles refer to when a protein in the body called tau actually twists into fibers. Again, this causes damage and death of nerve cells.

What the Cognitive Reserve Theory says is that a PET scan of your brain may reveal holes, plaques and tangles and yet you may have no symptoms of Alzheimer's because you have built up such a terrific reserve over the years. In fact, one Australian study cited by Carper showed that people with high cognitive reserve reduce their odds of being diagnosed with Alzheimer's by nearly fifty percent. So, your brain may have the physical signs of Alzheimer's (the "holes" in it) but you may not perceive any memory loss if you've sufficiently built up your cognitive reserve.

What builds up the reserve? Lots of stuff can help including having a good marriage, a healthy social life and a stimulating job, but a key factor in building up the reserve is having lots of leisure activities and learning activities in your life throughout your lifetime. The more education, new skills and fun hobbies that you have, the more of a reserve you are going to build up. If you haven't tried crochet, or haven't explored all there is to explore with it, then this could be one way to start adding to your reserve today.

Betsan Corkhill explains this in more scientific terminology in the Stitchlinks' Guide to Our Theories So Far: "Research in neuroscience and neurogenesis has shown that not only can new neural pathways be opened up, but new brain cells can be born and a leading neuroscientist working in the field of neurogenesis (birth of new brain cells) told me that "It's likely that learning in the motor cortex has a knock on effect in areas of cognition and memory." So this is really exciting. This could have implications for those suffering early memory problems as some researchers believe that the more neural pathways you have working the more reserve you'll have and therefore the more protection you'll have against symptoms of diseases such as Alzheimer's."

So, you want to keep learning as much as possible from the time that you are young to the time that you get old in order to build up your cognitive reserve. And there's something else interesting that has been shown to stimulate the brain – searching for things on the Internet. Out of all of the 100 tips that Carper suggests in her book, this was the one that struck me the most because it's so simple, so helpful and so surprising to me. We always seem to think of the Internet as a brain-draining or brain-numbing activity, but actually research shows that actively researching stuff online is a super helpful brain exercise that may be improving brain function. In fact, Carper reports on UCLA Center of Aging findings that show "that people ages fifty-five to seventy-eight who rarely used the Internet previously were able to trigger these key centers in the brain *after only one week of surfing the Web for an hour each day*." That's huge! And since there is a large amount of information about crochet online, along with a huge interactive crochet community through major sites like Ravelry, Crochetville, and (new in 2012) Hookey.org, this opens up a lot of potential research time for crochet enthusiasts who want to grow their brains with the web. I know that I can easily spend several hours each day doing crochet research online and still find new areas I want to explore!

Another thing to note here is that sensory stimulation is good for the Alzheimer's brain. As discussed in the chapter on depression, the craft of crochet appeals to many senses. The feel of the yarn, the luxury of the color that you're working with, even the smell of some yarn types … these are all things that stimulate the senses in a positive way. Deborah Mitchell notes that "exposing people to positive sensory stimulation not only helps improve mood, it can also reduce stress, evoke memories, and enhance quality of life." Read that sentence again – positive sensory stimulation can evoke memories! Crochet can help you remember!

Maintaining mental health with crochet

"Creating works of art, whether it is done with watercolors, oil paints, clay, charcoals, ink, paper or other media, has been shown to reduce stress and depression and improve a person's sense of well-being and self-esteem. Working with art materials also improves hand-eye coordination and stimulates neuronal activity in the brain, strengthening the gaps between nerve cells. Art therapists who work with Alzheimer's patients report that their clients are less stressed and depressed and more sociable than patients who don't participate in art activities." – Deborah Mitchell

Now we'll look at how crochet plays a role in the fourth category of Alzheimer's prevention laid out by Carper: self-care. What we can see from all that we've learned so far that is that crochet can be used to relax, build self-esteem and provide you with a positive leisure activity, all of which is crucial to self-care. And some of this brings us back to that very first chapter on depression because depression is a major problem for people with Alzheimer's and proper self-care for Alzheimer's treatment and prevention includes treating the depression.

It is important to note that research has come a long way towards identifying cause and effect in relation to depression and Alzheimer's. It was long believed that depression was a symptom or effect of Alzheimer's. It makes logical sense to those of us that have seen Alzheimer's in action that it's something that would cause a decline into depression. After all, if you can't remember things then you're going to start to feel useless and that could lead to depression. However, Carper reports on research done at UCLA, the University of Miami and the Rush Alzheimer's Disease Center in Chicago, all of which suggests that depression is actually a cause of Alzheimer's, not a symptom. People suffering from depression already are more likely to develop Alzheimer's and it is more likely to happen at a younger age than for people who aren't already depressed. It is unclear why this is but one theory posits that depression weakens the brain's neural reserve, creating an inability to resist Alzheimer's. Therefore, treating depression as early and thoroughly as possible before you reach your older years can have a clear benefit in terms of reducing the likely development of Alzheimer's. As discussed in the first chapter of this book, crochet alone is clearly not enough to dig you out of depression but it can be one utensil combined with therapy, medications, etc. to help deal with depression.

And it should be noted that depression can affect the elderly even if they weren't prone to depression in their younger days. Depression in the elderly is often due to a combination of loneliness, lack of activity and feelings of uselessness. Someone who chooses to join a crochet circle and to crochet blankets for charity would be battling all of these things and in turn possibly helping to prevent the onset of Alzheimer's.

Another major contributing factor to Alzheimer's is stress and stress-related disease. High blood pressure and the problems that come along with it, such as stroke, are major contributing factors to

Alzheimer's. If crochet can be used as a meditative form of stress reduction then it may help to prevent Alzheimer's in this way. We'll look at the physical benefits of reducing stress with crochet in a later chapter of this book but there's also an emotional side to stress to consider because of a personality trait called neuroticism. People with high scores on neuroticism tests are less emotionally stable and more reactive to stress, therefore they are more likely to experience negative feelings like anxiety, depression and guilt. Regular exposure to high stress levels causes your body to release cortisol around the brain and studies show that people with high cortisol levels are more likely to experience memory problems.

Wait, what exactly is neuroticism? It is the term for the type of personality that tends towards pervasive negative thinking. It can be a factor in other mental health illnesses like depression and anxiety. People with this problem respond poorly to stress and end up feeling anxious, upset and angry when their lives become stressful. Neuroticism is a personality trait and that means that you can't just erase it from your being but learning to recognize your vulnerability to emotional and environmental stress and to treat it accordingly can be a benefit. For example, you can learn to meditate or to distract yourself with a calming activity (like crochet!) when the symptoms of neuroticism present themselves. Why is this important? Well, according to Carper, research has found that people suffering from neuroticism are about forty percent more likely to experience Alzheimer's symptoms than are people who are easygoing and who score low on neuroticism tests. What's really fascinating from a medical perspective is that these people often don't actually show the physical signs of Alzheimer's on their brains (in other words, their PET scans don't show the holes, plaques and tangles associated with the disease) but they still have the memory problems associated with Alzheimer's.

In addition to the trait of neuroticism, another trait has been linked to Alzheimer's research: conscientiousness. There have been some interesting findings in Alzheimer's research that indicate that individuals who are conscientious are significantly less likely to develop Alzheimer's. Carper reports on studies done at Rush University Medical Center in Chicago that show that individuals with high scores on conscientiousness tests may be only half as likely to develop Alzheimer's than individuals with low conscientiousness scores. What is conscientiousness? It's a trait that describes a set of qualities including being thorough, deliberate and painstakingly careful. In other words, if you are someone who has perfectly even crochet stitches and rips out any crochet stitch that isn't perfect then you are probably conscientious. While conscientiousness is a character trait and not a byproduct of doing crochet, I wonder if it is possible to use your crochet work to actively develop a more conscientious approach to life. If in just this one area of your life you are able to focus on being more goal-directed, more disciplined, more organized and more deliberate then could the effects of this bleed over into other areas of your life and have the potential to delay the onset of Alzheimer's? I don't know the answer but I think it's a valid and interesting question.

This all comes back to the importance of self-care in Alzheimer's prevention. Learning to reduce stress and alleviate depression will help with overall improved health in later years. Properly taking care of yourself also means that you find a way to socialize and engage with others. This can be another key tool in Alzheimer's prevention and, as we looked at earlier in the chapter on anxiety, crochet can be a great tool to get you socializing with others if that is something that you find difficult to do. Numerous studies have shown that the more engaged an elderly person is in their community, the more connected they feel to their friends and the better their support system, the less likely it is that they will develop Alzheimer's. Carper reports that loneliness is not only a major predictor of Alzheimer's but also leads to more rapid decline over just a short four-year period. Moreover, having a large and strong social circle contributes to your cognitive reserve, meaning that even if your brain has signs of Alzheimer's you may not manifest the symptoms if you have a healthy connection to the people around you. Research even indicates that the more that the brain degenerates the more the person benefits from interacting with others to keep staving off the symptoms of Alzheimer's.

Being connected to others in your community doesn't just mean having a good group of friends around you (although it does mean that). It also means feeling like you have a purpose in life, something greater than yourself to live for. For some people this purpose is their family. For others, purpose can be found in volunteering. Either way, crochet can be a way that you use your skills, gifts and interests to provide care for others, helping you to stay connected to your community. This increases your sense of self-worth and your perceived value in society, making you feel like you have a purpose in life. Research has shown that scoring high on "purpose of life" tests is directly correlated with a lowered risk of Alzheimer's.

One key thing that I've noticed as I've been studying people who crochet for health benefits is that they feel a direct tie to others simply through the act of crocheting. They do not actually have to be sitting in a room crocheting with other people to feel this sense of connection nor do they necessarily have to be crocheting something for someone else, although these things do help. Merely being part of a craft that has been passed down from generation to generation and is now done by a large community of people helps you to maintain a sense of connection to others.

One of the people I asked about this was Em from nothingbutstring (see *Meet Em!*) who concurred: "Absolutely. Crocheting fills me with all the happy memories that I have of my grandmother. Spending hours with her around the kitchen table learning stitches or her explaining to me how to read a crochet graph. I think crocheting is one of the things that kept my grandmother and I close, it was a shared interest. My grandmother lived to be 102 and even though she had arthritis in both hands she still managed to crochet until she passed away."

Another person who shared her thoughts on this was Sherri A. Stanczak (whose full story is on the page titled *Meet Sherri*). She said: "I really miss my grandma whenever I make a new project. She and I used to create, change and share our ideas with each other. She was a perfectionist. She taught me a lot. Sometimes when I make something with the yarn or thread she left for me, I still feel that connection with her. It is almost as if I am spreading her memory to others. There is definitely something healing about that."

This sense of connecting to others through crochet can be profound for people of any age. And it may have the potential to benefit some people with Alzheimer's, particularly in the early stages. Nancy Pearce, author of Inside Alzheimer's, argues that the most important thing that we can do for the people in our lives who are suffering from this condition is to continue trying to connect with them. Maintaining a sense of human connection is what these people want all the way through to the end of their lives and it becomes increasingly difficult as they forget the normal ways of interacting and even who the people in their lives are. If they can come back again and again to crochet and re-learn how it can make them feel connected to others (maybe even through their early memories of learning to crochet) then perhaps this can be a great form of comfort and healing.

Crochet for diet and exercise

Crochet may also have a minor relationship to the second and third criteria of Alzheimer's prevention. The second criterion is physical activity. This refers primarily to aerobic exercise and maintaining balance, which obviously is not what crochet is about. However, Carper explains that scientific research shows that all types of activity do help a little bit to keep your brain functioning well. She says that even jiggling your foot and fidgeting with your fingers is an improvement over not doing anything and one can extrapolate from this that it is better for the brain if your fingers are moving away with crochet than if you're just sitting there, inactive. We saw something similar back in the chapter on depression when we talked about serotonin. You can boost your serotonin levels by engaging in out-and-about physical exercise but you can also do so with repetitive actions like crochet or even just chewing gum. This seems similar. Many people like to crochet while watching TV or listening to the radio, providing at least a small amount of physical activity for the brain that they wouldn't get if they were just sitting there in front of the tube.

The third criterion is the issue of maintaining a proper diet. Obviously there's not a direct correlation between diet and crochet. However, many people have said to me that they have used crochet as a tool for sticking to their diets because it keeps their hands and minds busy. This is especially important for people who are home with the fridge most of the day, which is often the case for older people. I'll discuss the issue of crochet as a diet tool in a later chapter of this book but wanted to note here that it, too, can be a way that crochet has the potential to help to ward off Alzheimer's.

In relation to diet and exercise, it is also important to note that smoking and excessive drinking are believed to be contributing factors to

Alzheimer's. A University of California, San Francisco study cited in Carper's book found that smoking can nearly double your risk of Alzheimer's. Likewise, research at the Wake Forest University Baptist Medical Center found that older people who drink more than fourteen drinks per week double their odds of developing dementia in comparison with those who don't drink. So, people who want to prevent Alzheimer's should consider quitting these addictions. Of course, quitting an addictive habit like cigarettes and alcohol requires a lot of hard work and various resources but as discussed earlier in this book crochet can be one way to keep your hands and mind busy so that you don't pick up the next drink or smoke when you're working on quitting.

Crochet for People with Late Stage Alzheimer's

So far most of what we have talked about here is how to possibly prevent Alzheimer's through crochet. But what about those people who already have the condition? Can crochet help them as well? That is tough to say. My guess, though this is not a very profound thing to say, is that it would be beneficial for some people with age-related memory loss and not for others.

One clear benefit of crochet is that if a person with Alzheimer's can do the stitches then it will help to keep the hands and mind busy. Many of the sources that I read about working with Alzheimer's patients mentioned the problem of "agitated hands." The Alzheimer's patient gets restless and fidgets and this is likely a sign of internal distress. It can also be dangerous because those idle fidgeting hands may get in to trouble that the individual doesn't even realize is trouble until something disastrous has happened. Oftentimes Alzheimer's patients will go rummaging through things, which is fine unless what they're rummaging in is dangerous. Sometimes they will start to pick at their own skin. Keeping the hands busy with something like crochet helps maintain the safety of the individual and anyone else in the home.

Keeping the hands busy with an activity that requires some coordination is also good for the individual's general quality of life. Gary Joseph LeBlanc, writing on the website for the Fisher Center for Alzheimer's Research Foundation says, "Keeping them active may or may not slow down the progression of the disease. What it will accomplish is to prolong the ability of their motor skills to continue to function. The fact that they're still working with their hands will help immensely in the battle to maintain coordination, which will only improve their quality of life." LeBlanc also notes that a focused activity helps significantly to reduce anxiety, which is a prominent and problematic symptom in people with advanced Alzheimer's. He specifically notes that knitting is a great craft for keeping people busy and says that even when the person can no longer knit they can roll the ball of yarn to create a calming feeling. Crochet is generally considered to be an easier craft than knitting (in part because it requires less coordination between the two hands since it uses only one hook instead of two needles) and therefore seems to me to be an even better choice!

Alzheimer's is a complicated condition that we still don't know enough about. Would putting a hook in my grandma's hand have answered her question, "what can I do?" I'm not sure that it would have, but it would have been worth a try. The nursing home that she is in now is a good facility that offers a lot of activities for the residents to keep them busy and socially engaged. While crochet isn't specifically offered at her home, I have read about many, many other nursing homes and hospitals that do offer knitting and crochet groups, something that I think is a positive thing to offer for the reasons outlined above.

In fact, if you take a look at good nursing homes for the elderly around the country, you will see that most of them offer art therapy, occupational therapy or both. A 1991 study by Ferguson and Goosman concluded: "Inclusion of art therapy in the residential nursing home and a day-care facility had positive effects on the elderly. Socialization, self-esteem, and memory retrieval were enhanced by the art experience." While their work was not specifically addressing Alzheimer's patients, it did address memory issues in the elderly in general. And, as we know, a diagnosis of Alzheimer's is terrifying specifically because of the fear of losing one's memory, a problem which plagues even those aging normally.

Crocheting Away the Ache: Pain Management Crafting

In my research for this book I learned that there are numerous people out there who are using crochet as a form of pain management. It surprised me when I first learned about it. Crochet as an aspirin? Seemed strange. But as I read more and more research about using crochet to take the mind off of physical pain, it began to make more and more sense to me. The majority of people that I read about who use crochet for pain are treating long-term chronic pain conditions. However, crochet has also been useful to people in short-term pain situations. We'll look at the short term first and then delve more deeply into how crochet is helping people to cope with long-term physical pain.

Short term non-narcotic pain management

Crochet is a tool that has been successfully used to treat various types of patients suffering from short-term pain. It is important to note, however, that there are different types of short-term pain. Acute pain is pain that comes on quickly and is very strong and you may or may not know the cause of it. Acute pain should always be taken seriously since it can be life threatening and you should always get it checked out. You certainly shouldn't say, "strange, my chest suddenly hurts uncontrollably, maybe I'll crochet and see if it goes away." But if you have chronic short-term pain, such as pain associated with a difficult third trimester pregnancy, and the problems have been diagnosed then you may be able to use crochet as a diversion for short-term pain management.

One of the best examples that I came across of people using crochet to deal with ongoing but short-term pain was a program at the Alta Bates Summit Medical Center in Berkeley, California that used crochet for short-term pain management in cases of women who are on bed rest for pre-term labor. {I should note here that I learned about this program from a 2006 article in Advance for Occupational Therapy Practitioners. I attempted to contact the program and received no response so I do not know if it is still active. However, I wanted to include the story of what they were doing because I think it offers some powerful insight into the possibilities of utilizing crochet for short-term pain management.}

Women who are on bed rest during pregnancy are experiencing two related problems that can be resolved in part with a craft like crochet. First, they are experiencing actual physical pain that they may not want to treat with a narcotic because of the risk that such a medication can pose to the baby. Second, they are experiencing high levels of stress due to the fears that they have about their higher-risk pregnancy. Gay Rose Soque, RN, who worked at the Alta Bates Summit Medical Center, explained in the Advance article how crochet helped some of their patients: "Some were in pain, using a PCA [patient-controlled analgesia] or getting an IV push every two hours. They were able to focus on their handiwork, and it distracted them from all of it. They felt better—this is a non-narcotic way to handle the pain and stress—and they were so surprised."

This story isn't the only example I've seen of crochet assisting with the anxiety, and even the pain, of difficult pregnancies and even childbirth. Kristine Mullen of Ambassador Crochet (see her whole story in *Meet Kristine!)* shared the following with me: "With my last pregnancy, as my due date came closer, I found myself growing anxious. After having several complicated deliveries in a row (my 5th was delivered not breathing with shoulder distocia), I was in major fear of what would happen this time around. It got so bad that it was all I could think about. And of course, the more I thought about it, the more worried I became. During one of my last OB appointments, my doctor said to try to bring something in the delivery room that would put my focus on something other than childbirth, and maybe that would help. I immediately decided to bring a crochet project. It definitely helped take my mind off of the pain."

Crochet is great for people who are suffering from short-term pain in a situation that requires them to stay on bed rest or have limited mobility. It doesn't require a lot of physical exertion. It doesn't require a large number of tools or cumbersome equipment. It doesn't even require much skill although the challenge of developing new skills can provide welcome mental relief to someone who is trying to distract themselves from attention to their pain. With just a small ball of yarn and an even smaller hook, you can sit up in your bed and follow one loop with another until you've forgotten about your pain and the stress it is causing you for at least a little while. It may not seem like much but glancing up at the clock and seeing that you've gone for one hour without focusing on your pain can be a huge relief to someone who is dealing with a short-term but continuous pain management issue.

One of the people I interviewed specifically about using crochet during a short-term pain problem was Katherine Dempsey of A Danish Heart blog (read her full story on the page titled *Meet Katherine*!). Life was going well for Katherine in her work as a Complementary Therapist with her own rural practice. Then in April 2011 she experienced a bad fall and everything in her life changed. She tore the ligaments and tendons in her ankle, causing excruciating pain. I can relate, with a wince, because I tore the ligaments in my ankle in March 2011 and although I was ultimately fine I felt like I was housebound for a month or two. Katherine's situation was worse. In addition to the ankle problems, she tore a disc in her back resulting in terrible sciatic pain.

I interviewed Katherine about the experience approximately six months after the accident and she was still unable to return to work. Even if she could have gone back to her job, many of her patients had moved on to other healers because they themselves needed care during the time that she was unable to be there for them because of her own pain. We saw earlier in this book, with Em's story, how becoming unemployed or underemployed as the result of illness or injury can lead to depression and other problems.

For Katherine, crochet proved to be what she calls "the right distraction" from everything else that was going on including the pain she was in. She says, "I have been doing embroidery for many years but for some reason I couldn't focus on it. Crochet became the right distraction. I didn't need to count small holes as in embroidery but the repetition of the stitches seemed to be good. I started to count the stitches and was able to concentrate on the simple movement of the hook. It felt a little like hypnosis."

Katherine "fell in love with all things wool." She got active in the online crochet community, which aided in providing her with a helpful, supportive, healing distraction during her time of need. Distraction is the key way that crochet helps in dealing with short-term pain where you don't want to take medication for one reason or another. You need to make your mind focus on something other than the pain or else the pain will feel intense. Crochet is one option.

Meet Katherine!

Katherine Dempsey took a bad spill that resulted in torn ankle ligaments and tendons, a torn disc in her back and sciatic pain. This left her bedridden and out of work, making her restless and frustrated in addition to being in terrible pain. She used crochet to help her get through this period of difficulty.

Up until April 2011, everything was going really well for Katherine Dempsey. She had been working for one dozen years as a successful Complementary Therapist specializing in Reflexology and Nutrition. She helped write a recipe book for people suffering with Candida. She had many repeat clients for her rural practice. Life was swell ... until that fateful day during a holiday when she took a fall.

In addition to the pain of a torn ankle (with both ligaments and tendons broken), Katherine tore a disc in her back and experienced immense sciatic pain. When I communicated with her six months later, she was still unable to work. Her patients tried to be understanding but they needed their own continuity of care and many had to move on to other healers while Katherine sat at home dealing with her pain.

While at home recuperating (homebound and taking tramadol four times per day for the pain), she was given the gift of a copy of the Mollie Makes magazine with the crochet apple cozy on the cover of it. She instantly fell in love with crochet. She shares:

> *"I have been doing embroidery for many years but for some reason I couldn't focus on it. Crochet became the right distraction. I didn't need to count small holes as in embroidery but the repetition of the stitches seemed to be good. I started to count the stitches and was able to concentrate on the simple movement of the hook. It felt a little like hypnosis ...*
>
> *I could make simple flowers with different colours and textures. I quickly became interested in all things wool. I love the colours and textures of wool and really enjoy finding new wool shops. I mostly use wooden hooks and love the feel of the chunky yarn and working with bigger hooks."*

One of the things that Katherine mentioned was the way that the online craft community aided in her healing.

> *"I had been on Facebook for some time and used it for friends etc. Suddenly I discovered Twitter and the crochet community there. I discovered Crochet Concupiscence as well as Laurie at the Crochet Liberation Front (*note: see the page Meet Laurie!*) through surfing the net but then used your followers to find more crochet friends. I'm now following over 200 people, mostly crocheters and bakers, and have nearly 100 followers. It's been wonderful to get to know other crocheters and to see their projects. A message tweet about not feeling great very soon brings in messages of support and care. Illness is a funny thing; your close friends only want you to be ill for a certain amount of time, then very much get on with it. Twitter seems more caring at this point. Ravelry is also fabulous as I've found patterns, forums, groups and people to follow."*

And, as a healer herself, Katherine knows how important crafting can be as a means of taking care of yourself. She says that it is something she has always suggested to her clients, encouraging craft as a form of creative expression. She especially recommends this to women who are busy taking care of everyone else in the family and could greatly benefit from something, like crochet, that offers them time and release just for themselves. Katherine's positive attitude in her healing is inspiring and I love her final thought from our interview:

> *"My ankle injury has caused so much upheaval but maybe it will end up very positively changing our lives forever. Crochet has played a huge part in this process."*

Visit Katherine Dempsey via her blog at adanishheart.com.

Meet Kristine!

Kristine Mullen had several difficult childbirth experiences including the delivery of her fifth child who wasn't breathing and had shoulder dystocia. Understandably, she was stressed out and fearful when it was time to deliver her next child. She brought crochet to the delivery room with her to reduce her anxiety and take her mind off of the pain. She ended up with a sweater for herself and healthy baby number six!

You might think that Kristine Mullen's sixth time in the delivery room should have been a snap. After all, she had done this five times before and had five beautiful kids to show for it. Unlike a first time mom, she should know what to expect. But also unlike a first time mom, Kristine had several complicated deliveries under her belt and she knew that what was to be expected could be terrifying. Her fifth child had been delivered not breathing with shoulder dystocia. Just thinking about what could happen with this sixth child had her increasingly worried.

During one of Kristine's final appointments with the OB/GYN before it would be time for delivery, the doctor said something that proved invaluable: "try to bring something into the delivery room that will take your focus off of the childbirth." Immediately, Kristine knew that she had to take her crochet work with her. Doing so not only decreased her anxiety but also helped take her mind off of the pain of the process.

Of course, any old pattern would not do to take her mind off of the baby coming. Kristine planned ahead and made sure to bring a crochet pattern that would truly challenge her brain. She needed something so hard that it would take all of her mental focus, turning her mind away from her body to the task at hand as the delivery progressed. The planning of the project helped take her mind off of the anxiety that threatened to engulf her and the activity of the project helped take her mind away from the pain.

Are you curious to know what it was that Kristine made during this time? It was a sweater for herself. Crocheters tend to fall into two camps: those who crochet for others and those who crochet for themselves. Kristine usually crochets for others. In fact, she's only ever made two items for herself and this sweater was one of them. It was a real treat to make something so detailed for herself and that surely added to the benefit of the project.

Kristine's sixth child was born and joined her adorable siblings in their happy home. Thankfully, Kristine hasn't had to take her mind off of any physical pain since that time. She does, however, still use crochet in a mentally healing way from time to time. She says, "it helps take your mind off your worries and troubles, and gives you a way to release that." As a mom of six she certainly must have times that she has to relax and crochet is a go-to way for her to do that.

As an aside to this story, it was another birth in her life that got this crochet designer started in making her own patterns in the first place. It was 2007 and a friend of Kristine's had just had a baby that was ten weeks premature. Kristine wanted to crochet a premie blanket for the new baby but she couldn't find any patterns that she liked for a blanket so small. She decided that she would just design it herself and she has been offering patterns to the world ever since.

You can visit Kristine at her website http://ambassadorcrochet.com/.

Long Term Pain Management and Chronic Illness

In addition to being useful for people who have short-term pain situations, crochet is also commonly (perhaps even more commonly) used by people who are dealing with long-term chronic pain conditions. This includes people with chronic pain conditions, such as fibromyalgia, as well as people with other types of chronic illness, such as cancer, that have pain as a side effect. In the case of long-term pain management, crochet does more than just distract the mind from the pain (although it continues to provide that service to the individual as well). It can also actually affect your physical ability to tolerate pain over time. Moreover, crochet can be a beneficial mental health tool for people who need help dealing with the depression and anxiety of living with a chronic illness. Chronic illness can take away a lot of who you feel you are as a person and crochet can be a way to give back, boosting your self-esteem.

First, let's talk about serotonin. Remember back at the beginning of this book when we looked at the way that the repetitive motions of crochet can encourage the release of serotonin? The majority of research and reporting that we know about serotonin levels are related to its role in depression. However, there is more to serotonin. Serotonin is also an analgesic. In other words, it is a natural painkiller. People who have low serotonin levels have a lower threshold for pain and therefore may be more uncomfortable during a chronic illness. In contrast, people who are able to raise their serotonin levels are able to increase their pain threshold. You may literally feel less pain or feel the pain less intensely as a direct result of taking actions, like crochet, that encourage serotonin release in the body!

Now, let's talk briefly about the mental health issues related to chronic pain conditions. The main one is depression, something that is often experienced by people dealing with long-term illness including chronic pain conditions. Stitchlinks (in "Why do we need the research") explained this, and the role that crafting can play in helping with it, very well in saying, "High self esteem also helps people manage long term illness more effectively – they stay positive and 'afloat' as apposed to being swamped by their conditions."

Stitchlinks further says, "Many who have long-term illnesses also suffer from low self esteem because they feel worthless in society. Being able to give something back by creating beautiful gifts for loved ones or charity, and a feeling of 'belonging' raises self-esteem and makes people feel worthwhile again. In a world full of daily challenges and pressures to conform, it's easy for self esteem to take a battering even in the healthiest of people, so here again knitting and stitching can benefit everyone."

One of the people who really experiences the benefit of healing from chronic pain through crocheting for others is Vicki Sulfaro. (See her whole story on the page titled *Meet Vicki!)* Vicki had a normal active life until the unfortunate day when she was stopped at a red light and her car was violently rear-ended by someone going about fifty miles per hour. The impact resulted in whiplash and spinal injury that causes her debilitating chronic pain to this day. It has been very difficult for Vicki to adjust to a new way of living, one in which her body feels broken and she can't do many of the things that she used to be able to do physically. It's important to Vicki, however, to maintain a positive attitude and to celebrate the life that she does have, and one of the ways that she does that is through crochet.

Vicki shared that crochet helps her deal with chronic pain in a number of ways. It gets her mind off of herself. It stirs up her creative energy, which induces positive feelings. But most importantly, it allows her to feel productive in this life even though her body isn't able to be active. Being physically limited by her pain, Vicki sometimes falls prey to the frightening feeling that she is taking too much from the world around her and not giving back enough. Crochet changes all of that. Vicki crochets for charity, giving comfort through her stitching to a number of different types of people including loved ones who have recently lost someone to tragedies and people who are going through treatment for illnesses requiring brain surgery. Vicki might still be in pain herself but it lessens it a little bit each time that she is able to use her crochet to do something useful, productive and healing for someone else.

Crochet can be beneficial to people dealing with many different types of chronic pain conditions. Remember that as we take a look at a few specific conditions, as these are meant to highlight the benefits of crochet as a healing tool and not to narrow down the conditions in which crochet can play such a role.

Meet Vicki S!

Vicki Sulfaro never goes a day without pain since the day that a car accident left her with spinal injuries. Nevertheless, she maintains an upbeat attitude about her situation and uses crochet as a healing tool to cope with the new difficulties of everyday life mostly by crocheting to give back to others and find purpose in her new world.

It was a normal day. Vicki was sitting at a red light with her daughter, waiting for her turn to cross the intersection. Suddenly, a crash came from behind. A kid from her daughter's school barreled into their parked car at nearly fifty miles per hour. The car pitched back and forth, resulting in life-changing spinal injuries for Vicki. She has two spinal fusions and she lives in severe, constant pain. In spite of this, Vicki maintains a positive attitude, due in part to the healing benefits she's experienced through crochet.

Vicki explains that her take on the situation is that it could have been a lot worse. She and her daughter survived the accident. She could have been killed, but she wasn't, and Vicki sees this as a second chance on life. She doesn't want to be someone who takes that for granted by whining and feeling sorry for herself. Of course, it's tough to live in constant pain and never get down about it, so Vicki uses her crochet as a tool to keep her mind in the positive place where she wants it to be.

Vicki says that crochet helps her in many ways. First of all, it helps her to relax, which is important when dealing with chronic pain since stress can exacerbate the experience of pain. Second, crochet helps Vicki to feel useful and productive in her life. Chronic pain can make people feel helpless so it's important to the healing process to be able to feel useful and crochet is a way that Vicki can give back.

Vickie crochets many items that she then donates to charity. Her favorite charity crochet work is making hats for people who have gone through brain trauma and surgery. There are many options to donate crocheted chemo caps to people dealing with cancer but Vicki points out that there aren't nearly as many focused on brain injuries. The spine and brain are closely linked so in a way Vicki is helping people like herself and that is healing for her as well.

Vicki also uses her skills in crochet to respond to situations in the community that would make anyone feel helpless. For example, when the Lakewood 4 were murdered, Vicki banded together with several other crocheters to make afghans for each of the families who lost someone to the tragedy. Similarly, when local deputies have been shot and wounded (sometimes fatally), Vicki and her group have reached out to comfort them with crocheted comfortghans. This type of charity work is a way to take control over situations and respond in a positive way, showing not only empathy for others but restoring some balance to the spectrum of good and evil.

This comes full circle as a way for Vicki to heal from her own chronic pain. She actually learned to crochet at a young age. Her third grade teacher taught her during recess and she has been crocheting ever since. In fact, one of the things that really worried her after the accident was that she might not be able to crochet anymore because of the physical effects of the whiplash. Vicki did undergo physical therapy to help with her injuries, though, and one of the first things that she crocheted was a baby dress and bonnet for her pregnant physical therapist.

Vicki has a tough time because she feels like her body is broken now. It hurts and it doesn't work the way that it's supposed to. She used to be able to ski, hike and run marathons and now she can't do those things. However, crochet takes her mind off of that. She says:

"When I crochet I don't think about how my body is now broken; I think about how I can create something beautiful and useful with my hook and either yarn or thread. I think the most healing part of crochet for me is I am able to take something simple, such as a skein of yarn, and turn it into something beautiful and useful. Crochet has turned my life around. I can't hike anymore but crochet can take me places."

So Vicki is able to make something useful and then give it to others who might need it, which is a really powerful part of healing for people in chronic pain. Vicki also helps others by teaching them to crochet. She recently passed along her skills to her son's girlfriend by teaching her how to make fingerless gloves. This sense of connection that comes from sharing her knowledge strengthens the feeling that she has a purpose in this life even if her body sometimes wants to resist. Vicki is also able to use the online world to connect with others, some of whom she's gone on to meet in real life.

Finally, Vicki also designs her own crochet patterns. She likes the way that this channels her energy into something positive and creative. She says that this is yet another way that she can give back to the world instead of feeling like she's just taking from it. And she adds, "crochet lets me be me".

You can visit Vicki on her blog at http://www.crochetqueenheavensent.blogspot.com.

Fibromyalgia

Fibromyalgia is a condition that affects both the body and the mind. The primary symptom of the disorder is musculoskeletal pain across a large percentage of the body. However, it is highly common for people suffering from fibromyalgia to also experience fatigue, memory loss and mood problems. The Mayo Clinic reports that women are more likely than men to suffer from fibromyalgia but that it can affect either gender. They also report that fibromyalgia sufferers are more likely than the general population to experience other health issues including tension headaches, TMJ, irritable bowel syndrome, depression and anxiety.

It is not known what causes fibromyalgia. It is a condition that can come on quickly following a trauma but it can also come on slowly over time. There is no known cure for the condition. Treatment consists primarily of rest, relaxation, stress-reduction and exercise.

One of the wonderful people that I interviewed for this book was Shelli Steadman, a woman whose fibromyalgia story is similar to many of the others that I've read. Shelli's life and health were basically normal until she reached the age of thirty. At that time, she began experiencing small, annoying health problems that weren't easily diagnosed, things like fatigue, unexplained weight gain and problems with her feet. Her experience with many medical professionals is the kind of horror story that none of us want to hear but many of us know all too well – one doctor would tell her that she was just gaining weight because she wasn't exercising enough while another would tell her that there wasn't even a problem, that it was all in her head.

Finally, after about three years she was told that she had hypothyroidism and she began taking a synthetic thyroid medication. She experienced relief of some symptoms, however, she continued to experience many other symptoms including increasing pain and exhaustion. She was basically sore and tired all of the time, which is a succinct way of explaining what fibromyalgia looks like. It took quite awhile but she was eventually diagnosed with fibromyalgia and got on the right medication, which has helped her greatly. Of course, she still does experience some pain, but at least now she finally knows what is wrong with her health.

Throughout this entire ordeal, Shelli found that crochet was a tool that she could use to help take her mind off of the pain as well as to assist her in dealing with the depression that occurs when you are suffering from an ongoing chronic illness. She had learned to crochet from an aunt when she was not quite a teenager and had been doing so off and on for years. As her physical problems increased, Shelli was no longer capable of being as physically active as she once was and that was when she really turned to crochet as a helpful tool. In relation to the pain, Shelli explains:

> "Crochet helps me put my pain on the back burner for a while. It takes my focus away from how I'm feeling and puts it in a more productive place. As I'm sure anyone who ever felt any kind of pain can tell you, if you are distracted from focusing on that pain it seems lessened somehow. I've realized that if I focus too much on how I am feeling it's as if the pain is magnified. Crocheting lessens my pain by distracting me with yummy, colorful yarns and stitch work.
>
> Crochet is definitely meditative due to the fact that it is a repetitive activity. In most of the projects I've done there's a part where I get to repeat the same stitch pattern over and over. At this point I can let my mind relax and my hands go on automatically. I don't necessarily think about anything because that distracts me from what I'm doing. I'm able to just relax, breathe, enjoy the feel of the fiber in my hands, and watch my project take shape. I'm sure it helps to keep my hands and fingers limber, too."

And she has a great take on the way that crochet has helped with the depression component of chronic pain conditions, which we looked at briefly in the chapter on depression but it's worth remembering again here:

> "I believe my depression evolved slowly along with my health problems. I'm sure my hypothyroidism has some of the blame here, but I know the depression also stems from not being able to feel like my "normal" self anymore. It's frustrating to deal

with the symptoms of fibromyalgia and hypothyroidism. I consider myself to still be young. My health issues began when I was about 29-30, and I'm only 35 now. I want to run and play with my kids and do household activities I previously had no trouble doing. No longer being able to do these things is depressing, especially when, on the inside, I still think like my old self.

Fortunately, I feel like I have a great perspective on life and don't give in to the depression. It's always there, but I refuse to let it get the better of me. I am also blessed with a great family and they make every day worthwhile. Crochet helps me beat depression because it is something that my health issues cannot take from me. It's kind of like getting to thumb my nose at my illness! Crochet gives me an outlet to create and make beautiful things. It gives me a sense of accomplishment."

It is also important to note that there is an important physical benefit to crochet for people who are suffering from chronic pain, especially people who find themselves sensitive to touch like those people who are dealing with fibromyalgia. Shelli Steadman illuminates this for us: "Fibromyalgia has made me overly sensitive to touch. Even a well-meant pat on the back can hurt. Feeling a soft yarn glide between my fingers is a luxury. I especially love the 100% alpaca yarn I indulged in buying. I love it so much that I've had a terrible time deciding what to crochet with it! I've frogged more than one project, and I'm beginning to believe it's because I don't want to be done with this sensuous yarn! Sometimes my wrists and hands get sore because I have been crocheting for too long at a stretch, but the benefits of the creative process with hook and yarn far outweigh the pain."

Unfortunately there is a frustrating irony for crochet-ers who are suffering from fibromyalgia, which is that the repetitive activity that takes the mind off of pain can sometimes also cause pain. This is well-illuminated in an article in Fog Magazine by Carol (*see the page Meet Carol!* for her full story):

"My Fibromyalgia eventually forced me to quit working. My life changed. Suddenly I had time on my hands and I needed to find some activities to keep my mind occupied. That's when I remembered my grandmother again. Unfortunately, now that I actually had time to learn the art of crocheting, my dear grandmother was in a nursing home 1,000 miles away. I would have to teach myself.

When I began crocheting I thought it would be something to occupy my time. But now, I feel it's become a passion. I want to crochet every day but it's not always easy. My Fibromyalgia attacks my wrists and hands so there are days that I just can't. And some days, by the evening, I can barely use my hands because I've crocheted all day. But I can't wait until the next day to get started again on my projects.

Isn't it ironic that the very thing that gave me the time to learn this craft – fibromyalgia – is the very thing that causes me so much pain that I can't do it sometimes? Fibromyalgia makes it more of a challenge, and when I finish a project I really feel that I've accomplished something."

Carol explained to me that she uses larger hooks to help defray the pain because they are easier to grip and so don't cause the pain of fibromyalgia to flare up as much as smaller hooks do. I've also read online that bulkier hook handles, such as the handmade handles crafted from polymer clay, are helpful for people with fibromyalgia. Carol also provided me with a lot of great insight into why it is that she continues to keep crocheting despite the fact that it can cause her pain. Crochet isn't just something that she does to keep her mind busy; it's something that she truly does to give to others. Being able to give to others is something that she has always loved to do, especially in the sense of being able to take care of her family. The fibromyalgia has taken a lot away from her in terms of what she can do for her family on a regular basis but crochet is something that she can do.

She explained, "Fibromyalgia stole my job and caused me to have to learn to be a different wife and mother. I have always been a person who does for others and I love cooking from scratch, making homemade gifts, etc. I now cook only a day or two a week, luckily my kids are 17, 19, and 21 so they are able to take care of themselves but I love doing things for them. My husband is a saint and does the laundry, shopping, and much of the cooking. Crocheting is something I can almost always do and I can do it for others."

Carol really enjoys the process of crocheting but especially enjoys seeing the joy in the face of someone she's giving a completed crochet project to. At the time that I interviewed her, she was working on a scarf for her oldest son and was happy because he would check in regularly to see if it was finished yet. The joy that he expressed about being able to get a handmade gift from her helps her to feel useful and special and not just like a "sick" person and in that sense it helps to heal her.

One key thing that Carol mentioned is that you don't have to know a wide range of crochet skills to be able to crochet something that is valuable to yourself and others. She really only knows the basic crochet stitches and so she sticks to crocheting scarves and afghans but that's plenty to keep her and her loved ones happy. She notes that both scarves and afghans are very comforting things and that she is thrilled to be able to provide her family with that comfort. She knows that all of her children love their crocheted afghans and she loves knowing that when they move away and grow older they will still have with them this homemade item that was created with love. Love itself is the healing factor here.

Crochet also helps to tie Carol to her family in a larger sense, across generations. Her grandmother taught her to crochet some basic stitches when she was a little girl and Carol is proud of the fact that she is able to carry on her grandmother's talent. Carol didn't really start crocheting until she was forty and when she returned to it, she had to re-teach herself, but her grandmother had planted that seed for her, the seed of something which has been very important in her life. Carol has taught her daughter how to crochet and although her daughter currently isn't all that interested in the craft, Carol knows that she, too, has planted that seed. Her daughter will know that there is a craft out there that can bring comfort to her and the others in her life if she ever needs it.

One thing I've learned about fibromyalgia is that there is a bit of a Catch 22 with the pain because the natural instinct that people have is to avoid doing things that will be painful so they limit their activities and then that, in turn, decreases their range of motion and makes moving even more painful. A 2010 post on the Rows Red knitting blog explains this: "Fibromyalgia, at least the way I experience it, has two pain components. There is the pressure point pain, where I have to be lightly pressed or rubbed to feel gasp-worthy pain, and the always present ache portion of the equation. That part of it is always there, to varying degrees. This is the (usually) dull or throbbing ache in various parts of my body, so many different parts that I usually just call it whole body pain. It's either apparent while I'm at rest (either laying or sitting) or noticeable when moving or stretching doing normal daily activities like reaching for something at my desk, or bending over. Your instinctual reaction is to restrict your movements since they either hurt right away, or will hurt soon afterwards, and this leads to a gradual inflexibility and a loss of range of motion. The blackly comedic note here is that exercise is the most common recommendation from your doctor to combat this. Fibro's final gift is exhaustion." So you're too tired to exercise but exercise is exactly what you need to be able to stay as mobile as possible despite fibromyalgia. At the very least crafting can help keep the hands moving even though it can sometimes be painful.

Fibromyalgia sufferers usually have periods where they are "okay" and then flare-ups during which the pain and other symptoms are especially pronounced. For many crafters, this is the time during which they must scale back on their crafts. However, others find that they can crochet as a form of relaxation to help them through a flare-up, especially if they take many breaks and incorporate the crochet into a general program of total self-care. It is also smart to take a proactive approach with self-care to prevent flare-ups in the first place. If crochet is a relaxing, stress-reducing activity then it can be an integral part of a preventative wellness plan. As with all things, moderation is key!

Meet Shelli!

Shelli Steadman was 30 when she started experiencing health problems that her doctors had trouble diagnosing and which turned out to be due to hypothyroidism and fibromyalgia. She couldn't be as active as she once was and found crochet helped her spirits remain uplifted as she adjusted to a new "normal".

Shelli Steadman had a normal life until right around the age of 30. Even then, the health symptoms she began to experience seemed more like annoyances than serious problems. She was fatigued. She gained weight and couldn't lose it. She had problems with her feet. For three years, the doctors failed to figure out what was wrong with her. They did tests, told her that the tests were all normal and said unhelpful things that ranged from "you should exercise more" to "the problem is all in your head, nothing is wrong".

One doctor finally did a test that showed that Shelli had hypothyroidism. She started taking synthetic hormone medication but that failed to resolve many of her symptoms. She was still tired all of the time. She was also sore and constantly hurting. After eliminating everything else, her doctor diagnosed her with fibromyalgia. She now takes medication for that as well.

Shelli had learned to crochet at the age of 12 when an aunt taught her the basics. She had crocheted off and on throughout the years but really came back to it when she started experiencing all of these health problems. No matter how tired she is or how much her body aches, she can pick up a crochet hook and be active in that small way. She didn't start doing it with the intention of it being a healing thing but she gradually began to realize that it was offering her many benefits.

The health problems caused Shelli to experience mild depression. She uses crochet to fight that problem. She says: "Being able to do something so meditative and the outcome be something beautiful is uplifting." When asked to share more about the meditative benefits about crochet, Shelli shared the following:

> *"Crochet is definitely meditative due to the fact that it is a repetitive activity. In most of the projects I've done there's a part where I get to repeat the same stitch pattern over and over. At this point I can let my mind relax and my hands go on automatically. I*

don't necessarily think about anything because that distracts me from what I'm doing. I'm able to just relax, breathe, enjoy the feel of the fiber in my hands, and watch my project take shape. Crochet helps me put my pain on the back burner for a while. It takes my focus away from how I'm feeling and puts it in a more productive place. As I'm sure anyone who ever felt any kind of pain can tell you, if you are distracted from focusing on that pain it seems lessened somehow."

Shelli explains that her depression is something that evolved slowly along with her other health problems. Part of the issue is likely to be related to the hypothyroidism, which is linked with depression. However, Shelli believes it had more to do with the fact that the illness stole so much from her in terms of not feeling like her "normal" self anymore. She says:

"It's frustrating to deal with the symptoms of fibromyalgia and hypothyroidism. I consider myself to still be young. My health issues began when I was about 29-30, and I'm only 35 now. I want to run and play with my kids and do household activities I previously had no trouble doing. No longer being able to do these things is depressing, especially when, on the inside, I still think like my old self. Fortunately, I feel like I have a great perspective on life and don't give in to the depression. It's always there, but I refuse to let it get the better of me. I am also blessed with a great family and they make every day worthwhile. Crochet helps me beat depression because it is something that my health issues cannot take from me. It's kind of like getting to thumb my nose at my illness.

Shelli also enjoys that there's always more to learn about crochet. She enjoys tackling new stitches and new crochet techniques. She was always a busy person and one of the frustrating parts about her illness was that she still wanted to be busy but the fibromyalgia would restrict her ability to do so. She can sit in a recliner and crochet, resting her arms on pillows while working if they are especially sensitive that day.

Shelli experienced what so many people do during an illness, which was the feeling that she was no longer able to help others as much as she used to. Crochet helped with that. She says:

"It makes me happy to make a baby blanket for a friend or scarves for my church to give to shut-ins. I have always been someone who likes to help others; I did not (and still do not) like the feeling of having to let others help me instead. Crochet helps me with this issue. It allows me to still be able to do nice things for others."

One of the things that makes Shelli's experience unique from many others is that she especially benefits from the touch of the yarn. Fibroymalgia is a condition that makes you very sensitive to touch so you end up lacking the benefits of normal every day tactile sensations. She shares:

"Even a well meant pat on the back can hurt. Feeling a soft yarn glide between my fingers is a luxury. I especially love the 100% alpaca yarn I indulged in buying. I love it so much that I've had a terrible time deciding what to crochet with it! I've frogged more than one project, and I'm beginning to believe it's because I don't want to be done with this sensuous yarn! I do love the colors, too. I am often surprised at the plethora of colors and textures of yarn! Sometimes my wrists and hands get sore because I have been crocheting for too long at a stretch, but the benefits of the creative process with hook and yarn far outweigh the pain. On another tangent, I usually get cold in the later part of the day (a side effect of hypothyroidism), and it's pretty cozy to snuggle into my big, soft recliner wearing my crocheted cowl and covering up with a pretty shawl or afghan that I made or am in the process of making."

One of the things that Shelli noted was that all aspects of the crochet process offer different benefits.

"I don't think I could separate the experiences. All three aspects of the process contribute. The planning and excitement that surrounds finding the perfect project to do next is uplifting. Actually crocheting the project is meditative. Having the end product completes the circle and feeds my need to accomplish something worthwhile."

Shelli is a fourth grade teacher. She is hoping to start teaching crochet as part of an after school program available in her school district. She hopes it will help the kids with fine motor skills and concentration development as well as providing them with a means to achieving a sense of accomplishment. Shelli wraps up with this thought:

> *"Crochet is a flexible activity that you can match to your current physical abilities. If you're having a tough day physically, you can crochet something simple that doesn't require much on your part other than repeating an easy stitch. On better days, you can work on something more intricate. I truly feel that crochet can be an outlet for someone in need of healing. Crochet is a relaxing, meditative art form. It's also portable! You can take your crochet projects with you just about anywhere. Crochet is something you can do for someone else. Any activity that takes your mind off your own troubles to help others aids in your own healing."*

If you are interested in connecting with Shelli, you can find her as Shelli34 on Ravelry or Shelli777 on Twitter.

Meet Carol!

Carol's whole life changed when she began to experience the symptoms of Fibromyalgia. Her job came to an end. Her mothering changed. The way she lived out her role as a wife changed. It wasn't an easy thing to cope with. Crochet helped.

Carol is a wife and mother of three who had devoted much of her time to caring for others. She had always been the kind of mom who loved to make homemade gifts, cook from scratch and nurture those around her. She also worked but after fibromyalgia came into the picture, everything had to change. She says, "Fibromyalgia stole my job and caused me to have to learn to be a different wife and mother."

After a period of time, the condition forced Carol to stop working. She shares,

> *"My life changed. Suddenly I had time on my hands and I needed to find some activities to keep my mind occupied. That's when I remembered my grandmother again. Unfortunately, now that I actually had time to learn the art of crocheting, my dear grandmother was in a nursing home 1,000 miles away. I would have to teach myself."*

And teach herself she did, learning to crochet around the age of 40. This not only gave her a way to spend her time now that she could no longer work but also gave her a way to continue to create for and nurture her loved ones. She explained,

> *"I have always been a person who does for others and I love cooking from scratch, making homemade gifts, etc. I now cook only a day or two a week, luckily my kids are 17, 19, and 21 so they are able to take care of themselves but I love doing things for them. My husband is a saint and does the laundry, shopping, and much of the cooking. Crocheting is something I can almost always do and I can do it for others."*

Carol does enjoy the process of crocheting (noting that seeing a project developing gives her a sense of accomplishment) but especially enjoys seeing the joy of someone she's giving a completed crochet project to. At the time that I interviewed her, she was working on a scarf for her oldest son and was happy because he would check in regularly to see if it was finished yet. The joy that he expressed about being able to get a handmade gift from her helps her to feel useful and special and not just like a "sick" person and in that sense, it helps to heal her. The fibromyalgia has taken a lot away from her in terms of what she can do for her family on a regular basis but crochet is something that she can do.

One key thing that Carol mentioned is that you don't have to know a wide range of crochet skills to be able to crochet something that is valuable to yourself and others. She really only knows the basic crochet stitches and so she sticks to crocheting scarves and afghans but that's plenty to keep her and her loved ones happy. She notes that both scarves and afghans are very comforting things and that she is thrilled to be able to provide her family with that comfort. She knows that all of her children love their crocheted afghans and she loves knowing that when they move away and grow older they will still have with them this homemade item that was created with love. Love itself is the healing factor here. And since Carol is teaching her daughter to crochet, she's passing on that healing love in a very tangible way.

Carol won't lie; crocheting with fibromyalgia isn't always easy. The same craft that brings her so much joy can also stir up pain in her body. She uses large hooks to help offset that pain because they are easier to grip and less likely to strain her hands. She says that with these types of minor adjustments, the drawbacks of any pain caused by crochet are outweighed by the health benefits the craft offers her.

Multiple Sclerosis

Multiple Sclerosis is an autoimmune disease that affects the central nervous system, causing a host of symptoms including painful muscle spasms, difficulty with leg and arm movements, tremors and weakness in the extremities, eye problems including vision loss, difficulty with problem solving and depression. Treatment of MS includes many different options such as medication and physical therapy but general medical consensus is that treatment also requires lifestyle changes including getting enough relaxation and avoiding stress and fatigue. It is here that crochet plays its role and of course it is also key in helping to deal with the depression that comes along with MS.

In his book *Multiple Sclerosis: Everything You Need to Know*, Paul O'Connor, MD, MSc, FRCPC cites studies that have been done to try to determine whether stress actually causes or worsens the symptoms of MS. The studies have been inconclusive to date but show that it's probably wise to avoid stress if you have MS. One of the symptoms of MS is muscle stiffness (called spasticity), which is worsened with stress so finding ways to calm your mind and relax your body can help with some of the physical pain of MS. If crochet is calming for you then by all means consider it a utensil in the kitchen drawer of your MS treatment plan!

O'Connor also cites the statistic that approximately fifty percent of people with MS suffer from depression at some point during their illness and that about twelve percent are seriously depressed (a number that is more than double that of the general population). Suicide is three to ten times more common among people with MS than those in the general population so it is clearly important for those suffering from the condition to get help with their depression. As you know from its many references throughout this book, I have suffered from depression and know firsthand both the devastation of it and the ways in which crochet can help with it.

Sherri A. Stanczak (read her full story on the page titled *Meet Sherri!*) suffers from MS and shared some of the ways in which it helps her, telling me: "When I crochet, it relaxes me, gets my mind off of my own problems, and when I am finished with a project, I get a certain satisfaction from it – just seeing something I made with my own hands. It makes me feel useful, when I am actually handicapped in some ways. There are a couple of things that are healing about my crochet work: the excitement of creating my own projects, making something for someone and seeing their face when I give it to them and just being able to complete something so pretty that just started out as a skein of yarn. Yarn comes in beautiful colors. When they are put together in a project, they take on a whole new personality. Just seeing the progress of a project is very healing. Being able to see the colors when there are times that I can't see – due to my M.S. – is a true blessing and nothing to be taken for granted. Feeling the yarn and the hook move between my fingers as if I am performing some type of magic, gives me a feeling of happiness and contentment. Also, the sense of pride I get when my work is completed. Crocheting is a great stress reliever. When I am upset, for some reason, my fingers work even faster; however, completing the project calms me down and makes me feel so much better."

Sherri's explanation makes it clear that there are many healing aspects of crochet for someone suffering from MS. Studies suggest that there may even be measurable benefits, sharing in their Guide to Our Theories so Far: "MS sufferers report ... having a functional capacity greater than their brain scans suggest they should have. Some neurologists in the US are suggesting to them that this may be down to their knitting." They're saying that their bran scans say they can only do so much but they actually feel like they are capable of doing much more and that their stitchwork may play a key role in the reason why!

Like with fibromyalgia, MS sufferers often experience flare-ups (also called exacerbation or an MS relapse) during which their symptoms are worse. These can be caused by a variety of different things. The flare-up may have physical effects, mental health effects or both, and the effects may be permanent or temporary. For example, Nessa (who we met in the chapter on depression) went through an MS relapse in August 2011. She regained much of her function but the relapse left her in a wheelchair, which is something that's new and obviously requires an adjustment. Nessa is using crochet to help her deal with the depression that has come along with that relapse, depression that has been her constant companion as long as she has had MS.

Nessa has experienced several relapses since her diagnosis in the late 1990's, and she said something that I found striking: "Finding the best way to live at every stage of this journey has had to be a proactive process of trial and error and of self-discovery and self-understanding." This truly conveys how important it is for anyone suffering from an illness to avoid victimizing themselves and instead to stand up and try to find the best way to live their lives that is possible given the limitations of their condition. Crochet was a part of that proactive process for Nessa, helping her to feel useful despite her increasing handicaps. Crochet was also very helpful in helping Nessa define her own identity that connected back to her family and the generations of needleworkers before her. Conditions like MS can take away your identity, or rather become the sole focus of your identity, if you let them and so it's important to define who you are outside of that and crafting is one way to do that.

Sometimes people with long-term health conditions find that they can no longer work at the jobs that they used to because of their illnesses. Thanks to the proliferation of Etsy and other opportunities for working from home, these people can now often make a living in spite of the limitations of their handicaps. One woman with MS who has done that is Heather Bolling, whose story was shared in a July 2011 news article by Chandra Harris-McCray.

Bolling was 28 when she blacked out while blowdrying her hair and ended up in a hospital for a week while doctors tried to figure out what was wrong with her. She was anxious, obviously, and she spent her time in the hospital crocheting headbands for all of the nurses that were working with her. The doctors finally figured out that Bolling had a severe case of Multiple Sclerosis and they told her that she might eventually have only about 30% mobility. Bolling decided that she would throw herself into the crocheting that she loved instead of feeling sorry for herself.

Bolling has two young children and she would previously sew clothes for them but she found that sitting down for prolonged periods for machine sewing was really painful for her condition. But she found that she could crochet without a problem (something she taught herself to do in part by watching online videos and in part by joining a local needlework circle). The craft quickly became a way to earn money. Bolling started a line of crochet headbands for all ages in a business she called Behind My Picket Fence. She then added other accessories like crochet bracelets to the mix, making some money for her family by selling the items she made at craft fairs and through local boutiques. She isn't necessarily trying to make a living from crafting but she does enjoy that she can earn some money for her family doing something that she enjoys … and she loves that it takes her mind off of the MS!

Meet Sherri!

Sherri A. Stanczak had to undergo spinal surgery that has left her coping with a significant amount of pain even half a dozen years later. Crochet helps Sherri to manage the pain. It also helps her to battle the feelings of depression that are often associated with chronic pain conditions.

Sherri was originally diagnosed with Multiple Sclerosis at the age of 25. As her health began to really deteriorate, her doctors came to realize that she had additional underlying problems. She explains on her website, "I had Spina-Bifida (spinal defect) and Diastematomyelia (split spinal cord). I had to start giving myself shots three times a week for the progression of the M.S. but I also had to have a very critical spinal surgery because my right leg went paralyzed."

The surgery left her in excruciating pain. Her right leg, which was her good leg, was damaged and now painful. Doctors have told her that they can't do additional surgery because it would leave her paralyzed from the waist down so she is on a number of different prescription drugs for pain management. She reports that the pain sometimes gets her down and this is exacerbated by the fact that she often feels like she can't do all that she would like to do because the pain leaves her bedridden much of the time. However, she also reports that crochet helps with these problems. In her own words:

> *"Getting out my crochet hook and a bag of yarn helps me feel better somehow. Crocheting is a great stress reliever. When I crochet, it relaxes me and helps gets my mind off of my own problems. When I am upset, for some reason, my fingers work even faster; however, completing the project calms me down and makes me feel so much better. When I am finished with a project, I get a certain satisfaction from it – just seeing something I made with my own hands. It makes me feel useful, when I am actually handicapped in some ways."*

As you can see, Sherri celebrates the healing aspect of all different parts of the crochet process. She elaborates:

"There are a few things that are healing about my crochet work: the excitement of creating my own projects, making something for someone and seeing their face when I give it to them and just being able to complete something so pretty that just started out as a skein of yarn. Yarn comes in beautiful colors. When the colors are put together in a project, they take on a whole new personality. Just seeing the progress of a project is very healing. Being able to see the colors when there are times that I can't see - due to my M.S. – is a true blessing and nothing to be taken for granted. Feeling the yarn and the hook move between my fingers as if I am performing some type of magic gives me a feeling of happiness and contentment. And then there is the sense of pride I get when my work is completed."

Being able to crochet is also something that gives Sherri a sense of connection to others. Specifically, she feels connected to her grandmother through her crochet work. Her grandmother taught her how to crochet when she was nine years old. Sherri shared:

"I really miss my grandma whenever I make a new project. She and I used to create, change and share our ideas with each other. She was a perfectionist. She taught me a lot. Sometimes when I make something with the yarn or thread she left for me, I still feel that connection with her, almost as if I am spreading her memory to others. There is definitely something healing about that."

You can connect with Sherri through her website at http://sherristanczak.webs.com.

Chronic Lyme Disease

I will admit that Chronic Lyme Disease wasn't on my short list of conditions that I specifically wanted to cover when I set out to do the research for this book. It just wasn't something that I knew a lot about. However, when I put out the call for stories of people willing to be interviewed about how crochet had helped heal them, I received a response from Tammy Hildebrand who shared with me the powerful story of how crochet helped her deal with this condition. That encouraged me to start learning more about it and what I learned was fascinating.

Lyme Disease, according to a popular website called Lyme Info, is a systemic infection that people get from tick bites. It is treated with antibiotics and it can be fairly well cured for many people. However, others find that their battle with the symptoms of Lyme Disease is lifelong, and most people call this "Chronic Lyme Disease" although that's actually a controversial name. The reason it's controversial is a complicated one and I'd encourage anyone with an interest to do further research because it's a huge topic that I can't cover in full here but the gist of it is that mainstream medicine doesn't generally accept the term "chronic Lyme disease" to describe the group of Lyme sufferers who continue to experience lifelong symptoms such as fatigue. Some doctors say that the people who have these symptoms have another autoimmune reaction or they really have chronic fatigue syndrome or even fibromyalgia.

The controversy has been legally complicated by the fact that a primary cure for Lyme disease is antibiotic treatment, and there are laws that limit or prohibit the use of antibiotics over a long period of time. The situation is further complicated by the health insurance industry and what they do and don't want to pay for in terms of long term treatment. The Lyme Info website links to a number of studies and trials that find that there is indeed such a thing as Chronic Lyme Disease, and they also quote Pat Smith from the Lyme Disease Association Website as saying that "10-15% of those with the Lyme bacteria progress to chronic Lyme disease." As for me, although my experience with this condition is limited, I tend to believe that if patients are saying that they are suffering from something, then they are. I have no reason to believe that the condition doesn't exist and there are ample personal accounts that say that it does. Whatever you want to call it, the symptoms are very real. Those symptoms include nerve pain, joint pain, short-term memory problems, difficulty concentrating, vertigo, fatigue and muscle weakness (which can lead to difficulty walking and loss of mobility).

As I mentioned before, I was encouraged to learn about this condition after I heard from Tammy Hildebrand. For those of you who don't know the name, Tammy is a crochet designer who is also very active in the professional crochet organization called the Crochet Guild of America (CGOA). She is on the CGOA Board of Directors and is the organization's professional development coordinator. Many of the people who find healing in crochet come to the craft or return to it from childhood only after dealing with an illness. In Tammy's case, crochet has been her life for as long as she can remember and so was a natural addition to her healing toolbox when she was diagnosed with Chronic Lyme Disease.

In fact, it's safe to say that Tammy doesn't really remember a time in her life when her hands have been empty of a crochet hook. She learned to crochet in second grade from a schoolteacher and has been active with it ever since. The one time that she can recall not having a hook in hand was when she broke her arm and literally couldn't crochet with her arm while it healed. Did that stop Tammy from crocheting? No. She devised her own method of holding her crochet hook with her feet and using her left hand to manipulate the yarn so that she could continue to crochet!

So of course Tammy wouldn't let Chronic Lyme Disease stop her crochet work. To the contrary, she turned to it to help heal her. The main role that it played for her was to help her in dealing with the depression that inevitably crept in as she dealt with this condition: "There were times I was completely bedridden with this disease. It can become pretty depressing when you can't walk or take care of your family or do anything you did in your "normal life". Crochet was the only thing that didn't change. My crochet was my constant companion. It kept me company. It gave me a reason to wake up each day. It made me feel like I still had something valuable to offer even if I had to do it from my bed. In a world spinning out of control and everything as you know it is gone, it is very comforting to have crochet remain the same. It was my anchor to reality when nothing else in my life was even remotely familiar. The greatest healing I find with crochet is that it is always the same. It feels like an old friend or your favorite pair of shoes. In an unfamiliar world of illness, crochet is my security blanket."

I have to add here that not only did crochet itself provide a comfort to Tammy as she dealt with this illness but so did the crochet community. Tammy's "crochet family" as she calls it immediately responded to the situation, using their crochet talents to raise money to help pay for her health care. While the money was certainly needed and appreciated, it was that show of support for a fellow crocheter that really touched Tammy's heart. In many cases, that can make all the difference in recovery from a chronic condition.

I read in the personal accounts on many Chronic Lyme websites that support groups, including online forums, were supremely helpful in dealing with this condition. Of course, groups specifically for Chronic Lyme sufferers are important because people can meet others there who are going through the same things as themselves, but it's also good to stay as connected as possible to others who share the same non-medical interests as you, too, and online crochet groups certainly provide a terrific opportunity for that. With any chronic medical condition, the patient runs the risk of becoming overly focused on their disease to the point that they feel like it defines who they are and this can be terribly limiting. Connecting to others around interests like crafting can help the person to feel whole, instead of limited.

Meet Tammy!

Tammy Hildebrand is well-established crochet designer, the professional development chairperson for the Crochet Guild of America (CGOA) and is on the CGOA board of directors. Crochet is her life. It has also been an important healing tool in her battle with Chronic Lyme Disease.

Tammy Hildebrand learned to crochet when she was quite young. Her second grade teacher taught her and Tammy still has that first floppy purple crochet hat she made. She obviously didn't know at the time that crochet would come to be her life's work but that's exactly what happened. (As a side note and a thanks to the great influence of teachers everywhere, Tammy tracked down her old teacher and shared with her the great role she played in her life. They are now Facebook friends so her teacher gets to see all of her crochet projects online.)

So for Tammy, crochet came first and illness came later. In fact, Tammy really can't remember a time before crochet.

> *"Crochet has been such a large part of my life for so long that I have a hard time pulling out specific aspects of it. It is just part of who I am. I am never without a hook in hand and really don't know if I could stop if I tried. It is like breathing to me and I really just don't even think about it. Years ago my husband and I owned a brick laying company. I would lay brick during the day and crochet in the evenings. I was tearing down some scaffolding one day and broke my arm. Rather than put my crochet on hold while my arm healed, I devised a way to crochet with my feet. I would sit "Indian style" on the floor and hold the hook between my toes with the soles of my feet placed together. Then I would manipulate the yarn with my left hand."*

Unfortunately, illness did come and it was in the form of something more long-term than a broken arm. Tammy was diagnosed with Chronic Lyme Disease.

Chronic illness frequently causes depression. Tammy experienced that and crochet was crucial in helping her to overcome it. She shared:

> *"There were times I was completely bedridden with this disease. It can become pretty depressing when you can't walk or take care of your*

family or do anything you did in your "normal life". Crochet was the only thing that didn't change. My crochet was my constant companion. It kept me company. It gave me a reason to wake up each day. It made me feel like I still had something valuable to offer even if I had to do it from my bed. In a world spinning out of control and everything as you know it is gone, it is very comforting to have crochet remain the same. It was my anchor to reality when nothing else in my life was even remotely familiar. The greatest healing I find with crochet is that it is always the same. It feels like an old friend or your favorite pair of shoes. In an unfamiliar world of illness, crochet is my security blanket."

Tammy has played a huge role in the CGOA, a professional crochet organization, so it should come as no surprise that the crochet community has certainly played a role in helping her through her illness. She shares:

"When I was diagnosed with Lyme, it wasn't just me, it was my entire family – husband and two teen daughters. (It is very common for entire families to be infected). My crochet family immediately set out to help us. One crochet friend set up an online auction using original designs donated by many of my designer friends. They raised almost $2000.00! Another designer friend heard about the auction and wanted to help, too, so she ran a 24-hour sale on her site with 80% of the proceeds going to us and sent over $3000.00! Sure the money was great but it was so much more. These people are my family. I love them! Without crochet, they wouldn't exist in my world. Many of us are so different and would never have come together if we didn't share the love of crochet. It crosses all boundaries. The late Jean Leinhauser used to say, "These are my people." That totally sums it up!"

Since being diagnosed, Tammy has become a Lyme activist. She promotes crochet to the other people she meets in the Lyme community, sharing how-to videos and tips to get them started in crochet, too.

You can connect with Tammy online. She is active in the online crochet community (find her on Ravelry, for example). And visit her blog at http://hotlavacrochet.blogspot.com/.

Hand Conditions

Fibromyalgia and MS are two conditions that feature hand pain as part of their symptoms. I wanted to make this a separate section, though, because of the unique issues for crocheters dealing with varying types of pain in the hands including those chronic pain conditions we've already talked about as well as others such as arthritis and Parkinson's. On one side, there's the fact that crochet can be tough for people with hand conditions because it obviously requires the use of the hands. On the flip side, however, there are many ways in which the physical stitchery of crochet can actually be beneficial to people with hand problems.

For example, Stitchlinks found that knitting and other types of stitching (presumably including crochet) served as a wonderful hand exercise for people including one woman suffering from Cerebral Palsy who used cross-stitching to improve her hand function by fifty percent. The woman had previously been unable to type on a keyboard or even hold a mug of tea in her hand but was able to do both of these things after improving her hand function through needlework. Cerebral Palsy is a condition with a number of different symptoms including muscle and joint pain, as well as shortening or tightening of the muscles, which inhibits range of motion. It can be more pronounced in the hands or in the legs (or both). Tina Matsunaga, a crocheter who blogs at Living with Cerebral Palsy, has noted in her blog that her mobility is even more limited during the cold winter months and that she tends to suffer from boredom as a result. She tries different things to keep her busy; last winter she learned Tunisian crochet.

Cerebral Palsy is just one of the many conditions that badly affect the hands, of course. A common one that always comes to mind is arthritis. Arthritis was actually the hand condition that interested me most in relation to crochet. Honestly, before I started doing any research into the health benefits of crochet, I assumed that crochet and arthritis were enemies. It was my understanding that arthritis causes crippling pain in the hands and it was my assumption that the actions taken in crochet work would be painful and difficult for people who are dealing with arthritis. I was pleasantly surprised to learn that crochet can be a balm for helping ease this pain rather than something that causes more pain to the arthritis sufferer.

In fact, I have read countless articles about elderly women who crochet that say that their crochet work keeps their hands limber. They believe that without their crochet, their hands would be in significantly more pain from the condition. Doctors frequently recommend hand exercises for people who are suffering from Rheumatoid Arthritis. Crocheting can be a positive type of hand exercise when it is worked in small periods of time.

The person who is suffering from arthritis does typically have to make some adjustments so that their crochet works for them instead of against them. In an article in Arthritis Today, author Margaret Littman reports on research by an occupational therapist into proper crochet techniques for people with this particular hand condition. She writes: "New tools and smart tricks can help you meld arthritis, knitting, cross-stitch and crocheting. You'll not only create sweaters and afghans, you also might increase hand dexterity, says Theresa Leto, an occupational therapist and instructor at the University of Findlay in Ohio. Leto suggests approaching needlework as an athletic event. "Warm up your hand in some way first." Soaking hands and wrists in warm water prior to picking up a needle helps some of her patients. "Then approach the activity like a sprinter, not a marathoner, and stitch in short sessions."

These days there are numerous tools on the market to make it easier for people with arthritis to crochet. This includes not only a variety of yarn choices but also ergonomic crochet hooks. With these tools, crochet not only becomes easier for the person with arthritis but can also be healing. Margaret Littman offers some additional tips for people who want to use crochet to help their arthritis:

- Trick #1. Use flexible, flattened and square crochet hooks. They are easier to hold than traditional round hooks.
- Trick #2. Add a foam sheath or wrap a rubber band around the hook handle a few times. It will prevent the hook from slipping your grip, and you'll use less force to hold it.
- Trick #3. Ask experts to watch your moves. Experts at a needlework shop can suggest adjustments for yarn tension and other

ways to ease stiffness and increase nimbleness.

And here are six more tips from a staff written article at freepatterns.com:

1. Don't try to crochet very early in the morning or very late at night, since arthritis pain and stiffness is more severe at these times.
2. Soak your hands in warm water before and after crocheting. This will help soothe the inflammation and relieve tension.
3. A gentle massage, with or without one of the good topical pain relief ointments on the market, will help. Be sure you use a non-greasy formula, so you won't defeat your purpose by having to work harder to control your yarn with sticky hands.
4. Choose a comfortable spot to crochet. If your body is relaxed, your hands will be less apt to cramp. Don't crochet for lengthy periods. Take a break now and then to stretch and move, and flex your fingers in a nice warm water bath.
5. Have a soothing cup of tea. Don't think about the arthritis; think about the lovely things you are creating and direct your energy toward that. You'll be amazed at what you can accomplish if you put your mind to it - arthritis or not.
6. Your condition will dictate when and how to pace yourself. Arthritis pain and inflammation are affected by weather and stress. On a particularly bad day, you might want to forego your project.

In this section on hand conditions, I also wanted to talk more specifically about one additional condition: Parkinson's. Parkinson's is a progressive chronic illness that affects the nervous system. Motor skills are highly affected with this condition and people suffering from the disease have tremors, lack of movement and slowed movement and speech. This can lead to significant amounts of pain as well as problems with depression and anxiety, all of which we know can be resolved in part through the positive distraction of crochet.

So can you crochet when you have Parkinson's? Marian, who blogs about her experience living with Parkinson's at http://marian-pathwalk.blogspot.com/, mentioned in one post that she feels like her hands shake too much to knit but she can handle crocheting and it's one of the things she does on planes to stay calm when dealing with the difficulties of traveling. So yes, people with Parkinson's can crochet although they may have to make adaptations for comfort like people with arthritis sometimes do.

Restless Legs Syndrome

So we've looked at how crochet can help people with hand conditions. But what about conditions of the legs? It seems odd to think of using crochet to help with problems related to the legs (unless you're like Tammy Hildebrand and can learn to crochet with your toes!) but I interviewed a woman named Sara-Jane (see *Meet Sara-Jane*!) who shared that crochet has been very helpful in helping her cope with the symptoms of Restless Legs Syndrome.

Restless Legs Syndrome, according to WebMD, is a nervous system disorder that causes the legs (and sometimes other parts of the body) to twitch and move. The sensation ranges from prickly and itchy to intolerably twitchy. The feeling is usually at its worst when the person is sitting or lying down. The most significant effect is that it disturbs sleep and so RLS is actually considered a sleep disorder, not just a nervous system disorder. It is unknown at this time what causes RLS although studies indicate that genetics, certain medications and having certain other chronic conditions may be causes.

There are medications available to treat the symptoms of RLS although they work only for some people while others find that they offer no relief. RLS is typically treated mostly with lifestyle changes including eliminating certain things, like caffeine, and adding others, like exercise. Sara-Jane has done many of those things, including limiting caffeine to morning hours, eliminating red dye from her diet and staying busy during the day. At night, she obviously needs to slow down and get ready for bed. That's when her legs start to shake, often to the point of pain.

Sara-Jane shared that she uses crochet to help her relax during these evening hours. She has found that if her hands are busy moving and her mind is focusing on her stitchwork then she doesn't have so many problems with her legs. They will relax and she won't feel like she is in so much pain. She has learned to use crochet as a tool not only at night but also whenever she has to be seated for long periods of time during the day, such as when she's on a long car or bus ride.

Restless Legs Syndrome is sometimes a temporary condition experienced by pregnant women. In fact, the National Sleep Foundation reported recently on a study that showed that more than one in four women will experience RLS symptoms during pregnancy. They go on to say that sleep problems during pregnancy are directly correlated with labor complications so it can be really important to get those symptoms under control. Many pregnant women don't want to try drugs since they may affect the baby so they have to just use lifestyle changes to reduce their symptoms. One of the things that National Sleep Foundation recommends for women in this situation is to not force sleep during periods of sleep disturbance but instead to get up and knit or crochet something for the baby until your legs calm down and you may be able to fall back asleep.

Meet Sara-Jane!

Sara-Jane suffers from Restless Leg Syndrome (RLS). She has found that crochet stops her painful leg twitching and helps her to relax.

It was about five years ago that Sara-Jane began to feel the effects of Restless Leg Syndrome. She would go to bed and her legs would still be moving around. She would lay there doing leg lifts to try to get relief but eventually she would need to stand up to get rid of the feeling. This prevented her from getting any sleep. She went to a doctor who prescribed her the right medication to get her back to a normal sleeping pattern but she has also had to make many lifestyle changes to improve her condition.

One of the key things that Sara-Jane had to do was to cut out all caffeine after about four o'clock. She no longer has any tea, diet cola or chocolate in her afternoon or evening diet. She also discovered that red dye would exacerbate the problem so she can't eat things like Twizzlers without feeling the effect.

Sara-Jane tries to stay busy during the day so that she doesn't have problems with her legs. However, at night she does have to settle down. She's a teacher and has to correct papers and plan for the next day. So after about eight pm, she's seated, and that's when her legs start to wiggle. She just wants to sit down and relax but her legs refuse, sometimes shaking to the point where it's painful.

Sara-Jane has found that crocheting can actually help stop the shaking in her legs. She had learned how to crochet from her mother when she was a child but hadn't done it in a long time. She shares:

> *"I have always been a crafty person, it's in the blood. My mother created beautiful Irish knit sweaters and after she retired (as a principal, so that runs in the family as well!) she took up quilting, all hand done – she never liked sewing machines. When I was younger I did needlepoint and crewel and after I had children I picked up scrapbooking and card making, but nothing compares to crocheting. It's affordable and I can always manage to find something to make."*

Sara-Jane picked up crochet again after another teacher at her school showed her the crochet that she was working on. She was immediately "hooked." She would crochet between classes, at night or in the car, and she found that if her legs were twitching they would stop when she picked up her crochet work. She says:

> *"When I sit at night, or in the car, if I'm at all tired – the legs start twitching. I will pick up my crocheting and the legs stop. I'm not sure if the same part of my brain that tells my legs to twitch also tells my fingers to move in a certain way, but that's the way I think about it. Just knowing that I can alleviate the wiggles gives me great emotional relief."*

Crochet has allowed her to be able to do things that she wouldn't be able to do if she couldn't get her RLS under control. For example, she goes on an annual trip with students to Washington, D.C., which is four hours away from her Boston home. That bus ride could be impossible with her RLS but she takes her crochet and a reading light to crochet at night on the bus and she makes the trip without incident.

Sara-Jane's favorite part of crochet is the feeling of accomplishment that she gets when a project is finished. But it's the actual process of working the stitches that brings her the most relief for her health issues. She loves that it's an affordable craft that she can do alone to get some rest while healing herself.

Menière's disease

The final chronic condition that I want to look at in this chapter is Menière's disease. This condition isn't characterized by chronic pain, per se, but it's a progressive incurable condition with devastating life consequences and it's important to look at how crochet can help with the depression that can result from receiving such a diagnosis.

Many people aren't familiar with this condition so let me explain it as best I can. Menière's disease is a condition that affects the inner ear. The inner ear gets damaged and it worsens over time. The most obvious impact is on hearing; sufferers of the condition slowly begin to go deaf. Equally debilitating, however, is the fact that the inner ear is what allows us to have balance and coordination and this disease interferes with that. People with Menière's, especially those who have it in both ears rather than just one ear, experience extreme vertigo which means that the world can constantly feel like it is spinning.

Menière's disease is a complicated disease. For one thing, no one is quite sure what causes it. Worse, though, no one is sure how to cure it. The condition just worsens with time. The only thing that sufferers can do is to make changes to their lifestyle to adapt to the effects of the condition and to minimize the symptoms as much as possible. A healthy diet, proper exercise, resting during times when the vertigo is high and other common sense actions are the most recommended courses of action for this disease without a cure.

Another major tool that sufferers rely on is the use of a variety of different relaxation techniques including yoga, meditation and breathing exercises. Relaxing allows the body to come to more of a state of rest, which can reduce the symptoms of the condition. It also helps with side effects of the disease including depression and anxiety. Just imagine if every time you tried to do something you risked falling down, feeling nauseous or getting dizzy all while experiencing increasing deafness. This would understandably result in anxiety, depression, fear and perhaps the feeling that you couldn't be useful to the world around you as we've seen often comes along with chronic illness of all kinds. Learning to relax through a variety of different techniques is a way to cope with these side effects of a condition like Menière's disease.

I interviewed blogger and crafter Elisabeth Andrée (see her whole story on the page titled *Meet Elisabeth Andrée!*) who was diagnosed with Menière's at the age of 32. Throughout her thirties she managed to get along well enough despite the condition. However, around the age of 40 her illness took a major turn for the worse. She was unable to work anymore because of her condition. She was increasingly deaf, felt ill all of the time and also had the stress of having no income because of her condition. She started to fall into a deep depression but was opposed to taking medication. She decided to embark on a comprehensive plan for self-healing, focusing on integrating a myriad of relaxation techniques.

At this time, Elisabeth Andrée started doing many things to heal herself. She began taking regular walks. She began doing yoga. She learned counting and meditation exercises. And yes, she crocheted. She actually hadn't done a lot of crochet before that point but felt instinctively drawn to pick up the hook as she got more and more ill. She explains: "Crochet helps me to calm down and relax, shifts my focus from misery to something interesting and pleasurable, and gives me the ability to create and thereby keep myself mentally healthy."

She went on to explain that she knows that her condition could allow her to easily fall back into depression at any time. After all, this is a progressive disease and thinking about what that means for her future can be frightening and could easily lend itself to despair. When she starts to feel that coming on, she turns to the healing power of crochet to snap out of it. She says that she can generate satisfying, calming feelings fairly quickly just through crocheting.

Menière's disease may have stopped Elisabeth Andrée from having a regular job but it hasn't stopped her from contributing to the world around her. She believes strongly in the value of passing on domestic craft skills from generation to generation. She, like many of us, has reverence for the women of generations before us who did not have the Internet and the library of resources that we have today to learn old-fashioned skills like crochet. And she wants to do her part to honor that by expanding on the craft by sharing her knowledge and experience of it with others, which she does primarily through online publication. Take that Menière's!

Meet Elisabeth Andrée!

Elisabeth Andrée suffers from an inner ear disease that will only get worse with time. It not only makes it difficult for her to hear but also gravely affects her balance and coordination. Over the years this has resulted in a job loss which might have caused her to spiral into depression. However, through sheer self-determination to celebrate her life, and with a little bit of help from crochet, this crafter has managed to learned to enjoy the little things.

Elisabeth Andrée was only thirty three years old in 1992 when she was diagnosed with Menière's disease. An ENT explained to her the frightening news that the disease is an irreversible process of destruction of the inner ear. This meant that she would experience increasing deafness. Many people who have this disease only have it in one ear and their bodies can more or less compensate for the damage in terms of how it affects the balance that the inner ear helps with. Unfortunately, this was not the case for Elisabeth Andrée who suffers from it bilaterally. This means it's in both ears, increasing the deafness as well as increasing all problems related to balance and coordination. The diagnosis was frightening but she went on with her life.

Eight years after her initial diagnosis, the illness suddenly worsened. In her own words:

> *"Because of that I lost my job. I was very ill, was suddenly deaf on one side and the other ear did not work properly and I had no income. I became depressed, but did not want to take medication so I invented my own plan to get me back to feel better."*

She was living far away from home and the process wasn't easy but she was determined to stave off depression and improve her life. To that end, she implemented a variety of different techniques. She started walking, a lot. She started doing yoga. She read many books on chronic illness and learned a variety of relaxation techniques from them. For example, she shares a "simple and a little bit silly counting exercise":

> *"Count from 1 to 10, but once you notice that a thought comes through, start again at number one. Do not get irritated; just start again. Keep trying until you reach 10 without additional thoughts ...*

and then do it in reverse from 10 back to 1. I did this exercise anywhere, in the shower, at bedtime, in the supermarket, in the train. It doesn't take the problems away but it does give you a break."

And of course, she also crocheted. She explains that in the years prior to that she didn't crochet very much at all although she did learn the craft when she was young. She notes that she comes from a time and place when girls would learn the domestic arts in school. Her mom tells her that she learned to crochet around age six although she doesn't recall it. She does recall making a round crochet cushion cover for her dog's bed when she was young, though. Both her mom and aunt crocheted. She herself hadn't done much of it in her adult years but then ...

"when I was so down and out, I almost instinctively grabbed my hook and yarn. Crochet helps me to calm down and relax, shifts my focus from misery to something interesting and pleasurable, and gives me the ability to create and thereby keep myself mentally healthy (sort of). It helps me not to fall back into depression and prevents me from being in despair about my future and if I do have a gloomy mood (hormones) than I can, just by crocheting, generate (fairly quickly) satisfying and calming feelings."

One of the words that Elisabeth Andrée used to describe crochet is "hypnotic." She loves the act of creating something through the process of counting, feeling the yarn in her hands, seeing the colors coming together. When you start to lose one of your senses, such as hearing in her case, you have all the more reason to indulge in the other senses that you still have and crochet is certainly an indulgence in both touch and sight. It is also emotionally satisfying for Elisabeth Andrée who loves everything from buying yarn and seeking out new inspiration to making new designs and sharing her crochet ideas with the rest of the world through her online activities. She says:

"Mastering a craft technique that has existed for so long I think is fantastic. We have it easy these days with the Internet, books and magazines. Considering that women - long and longer ago - used to create everything purely out of themselves, that makes me humble. It reminds me of the need for crochet to be passed to all generations

coming next to us. I therefore hope that my website can help, however minimal that it may be."

Elisabeth Andree doesn't know how her craft work will be affected by her illness in the future. She sometimes has problems with reading now, which includes reading patterns, and she has to adjust the way that she holds her crochet sometimes because of her vision problems. But she doesn't dwell on it. She realizes that today is the only day we have and she focuses on celebrating what's right in front of her right now.

You can visit Elisabeth Andree on her blog:
http://elisabethandree.posterous.com.

Improving Physical Health by Reducing Stress

While most of this book has covered the mental health benefits of crochet, I think it is important to point out that crochet has several potential benefits for your physical health as well. We've looked at pain management, for example. But there are other ways that crochet can help with physical health, too. These ways may not be as obvious or as direct as the benefits for mental health but are clearly just as important.

As I've mentioned previously some of the most detailed studies completed about the health benefits of needlework have been done since 2005 by Betsan Corkhill and the Stitchlinks organization. These studies have looked primarily at the role of knitting in health. Many of the results of that research can be extrapolated to apply to all needlearts, most certainly including crochet. These results indicate that there are numerous ways in which needlecrafting can improve physical health. This starts with lowering blood pressure and reducing stress since stress is a cause of so many serious (as well as less-serious) health problems. Physical benefits of crochet also include immune system boosts and an increase in energy levels. Let's take a closer look at all of that …

Understanding Stress

Stress is a known or suspected cause of countless health problems. We know this not only because it's something that we've been told again and again in the health headlines but also because each of us has experienced it in one form or another. Think about the last time that you "caught a cold" and what was going on in your life at the time. Was your schedule too hectic or your work environment particularly crazy or your relationship in the middle of a rocky period? When stress enters our lives, our bodies begin to break down. Stress over a long period of time is linked with fatal conditions including heart disease. It exacerbates most other medical conditions, sometimes taking them from minor to life threatening very quickly. In other words, if you want to be healthy, it is crucial to reduce stress in your life as much as you can. Crochet can be one way to do that.

You do not have to have a medical degree to know that crochet can be a stress-reducer. In fact, according to the Craft Yarn Council of America, more than two thirds of people who knit or crochet report that they do so because it helps them to relax and reduce stress (Fiedler). You can feel it happening when you get lost in your project. Your breathing slows down, your mind calms itself and your body comes to a place of more peace. This break that you are giving your mind and body allows the body to soothe itself, to recuperate and to erase some of the effects of stress in your life.

Although you do not have to do medical research to understand this correlation, there are many people with medical degrees who have done precisely this type of research. Because stress causes so many health issues for so many different types of people, extensive research has been done into the ways that we can reduce stress in our lives. And it turns out that there are medical reasons to explain why a craft like crochet can reduce stress and therefore improve physical wellbeing.

For example, a press release put out by FaveCrafts in 2009 titled Knitting and Crochet Offer Long-Term Health Benefits shared, "Pain specialist Monica Baird explains that the action of knitting actually changes brain chemistry, decreasing stress hormones and increasing feel-good serotonin and dopamine." Additionally, "Dr. Herbert Bendon, Director of the Institute for Mind, Body Medicine at Massachusetts General Hospital and Associate Professor of Medicine at Harvard Medical School notes that knitting is one method to create a "relaxation response" in the body, which can lower blood pressure, heart rate and help prevent illness."

Crafters concur with these experts. For example, Em from nothingbutstring reports that all of the stress that she went through created problems for her with high blood pressure. This is a situation that runs in her family and so she knows that it can cause serious physical danger when not properly taken care of. She noticed that when she started crocheting her experience of high stress levels decreased, and she noticed a corresponding decrease in her blood pressure levels. For Em, and many others, crocheting helps to alleviate stress and produces a physical result in the body that can be lifesaving.

People believing that crochet can reduce stress-related disease isn't something new. A newspaper article dating back to 1949 tells the story of a man who felt certain that his ulcers had gone away because of his crochet work. In recent years medical studies have found that most ulcers are not stress-related but instead are caused by other things, usually bacteria. However, stress can cause some ulcers and for many, many years (including back in 1949) it was believed that stress was the cause of all or most ulcers.

Joseph Dolinaj had been crocheting for about five years when he won the 1949 annual crochet contest hosted by the National Needlecraft Bureau for a 6' x 8' filet crochet tablecloth that was worked in one solid piece. The 200+ pound, 37-year-old man was a railroad signal tower operator by day but a crocheter by night. He is quoted as saying that before crochet he was always "jumpy and cranky" but that crocheting had calmed his nerves. He had actually started the craft as part of a bet; he was tired of watching his wife crochet every night and he bet her $5 that he could do better than her at the craft. He says that the relaxation it induced in his life got rid of his ulcers and he recommended that other men learn how to crochet to heal from ulcers too.

The sad thing about stress is that we cannot always eliminate the cause of stress in our lives. Sometimes we can and that is certainly something that we should do. But there are times when we just aren't in a position to quit the job that is making us stressed out or to heal the ailing parent whose health is causing us stress. What we can do is to control our own response to stressful situations so that we minimize the impact that they have on our lives. We do this with self-care and one form of self-care for many people is engaging in a relaxing and meditative hobby that takes the mind and body away from the stressful situation. Hence, crochet for stress!

Asthma and Stress

I'll be honest in saying that I really wasn't sure where to include the section on crochet for asthma in this book. Asthma is such a tricky illness. There are many different kinds of asthma as well as many different causes of asthma. In fact, there are so many possible root causes that patients and their doctors often don't know exactly what makes their asthma a problem. I know this from firsthand experience, which I shared with you a bit in the chapter on anxiety and panic attacks.

I started developing signs of asthma when I was a teenager, but it usually only came on when I would get my annual "winter cold." The cough would linger forever and so would difficulty in breathing. Asthma runs in my family. In fact, the entire reason that my mother was relocated to Arizona from Minnesota when she was a child was because she and her brother had asthma and the dry desert air was believed at that time to be a cure for asthma. Between Mom and my uncles and me and my siblings I had seen my fair share of albuterol inhalers, steroid treatments, nebulizers and hospital visits.

When my own asthma got worse, I did extensive research into possible causes of asthma. I went through the irritating process of having my back pinpricked five dozen times to see if the breathing problems were caused by an allergy. I manipulated my diet. I kept health diaries to track my symptoms in the hopes of sussing out an underlying cause. I asked the man behind the counter at the tea store in Chinatown what would be a good tea for asthma. Despite my own attention and research and visits to several doctors, I never did find out the underlying cause of my asthma. I don't have any known allergies and no particular diet seems to stop asthma attacks from happening. My breathing gets worse when I have a respiratory infection, which seems obvious, and I have difficulty breathing when I exercise, which is common. The condition is controlled with the use of a steroid inhaler and I am protected with an emergency albuterol inhaler but we aren't sure what causes the actual problem. And although there are some people who do have specific causes of their asthma, it is often the case that asthma sufferers are like me; they can control the symptoms but never do find an underlying cause. What we almost all find, however, is that asthma is exacerbated by stress.

If you have ever had an asthma attack, you know that being unable to breathe is one of the worst physical feelings that you will ever experience. The very thing that you do every day just to stay alive is suddenly almost impossible and every instinct inside of your being wants to fight to stay alive. You can see it in the eyes of someone that is in the midst of an asthma attack – the body thinks that it is about to die. Their eyes widen, their throats try to suck in as much air as possible, their bodies heave with both fear and effort. Unfortunately, the body's natural reaction to the problem tends to exacerbate the problem. The panic that you feel when you can't breathe, and your subsequent attempts to gasp in air, actually make it more difficult to regulate your breathing.

In the middle of such an intense panic attack, I typically find that there are two options. One is medication. If I'm lucky, I reach for an albuterol inhaler and soon my breathing has been regulated. In the instances where I have been less lucky (meaning I either didn't have an albuterol inhaler or the inhaler didn't work) the end result was a trip to the emergency room where I was given a breathing treatment and usually a pill. When I was younger, I used to think that this pill somehow traveled down into my lungs and opened them up properly. Now I know that the pill is designed to relax the body. Stress exacerbates asthma. Relieving the body's stress helps to minimize and eventually end the asthma attack.

That brings us to option number two, which I've learned to rely on more and more as I've gotten older and gotten to know my own body: finding a form of stress relief. When I feel the wheezing, gasping breath begin to come on, I try to stop what I am doing and refocus my body and my mind. If I can catch it early enough and divert my energy to a soothing, stress-relieving task then I can manage the attack without medication. Crochet doesn't solve the underlying problems that cause asthma, whatever they may be. And it certainly doesn't work in all situations or for full-blown asthma attacks as I've already related to you in my own experience. But it can work to soothe and de-stress the body enough to reduce the need for medication.

As a regular form of stress-relief, crochet can also reduce the intensity and frequency of asthma attacks for some people. Ongoing stress in life makes health problems worse for many asthmatics. Katherine Kam has reported that a senior medical officer at the National Institute of Allergy and Infectious Diseases confirms that, "During periods of stress and anxiety, asthma attacks occur more frequently, and asthma control is more difficult." Reducing the stress levels on a steady basis keeps the body in a calmer state and significantly less likely to experience a stress-related asthma attack.

Immune System and Stress

Stress wreaks havoc on the immune system. To make matters worse, when we are stressed out we often make poor choices in terms of diet, exercise and getting enough sleep and this weakens the immune system even further. The weaker the immune system, the more prone we are to getting a diverse array of illnesses from the common cold to deadly infections and heart disease.

The main thing that you need to know to understand the effect of stress on the immune system is that chronic stress can increase cortisol levels in the human body. Cortisol is a hormone, sometimes called "the stress hormone", that has a direct relationship to the body's immune function. Cortisol gets released in higher levels when the body is under stress. The evolutionary function of this is what we know as the "fight or flight" response, which can help save us in situations of immediate potential harm. However, if your fight or flight response is constantly turned on then your body begins to break down. High levels of cortisol can lead to problems with glucose metabolism, blood pressure regulation and inflammation in the body. It can also lead to significantly lowered immunity, putting you at risk for any number of different health problems.

One of the key ways to manage stress levels is to learn how to induce what is called "the relaxation response" in your body. In a healthy body this is the state that naturally follows the "fight or flight response." Basically, once you are out of harm's way, your body relaxes and goes back to normal, allowing it to properly function despite the momentary experience of stress. In people whose lives are filled with chronic stress, the relaxation response never comes and the body and immune system break down. The positive thing about this is that there are numerous things that you can do to intentionally induce the relaxation response in order to heal and restore your body. Meditation, journaling, exercise, breathing exercises and yoga are common methods that people use to restore their sense of relaxation. A repetitive hobby like crochet is another option.

In the same way that learning to reduce stress in the body can help in dealing with asthma, learning to reduce both physical and emotional stress can help reduce negative impacts on your immune system. This improves your chances for better overall health. And yes, there is at least one study out there that supports this. Anndee Hochman wrote in a 2004 Time Health Inc. article about a study done by Gene D. Cohen, M.D., Ph.D. that followed a group of people for a year, half of whom were involved in creative pursuits like taking painting and jewelry-making classes, and half who were not. The study found that after one year "the art students logged fewer visits to the doctor, took fewer prescription drugs, reported better morale and spent more time socializing".

Cohen argued that "creativity is a part of being human, and it has profound implications for our health." There may be many reasons for this. It may be true that there's a profound need inside of us to be creative and that doing so boosts the immune system. Or you may believe that being creative just takes your mind off of your problems so that you aren't so focused on going to the doctor every time that you get the sniffles. Either way, the research indicates that doing creative things, like crochet, will make you feel less stressed and generally healthier.

Energy Levels

A significant side effect of a high-stress lifestyle and a decreased immune system is a lack of energy. When you have a low-stress, healthy lifestyle, your body is able to regulate itself properly. You have high levels of energy throughout the day and then relax at night. But the stressed out body doesn't ever relax enough and therefore never properly restores. The result, as you certainly know from your own experience, is that you feel tired and fatigued a large percentage of the time. Some of us can't even remember the last time that we felt like we had a lot of energy!

The cycle of flagging energy can feel endless. You know that you need to get your body up and moving and your mind engaged in an activity if you want to feel energetic. However, you are so mentally and physically tired that the very idea of being active makes you want to go to bed. When you try to go to bed, you aren't worn out enough to actually sleep properly, so you toss and turn. You never get a proper night's sleep so the following day you feel like you have even less energy and then the cycle continues. Because your body is constantly stressed, your immune system is lower and you are more likely to get colds and other illnesses, which decrease your energy levels even more.

The study that Cohen did also found that the people who were engaged in creative activities were also more likely to feel like they had energy to do other things such as taking classes, doing volunteer work or even working part time. Writing about this finding, Hochman says, "This research proves what many creativity experts have long observed anecdotally: Learning something new is a catalyst for doing even more. When you are actively, creatively engaged, your body releases a chemical called adrenocorticotropic hormone, or ACTH. This neurotransmitter fosters communication between the two halves of the brain – a connection researchers believe is central to creative thinking – and also helps produce the "high" that keeps you doodling on a scrap of paper or mixing compacts discs of your favorite songs, unconscious of time and bursting with ideas and enthusiasm." Creativity begets creativity; doing something inspiring increases your energy levels.

The great thing about crochet is that it is something relaxing that you can to decrease stress in your life, which will ultimately increase your energy levels. At the same time, crochet itself can be a stimulating activity because it engages your brain and your creativity. This can help you to feel more energetic for a short period of time while you are excited about your project. The more you use your brain and feel active, even if you aren't out there running a marathon, the more capable your body is of regulating its energy levels, thus helping to break that negative low-energy cycle! Personally I find it interesting that doing a low-key, relaxing activity can actually enhance your energy. I've also found it to be true.

Insomnia

One of the most frustrating aspects of chronic stress that I've personally experienced is insomnia. Before I had ever experienced insomnia, I didn't think that it sounded like such a bad thing. I desperately wanted to not have to sleep so much. I loved the idea of being able to stay awake all night, writing and creating art and dreaming up new big ideas. But this is not the reality of insomnia.

With insomnia, you aren't physically tired enough to sleep but you are too tired to do anything except lay in bed so you just lay there awake and stressed out, making your health worse and worse. Insomnia is made worse by stress and anxiety. The more your mind whirs and whirs with thoughts and fears, the less likely you are to fall asleep or stay asleep. It's frustrating as you lay there in tears just wanting a break from the stress that you feel.

One of the key ways to reduce problems with insomnia is to reduce stress in your every day life. It is specifically important for most people to develop an evening and nighttime ritual that is conducive to mental and physical relaxation. Crochet can be a key part of that relaxation ritual if you find a way to make it work for you. Imagine an ideal scenario for a moment as to what your evening would look like if you were alone in your home and dedicated just to relaxing. You might take a long, hot shower and then lather yourself with scented moisturizing lotion before slipping into your most comfy pajamas. You might make yourself a cup of rose-flavored tea and put some quiet, soothing music on in the background. You might cozy up in your favorite chair, wrapped up in a much-loved vintage afghan. With a fire in the fireplace and a soothing light behind your chair, you might crochet for forty five minutes, working on a meditative pattern. As the fabric develops beneath your fingers, your body relaxes. When the last drop of tea is gone and the last ember has burned out in your fireplace, you work your last row for the night and go to bed. You fall asleep and you dream and you don't wake up until morning.

Sound appealing? Certainly.

A Quick Note on a Healthy Diet

One of the things that almost all of us need to do if we're interested in improving our physical health in any way is to make changes to our diet, choosing a proper healthy diet that can be maintained over the course of a lifetime. While crochet can't force you to make smart eating choices, it can help to provide you with something to keep your hands busy so that you aren't snacking in between meals if you aren't hungry. Crochet gives your mind a focus so that you aren't just thinking about food. It serves as a distraction in the same way that we saw it used when we were looking at crochet for addictions. Plus, it helps you to burn a few more calories during sedentary activities (like watching TV) than if you just did those activities alone.

I haven't been able to locate a significant amount of writing on this topic but I've seen it mentioned (often half-jokingly) here and there around the web. The most significant support I've seen for this is the work of Dr. Katherine Applegate, Ph.D. of the Duke Center for Metabolic and Weight Loss Surgery. I first found out about this doctor through an October 2011 post on the Crochetbug blog. Crochetbug explained that Applegate provides psychological services for bariatric surgery patients.

(In case you're not sure, that encompasses a variety of different types of weight loss surgery that reduce the size of the stomach either through a partial stomach removal or through a gastric band implant). Crochetbug explains that the surgery is just half the battle; the rest of losing weight is up to the patient in making lifestyle changes to avoid the things that trigger overeating.

She writes: "Dr. Applegate (who is herself a knitter and crocheter) said that crochet and knitting are not silly hobbies to be pooh-poohed, but can be helpful tools that should be considered for inclusion in a weight-loss plan. Either will keep your hands occupied, and if you're doing one thing (crochet), you can't be doing another (eating)." She also explains that there are four major reasons that people overeat (boredom, stress, anxiety/ depression and for comfort/ reward) and that crochet can resolve each of these four things.

Incidentally, my additional research into Dr. Katherine Applegate suggests that this crafting doctor believes in the power of needlework for resolving many issues, not just dietary ones. In early 2007 she taught a workshop at the Duke Diet & Fitness Center titled "Crafting to Stress Less: How Knitting and Other Crafts Can Help you Relax While Keeping your Hands Busy." This comes full circle to her work with weight loss patients because she notes that extra stress increases problems with weight gain so taking up a hobby that relaxes you, like knitting or crochet, can help you with weight loss through stress reduction.

Working It! Crochet as Occupational Therapy

Occupational therapy is a significant part of healing in the treatment of a diverse range of conditions including physical problems, mental health issues and developmental disabilities. The Bureau of Labor Statistics describes the work that occupational therapists do as treating "patients with injuries, illnesses, or disabilities through the therapeutic use of everyday activities. They help these patients develop, recover, and improve the skills needed for daily living and working." The "everyday tasks" that are used as tools by occupational therapists are as diverse as the conditions for which the treatment is used and yes, one of the tasks in some settings can be crochet. An article by Erin Morton about therapist Mary E. Black goes further in defining the occupational therapist as "part nurse, part social worker, part psychologist and part craftsman." That's right, craftsman (or craftsperson if you prefer).

Crochet is a craft that is great for use in occupational therapy settings. It can be used to help develop neuromuscular skills, fine motor skills and cognitive skills and it is something that can be done by people of almost any age. This, along with its affordability, makes it a great option for occupational therapists to consider. In fact, in the 1970s when alternative therapies were commonly explored and crafting was popular some instructors at Occupational Therapy schools required their students to create files of instructions for crafts including crochet and macramé to use as a resource for their future patients (Rockett).

Art therapy is useful as a therapeutic tool for many reasons. I think one of the major reasons is that with art there is no "right" and "wrong." This is true with crochet, as well, of course. Sure, there may be patterns you can follow and basic rules that make crafting easier, but in the end, crochet is a craft of self-expression and you can do with it what you please. I think this is a relief for many people who are having trouble doing regular things, like eating or walking, in the "right" way. Crafting relieves the pressure of doing something "right" and lets you just do something beautiful in whatever way you can.

Additionally, I think it helps a lot that crochet is such a stress-relieving activity. Trying to learn new skills or re-learn skills that you've lost to injury is stressful and frustrating. And of course, the more frustrated that you get, the harder it is to relax and learn those skills. So it's terrific if you can find a way to just relax and feel less stress. With more relaxation, the patient is going to feel more comfortable continuing therapy.

Crafts can be widely used in occupational therapy because they're appropriate to all ages, developmental levels and institutional settings. Sara Gormley, OTS, writing for StuNurse Magazine, says, "Crafts are an appropriate medium across the lifespan from toddlers stringing cereal necklaces to the elderly crocheting pot holders. Settings appropriate for use to assess or treat disability include, but are not limited to: early intervention programs, school based settings, mental health and rehabilitation, hospitals and nursing homes." And in an article by Bissell and Mailloux that reviews the history of crafts in occupational therapy settings for the physically disabled it was found that "the use of crafts has been a central concept in occupational therapy since the founding of the profession".

The study done by Bissell and Mailloux is actually a really fascinating one because it shows the ups and downs of how crafting was used over time in therapeutic settings and how the waxing and waning of its use tends to have a lot to do with the politics of occupational therapy as an industry rather than the way patients may perceive its benefits. The authors share that the very first professional journal of occupational therapy included an article recommending crafting in OT settings and go on to talk about how crafting was first used as a treatment for the mentally ill and then after World War I it was extended to use in physical therapy settings for war-injured veterans.

But things get tricky over time when it comes to crafting in therapeutic settings because of the changing philosophies surrounding "best practices" in the field. This is something you can see in any field, of course. It was something I studied in juvenile criminal justice classes where we see that during some periods of history the primary purpose of juvenile facilities was to punish child offenders and during other times it was to rehabilitate them, depending on the socio-political beliefs of the era. A similar thing is seen if you look at the history of psychological treatments. With occupational therapy, according to Bissell and Mailloux, "occupational therapy during the early twentieth century grew from a philosophy known as moral treatment." The basis of moral treatment was "respect for human individuality and a fundamental perception of the individual's need to engage in creative activity in relation of his fellow man".

So from 1900 - 1930 or thereabouts occupational therapy included an emphasis on crafting to encourage individual self-expression as part of the treatment process. In fact, from 1920 - 1930 there was a lot of momentum in spreading the word about the benefits of occupational therapy including crafting. The authors say that, "the use of crafts was discussed in terms of physical factors such as strength, coordination, and endurance, as well as psychological and social aspects such as problem solving, decision making, self-esteem development and group socialization." This was, in many ways, the heyday of crafting as a form of occupational therapy with many strides being made in celebrating how crafts can heal in both physical ways and psycho-social ones.

Things were to change quickly, though, as a result of The Depression. When money goes away, social programs often change their emphasis and focus. Although crafts were still used in occupational therapy settings, there was a definite transition towards focusing only on crafts that could improve physical skills for the disabled, such as developing more strength, and much less emphasis (where there was any) on the emotional and social benefits of crafting. At this time, the occupational therapy community was really aligning more with the medical community, primarily for financial reasons, so the emphasis had to be on medical benefits of all aspects of OT. After The Depression ended, there was more emphasis on occupational therapy services again, but the change had been made and the community continued to focus primarily on using crafting for physical therapy and not psychological therapy.

There was yet another shift in the occupational therapy community around the 1960s (a ripple effect from all of the changes happening in the culture at the time, surely). In places that treated individuals with disabilities there was an increasing focus on not only improving their physical wellbeing but taking a holistic approach to healing their minds and improving their social options as well. Oddly, Bissell and Mailloux say that there still wasn't much written about crafting during this time in the OT community and it seems that there continued to be more emphasis on physical treatments, like exercise, rather than crafting as an option. This had begun to shift a little bit by the time that Bissell and Mailloux completed their own study in the early 1980s.

As an aside, I just want to interject here that if the history of crafting within occupational therapy settings is of any interest to you, I'd absolutely recommend learning about the life and work of occupational therapist and weaver, Mary E. Black. (I mentioned her above because I read an article about her by Erin Morton; you can find that article's details in the reference section of this book. I don't know of any books specific to this crafter but the Morton article is a good one and there is additional information about Black in various places online.) Black was born in the late nineteenth century and worked as an occupational therapist in hospitals and sanitariums throughout the U.S. and Nova Scotia beginning in 1919. It was always her focused goal to utilize her love of weaving as a tool in her therapy whether she was working with post-war veterans or the mentally ill. She was willing to relocate as needed to be able to do this work and often had to do so because of the changing nature of crafts within therapeutic settings.

Getting back to craft in therapy today ... Bissell and Mailloux found that out of all of the therapists that they surveyed, nearly three out of four "stated that they used crafts as part of their treatment plan to achieve therapeutic goals." However, more than half of the therapists that were using crafting were doing so only about twenty percent of the time. The number one reason that they gave for not doing more with crafting was that it wasn't something that was measurable and therefore couldn't be documented and reported on. Although Bissell and Mailloux don't say it, I have little doubt that this has a lot to do with funding. I know from my own experience in various non-profit and government agencies that it is often tough to balance what is best for a patient or client with explaining why it is best to the people who are funding the organization that is offering the services. Occupational therapists might see huge benefits to crafting but if they can't offer measurable proof that their methods are working than they may not be able to get the money they need to keep their methods going.

Interestingly, Bissell and Mailloux found that there was a significant increase in the use of crafting in physical therapy settings that employed people who were specifically trained as Certified Occupational Therapy Assistants. Although most therapists were reporting that they used crafts in therapy less than twenty percent of the time, those places that did have certified OT assistants working with them were using crafts as therapy more than eighty percent of the time. This suggests that there was clear acceptance of the value of crafting within the specific niche of occupational therapy even if it wasn't so widely accepted in the larger physical therapy community.

Bissell and Mailloux published their findings in 1981. I'd like to think that since that time there has been a revival in the celebration of crafting as a therapeutic technique. There has certainly been a revival of the handmade / DIY movement in general and there is wide celebration of crafting in many other settings so it seems like there would be a cultural shift towards more of that in OT settings as well. I wasn't able to locate any specific recent studies updating the work that Bissell and Mailloux did, though, so I can't say for sure whether or not it's just wishful thinking on my part to think that crafting is in a time of revival in therapeutic settings.

In fact, the related recent studies that I did find seem to indicate that there continues to be a chasm between the general belief that crafts can be helpful in therapeutic settings and the ability to justify that to the "powers that be" controlling the purse strings in those settings. For example, a 2009 study by Sinikka Pollanen, PhD, titled Craft as Context in Therapeutic Change, states that there is "ambivalence felt by occupational therapists with respect to craft as a valuable modality" and that "recent discussions by occupational therapists suggest that although craft is relevant to occupational therapy, there are uncertainties about its position in the contemporary practice."

However, a few things give me a bit of hope that we're in or entering a period of history where craft is celebrated as a beneficial part of an occupational therapy treatment plan. First of all, the fact that studies continue to exist, all showing at least some benefit of crafting in OT settings, shows that an interest in this prevails despite ups and downs in the use of crafts in those settings. Second, Pollanen cited a 2008 study that found that "occupational therapists suggest that while craft-making has therapeutic value and that reasoning about the therapeutic use of craft is similar to reasoning about other therapeutic activities; the personal experience of craft-making has a strong influence on the selection of craft as activity." In other words, a therapist is more likely to choose crochet or another craft as a tool for therapy if he or she has had a positive experience of crafting in their own lives. This gives me hope because the resurrection of the handmade movement means that more and more people are crafting and suggests that more and more therapists would then have a personal experience that makes them likely to consider using craft in therapy. A third reason I have hope that crafting will be used more in therapy in the years to come is because I can say that I do know of at least some occupational therapy settings (including both mainstream settings and alternative / holistic settings) that utilize crafting for physical and mental skill development. It's been done in different ways for more than a century, it is being done now and it will continue to be done in the future!

Hand Injuries / Fine Motor Skills

In the chapter on pain management, we looked at how some people use crochet to help them deal with chronic pain in their hands from conditions such as arthritis. Crochet can also be used to treat the hands when they have sustained some type of injury, in which case it is considered a form of occupational therapy. Types of injuries that might require this type of therapy include disabilities caused by strokes and repetitive stress injuries like those seen in carpal tunnel syndrome. In many cases, what you're trying to do here is rebuild the fine motor skills, which we'll talk about in more depth in just a minute.

But first, I wanted to say that hand exercises can also be used as a preventative measure for preventing hand injuries. People who crochet a lot might find that the crochet itself leads to repetitive stress injury in the hands and wrists, which can be prevented simply by pausing periodically during a crochet project to stretch and exercise the hands. *You can find a series of hand and wrist exercises in Appendix B at the end of the book.*

Okay, so now let's talk about fine motor skills and how crochet can be used to help develop them. The fine motor skills are the physical skills related to the hands and arms (and some other body parts like the mouth). Being able to grip a pencil is an example of a fine motor skill that kids learn as they start to become school-aged. To do that, the body has to have several muscles working together in coordination and that's something that the body has to learn.

Crafting is used in occupational therapy settings to help develop fine motor skills. In fact, the aforementioned 1981 study by Bissell and Mailloux on the use of crafts in occupational therapy for the physical disabled ranked the number one reason to use crafts as the fact that it improves fine motor control. Crafts can be used in occupational therapy treatment for patients of all ages. Young patients suffering from developmental disabilities may be behind in their motor skill development and can use crochet to practice those skills. Older people may lose some of their fine motor skills due to other health conditions, such as strokes, and they can also use crochet as part of their occupational therapy program.

Crochet may look and even feel like a very sedentary craft to most people. But if you pay close attention (practicing that mindfulness that we talked about at the beginning of the book!) then you will notice that crochet actually utilizes a large number of muscles in the body. Humor me and try this exercise. Gather your crochet work and go sit in the middle of a room without any distractions; if that's not possible, sitting anywhere is fine, but the exercise works better if you're sitting cross-legged in the middle of an empty space so that you can really pay attention to what's going on with your body. Now crochet something simple that you already know how to do by memory, such as a granny square or a simple back-and-forth set of single crochet rows. As you work, pay close attention to every single motion that you put into each stitch. Notice how your eyes work back and forth across the row. Notice how each finger moves, how your thumb moves to support the work, how your arms move slightly. Notice if there is tension in your neck or shoulders (something that crocheters often find causes them pain if they don't have good crafting posture!) Ask yourself where your weight is distributed.

After doing that exercise, you should have a much better understanding of how many fine little movements go into just crocheting a small square for a blanket. While crochet may seem like an easy task to an able-bodied person, it can actually be difficult for someone who has problems with fine motor control. That difficulty, or more specifically the work done to overcome that difficulty, is what makes crochet useful for developing the fine motor skills.

Some of the fine motor skills that crochet can help with as part of an occupational therapy plan include finger flexion and extension and range-of-motion in the hands and lower arms. Crocheting requires being able to grip onto a hook, move it in something of a circular motion, grab and release the yarn and other little motions that help to strengthen and develop the fine motor skills in the hands. Crocheting can also help with oculomotor control, which relates to strengthening the muscles around the eyes, as well as with hand-eye coordination.

Cognitive Skill Development

Cognitive skills form the foundation of how we learn anything and so are clearly important for people of all ages. Unfortunately, developmental problems and injuries can inhibit a person's natural cognitive skills and they then need to re-learn and practice those skills to help them in learning for all areas of life. Crochet is terrific for cognitive skill development because it is a fairly easy-to-learn task that helps with working memory, problem-solving, attention skills, planning and strategizing and visual processing, all of which are major cognitive skills.

To start with, crochet can help develop working memory. The crafter needs to remember how to do a slip knot, then a chain stitch, then a row of chains, then a few different stitches like single crochets and double crochets. As the working memory develops, the crafter can stretch their memory further. One of the common phrases I've heard when people are talking about crochet patterns is that they may have an easy or difficult "stitch repeat." By this, the crocheter means that there may be several stitches or even several rows of different stitches that are then repeated chunk by chunk. For example, the crochet pattern might require that your row be made up of three double crochets followed by two double crochets in the next stitch followed by three double crochets and then a single crochet and this may repeat many times across a row. When you first start the pattern, you may need to read that again and again but eventually it becomes automatic; you remember it as you work. This stretches your memory.

Crochet is a task that you can get immersed into, which means that it can be used to develop skills with attention. The Serendip website provides an "incomplete list of cognitive skills" and notes that there are three different types of attention to be developed: selective attention, sustained attention and divided attention. People need to be able to filter out distractions, using selective attention to ignore irrelevant information. They need to learn to allow something to hold their attention for long periods of time. And they need to learn how to focus on more than one thing at a time, or multi-task, for certain situations. I believe that crochet can help people practice all of these types of attention skills. When you do get lost in a project, you're practicing sustained attention. If you find your mind wandering, you can switch to a pattern or stitch that's more complicated and therefore requires you to pay more attention to it. If you crochet in public then you can practice selective attention, focusing on your project instead of the distractions in the public space around you. If you crochet while caring for a baby, you'll probably practice divided attention, tending to the child as needed and focusing on your project when you can. Of course, in an occupational therapy setting these skills might be practiced in more specific and structured ways but this gives you an idea of how attention can be developed and honed through crochet.

One of the major things that crafts are used for in occupational therapy settings is developing skills in plan-making, goal setting and the execution of ideas. Crochet is excellent for this because it requires you to choose a pattern or project, plan out certain aspects (like how much yarn you need to complete the project), and then proceed through the steps to finish the project. More often than not, some type of problem arises (the stitches don't look right, there's something that you don't understand, you planned incorrectly and run out yarn ...) and when that happens, you also get to practice problem-solving and creative thinking. By learning to do this in crafting, you learn how to do it in the bigger world around you. And by doing it successfully in crafting, you gain the self-esteem that you need to be willing and able to practice it in the larger world around you.

Social Skill Development and Communication

Crochet can be used in occupational therapy settings to help not just with the physical therapy but also with some of the other issues that can be a barrier to treatment success – such as problems with social skills and communication. It may help simply by serving as a way to connect the therapist to the patient using the safe medium of crochet. Or it can be introduced in group therapy settings to create a safe environment for learning how to socialize in larger groups.

The study I mentioned previously titled Craft as Context in Therapeutic Change drew a distinction between "craft as therapy" and "craft in therapy", pointing out that crafts can be used in both ways in occupational therapy settings. Craft as therapy refers to how crafts are used to actually facilitate healing, such as using crochet to improve motor skills. In contrast, craft in therapy refers to the use of craft as a tool to enhance the therapeutic setting, for example, helping to establish or improve the patient / therapist relationship. When we look at how crochet is used for development of social skills and communication skills, we're looking mostly at "craft in therapy."

It works in occupational therapy in much the same way that we've explored already how it works in group settings in elder care homes and in substance abuse treatment centers. People who don't feel safe or comfortable or secure talking to one another or helping one another in big ways can come together in a room while working on crochet and it creates a bond and a safe space and a pleasant shared activity that leads to a deeper connection over the long haul. Whether it's elderly patients meeting together for the first time in a residential setting that's new for them or patient and therapist working on occupational therapy goal development in an outpatient setting, crochet becomes the medium through which other healing can begin to occur.

Sometimes crochet is the tool to help reach other occupational therapy goals but in other cases, it may be the goal itself (craft as therapy). For example, it has been found that enjoyment of leisure activities is a worthwhile occupational therapy goal in such settings as elderly communities. I read a really interesting 2008 article by Pereira and Stagnitti that researched the purpose and benefits of leisure in a small community of aging Italian adults living in Australia. It was not just about the importance of leisure to keep the elderly occupied, productive, happy, etc. (as they say, "meaningful leisure occupations can provide quality of life during aging") but also about the importance of occupational therapy recognizing this as a goal. They note that "achieving positive health and well-being through meaningful occupations for older people is congruent with occupational science and occupational therapy philosophy." But they note the same problem in their research that I mentioned in the beginning of this chapter was found by Bissell and

Mailloux: there wasn't enough research done into the health benefits of leisure in occupational therapy settings because, like with crafting, it wasn't seen as measurable. Like Bissell and Mailloux, Pereira and Stanitti explain that the mid-twentieth century found, "practitioners becoming increasingly concerned with scientific and technical aspects of intervention, whereas play and leisure were thought to be unscientific and inappropriate for use in practice."

But what Pereira and Stanitti say, and I'd agree, is that there is an immediate need to do more research into the health benefits of play and leisure (and therefore crafting) in occupational therapy settings, especially with the elderly. These authors were writing about an aging Italian population in Australia but they noted that the Australian social demographics in general were leaning towards an older population and of course this is true in the United States as well and is becoming even more of an issue as the oldest Baby Boomers begin to get into their elderly years. As a society, we need to encourage therapy settings for the elderly to offer a range of services including occupational therapy options, like crafting, that have multi-dimensional benefits.

The study done by Pereira and Stanitti consisted of interviewing the elderly. As you can tell from my collection of other people's stories throughout this book, I find it really valuable to hear what individuals have to say about their own lives and experiences, which is certainly a major reason this study caught my attention. What their interviews indicated was that the elderly people who engaged in leisure activities associated those activities with improved health. One specifically said that her knitting and crocheting helped her to relax. Another said that keeping active with various leisure activities helped to reduce the need for so much medication to deal with age-related diabetes. And one summed it up nicely by saying, "I'm 74 and I have to do something to live longer".

The study by Pereira and Stanitti found that the most popular leisure activity in the group they studied was playing bocce. Now, you might think that playing bocce has no correlation to crocheting for leisure, but hang in here with me and I'll explain. They found that there were six reasons that the participants felt like they received health benefits from this activity:

1. "An opportunity to enjoy and continue a cultural leisure tradition."
2. Physical activity/ exercise.
3. Being with friends in a social setting.
4. "Increased mental health by being completely focused on the task at hand."
5. Feeling self-esteem from using and teaching skills to newer players.
6. Experiencing competition.

Now crochet doesn't give you all of these things. It isn't a competitive sport and it doesn't really give you all that much physical exercise. But I would argue that it offers four of the six benefits on the list. It is a traditional craft that many people, women especially, feel is important because it links them to the generations before them and although that's not specifically "cultural" I think it does relate to that same basic experience of continuing something that might otherwise be lost to future generations. When practiced in groups, especially as it applies to occupational therapy settings, crochet can certainly be a social thing. And in those groups, people often help each other with new stitches and techniques, which allows the individuals to get those self-esteem boosts from passing knowledge on to others. Finally, the bocce participants felt that their mental health was improved because they were completely focused on the task at hand and crochet is something literally in your hands that you can focus on! So, although the leisure study was specific to a different type of activity, I think it shows how crochet and other crafts can be beneficial in occupational therapy settings where the main goal is to encourage the benefits of leisure for a specific population.

And incidentally, the social benefits of leisure in a therapy setting aren't limited to the elderly. I had a great-aunt who had Down Syndrome and I remember when I was little that she would always go to a day program during the day. I don't know a lot of the specifics about it but I know that she did a job there and I would guess that it involved tasks similar to those involved in various occupational therapy crafting groups. I would surmise that doing so offered her joy and an opportunity to socialize with others outside the family. The same could be true of the benefits of crafting as occupational therapy in a diverse range of settings.

And just as an aside, it can work equally well with people whose IQs are at the opposite end of the spectrum from those with a condition like Down Syndrome. In Pollanen's study, the author writes that craft is "useful when the client has challenges in verbal or cognitive processing, as well as for those with a tendency to over-intellectualize their experiences. In these cases concentrating on making by hand may create a symbolic distance or a certain kind of metaphor." I can appreciate this since I fall into the latter category; I constantly over-intellectualize my emotions. That was definitely a barrier for me in therapy, as I spent many therapy sessions saying, "here is what I feel but here is what I know I'm supposed to feel and here are the reasons I feel this way and, and, and" instead of just being in the feeling. The whole concept of just being in a feeling instead of thinking about the feeling still remains mostly mysterious to me. And I can see how using a hands-on meditative craft to get "in the moment" can help break that down just the tiniest bit and make room to effect real change. Margaret Mills mentioned something like this in her interview as well, saying, "I tend to spend too much time inside my head (writing, researching, etc.), and find it helps to do "hands-on" work to balance that – crochet, of course, but also gardening or sewing or cooking".

So I think that this chapter on occupational therapy brings us full circle because crochet may be used in physical therapy settings to help not only with the physical aspects of the condition but also with developing social skills related to the mental health of the patient. The aforementioned study by Pollanen reported that research bears out that craft can be useful to achieve therapeutic change in all of the following areas:

- Physiology including heart rate and respiration
- Psychophysiology including pain and level of consciousness
- Sensomotory development including fine motor skills development
- Perception including "discrimination of differences"
- Cognition including skill learning and memory retention
- Behavior including activity level, accuracy, and safety skills
- Craft-related skills (such as the specifics of using a crochet hook)

- Emotions including anxiety and depression (but we already knew that by now, right?!)
- Communication, both verbal and non-verbal
- Interpersonal skills including relationship patterns
- Creativity including artistry and inventiveness

This all reiterates that crochet can be used to heal from health issues of all kinds – physical or mental.

Me, My Hook and I: Crochet for the Caregivers

We have explored how crochet can be healing for people with a variety of different mental and physical health conditions. But in doing so, we've left out a large group of people who can also benefit from crochet: the loved ones of those who are ill. Illnesses of all kinds can wreak havoc on family members and other people who love them. Sometimes living with a loved one who is ill can cause us our own health problems. We might get fatigue and headaches from the stress of worrying about a loved one. Or we may experience our own depression and issues with codependency as we help someone we love work through their mental health issues. Often, the health of everyone else takes a backseat to concerns about the sickest person in a family. However, it is very true that if we don't take care of ourselves first and foremost then we can't take care of those we love. For that reason, it's important that anyone with a sick loved one takes special care to make sure that they themselves are not suffering health consequences as a result. And crochet can help with that.

One of the biggest benefits of crochet for people with ill loved ones is that it is a craft that can build self-esteem. Having a loved one who is ill can make you feel helpless and eventually even worthless. You can't help them to feel better or get better. And sometimes you get mad at them for being sick even though you know that they typically can't help it ... then you feel bad about yourself for not being more patient with them and with the situation. In some cases, the ill person's behavior (especially in cases of their mental illness) can specifically cause you to doubt your own sanity and this can lower your self-esteem. Crochet can be a gift that you give to yourself to maintain your own sense of who you are and what you can do as an individual. You can create things with your own two hands and be proud of that. You can create items that comfort your sick loved one, which is a way to give to them even if you can't fix their health problems. You can crochet things for other people in need, making yourself feel useful and valuable once again. And you can crochet special things just for yourself as a way of treating yourself well and showing yourself love.

As we've discussed previously, crochet is also a great form of stress relief and a way to reduce anxiety, feelings that we know all too well if we have someone in our lives who is ill. Our brains often whirl around on themselves with fears about what is going on with the sick person in our lives and attempts to puzzle a logical way through what is essentially an emotional experience. Taking the time to sit down to crochet, focusing on the process of forming stitch after stitch, can help to ease your mind. It gives you a much-needed mental health break when dealing with the difficulties of having someone in your life who is very ill.

Additionally, crochet offers the opportunity to feel like you are in control of something in your life. Sinikka Pollanen writes, "It can be said that craft can appear as an area of life that individuals can fully control according to their own terms, so that it supports the sense of control in life. Craft can help in attaining a feeling of life management and fully functional personality in situations where all the other areas of life are uncontrollable." This healing aspect of craft is certainly relevant to individuals who are going through a health crisis. But it can also be relevant to the caregivers in various situations. You can't stop your alcoholic husband from drinking, your sister's cancer from coming back out of remission, your anorexic daughter from starving herself thin, your parent's mind from deteriorating. You can't control any of it. But you can control every choice inside of your crochet project and while that's not everything, it's something, and sometimes something is enough to get you through to the next day.

If used properly, crochet can also be a way to just get time away from the entire experience of illness that sometimes seems to consume your life when you love someone with a serious health problem. When things get too intense at home or in the hospital, you can walk away and take a little time to yourself to crochet something and get your mind back into a peaceful state of being. You can even join a local crochet club where you might find a group of people to talk to about something other than illness for a change. It can be a refreshing and beneficial part of your life, even if you don't consider yourself "the sick one" in your family.

I know that this all sounds nice in theory but is harder to do in practice. And I know this because I've experienced it myself. Let me share a little bit more of my story with you, because not only have I used crochet to help me deal with my own depression and anxiety but I also have firsthand experience of using it as a healing tool for myself when dealing with other people in my life who suffer from an illness.

At the beginning of this book, I wrote about my most recent experience of spiraling down into a suicide-level state of depression. What I didn't go into detail about at the time was how this was triggered in part by the state of the romantic relationship that I was in at the time. (Oh come on, you had to know there would be another man, right? The one with the lost puppy dog look.) In all seriousness, the man that I was dating was a wonderful man and I treasure our connection to this day, but he was ill, too. What I've come to believe over the years is that we often subconsciously seek out romantic partners who will trigger things from our pasts and hopefully help us to resolve them. It's actually a really neat feature of the human process, but it can be terrifically painful as you're going through it, especially when you are young and don't really understand what it is all about. This man and I triggered huge emotional waves in one another, causing each other extensive amounts of pain even though we loved each other deeply.

We met in early 2007. I was already in the throes of a small-but-seemingly-manageable period of depression. So was he, although of course I didn't realize that at the time. For awhile, we were the bright spot in each other's lives that made depression lift. But of course if there are underlying problems within a person, they will resume eventually, and that was the case for both of us. In late 2008, we went through a breakup. All of my fears of abandonment and not being lovable and being alone forever came to a hilt; and all of the distraction of having a troubled boy around ceased so that I was left only with my own mind. That was ultimately the trigger for the final spiral that caused me to end up on my bathroom floor thinking about the right combination of vodka and pills to end my life ... and finally choosing the life-saving creativity of my crochet hook instead.

During the year following our breakup, we were on again, off again, never really together and never really apart. I spent a lot of time trying to figure him out and a lot of time trying to figure us out and a lot of time trying to make things work. We officially got back together again at the end of 2009 and stayed together for another two and a half years. During that time, I got healthier and happier. Crochet became a staple in my life that I could always turn to for myself. I went through therapy, developed stronger friendships, took better care of myself and certainly was doing considerably better during that time than I'd been doing before that. In fact, despite its many ups and downs, that relationship taught me more about how to take care of myself than anything else in life ever had and I'll forever value it for that.

But it wasn't easy. While I was getting better, this man that I loved was getting worse. His depression deepened. His anxiety heightened. And it all nearly pulled me back under despite the personal progress that I felt like I was making with my own illness. In fact, because I was doing better and he was now doing worse, I found it easy to justify focusing on his problems and trying to solve them. You already know that this was dangerous territory for me. And it's something that can be fatal to a girl who is just learning how to take care of herself.

I was definitely at risk of falling back into the pattern I'd been in with men since I was fourteen – trying desperately to take care of one that I perceived as being in more life-threatening danger than myself as a subconscious way to stop focusing on taking care of my own problems. By this time, though, I finally knew that this was what I was doing and knew without a doubt that my own life was at risk if I didn't take care of me first. Old habits die hard, though, and there is definitely a part of my fourteen-year-old self that is still stuck inside of me. I tried to focus on taking care of myself and not on this man I loved but I did not do it perfectly.

He was genuinely troubled. He was often suicidal. He was in a lot of pain. And I did really want to make it better, and I did genuinely believe that I could (or at least that I owed it to both of us to try). But sometimes it was a mess. He would go through these awful periods of just flat out disappearing because he couldn't deal with everyday life. He wouldn't answer the phone. He wouldn't respond to email. I should have understood this (remember me back in the chapter on depression, hiding in my bed as a friend threw pennies at my window trying to get me to not ignore the fact that he was out there?!) but when I wouldn't hear from him for a day or two I'd worry incessantly. I'd constantly check my phone to see if he'd called or messaged. I'm embarrassed to say that at 30-something I would be looking for him on Facebook and Googling recent entries of screen names that I knew he used just to make sure that he was alive, to quell the rising anxiety that this time he had needed me and somehow I wasn't there and now he was dead in his apartment alone. I am embarrassed to say that in my very first phone conversation with a therapist I had said that I thought I was co-dependent and then months later I would be in her office spending more time talking about this man's problems than my own, recognizing the irony of that all the while but so incredibly worried about him that I could not help it. We eventually figured out how to deal with each other's craziness. He learned to let me know with a text message that he needed to disappear for awhile. I learned to ask for such things. But more importantly, I learned (slowly, painfully, often with one step forward and two steps back) how to put myself and my health and my needs first in my own head and my own heart even when he was sick, even when he did need taking care of, even when I wanted to help him.

During this time, I remembered crochet. I had been crocheting all along ever since I discovered its benefits, but I really deeply remembered that it was something that had saved my life. And I clung to it as I dealt with the waves of being in a relationship with someone who was sick. Although he was never diagnosed, I believe that this man has Borderline Personality Disorder or something akin to it. And although I was never formally diagnosed with it, I know that I tend towards codependency in my relationships. And this is a terrible combination. I know firsthand the things that I described in theory above – the way that your own self-esteem drops when you're in a relationship with someone who is sick, even if they love you and you both mean well. And having read countless books on co-dependency and addiction and relationships, I know that I'm nowhere near alone in this. I think even people without severe mental health issues go through a huge struggle to balance putting their needs first with giving enough to their partners. Add in a dose of addiction or depression or disability or chronic illness and it is no surprise that maintaining that balance is often nearly impossible.

But I remembered crochet. I remembered crochet and I would take it to bed with me when I knew that it was healthier to go to bed alone than to keep fighting and puzzling through life with this man that I so desperately wanted to help. The sicker he got, the more I wanted to help him, and ironically, of course, the less that I could. I couldn't always be mature about the situation. I couldn't always know that he was behaving in mean ways because he was sick and not because of something I had done. I couldn't always remember that I had a wonderful life with or without this relationship. I couldn't always see that even if the worst did happen I would somehow find my way through to the other side. But I could always crochet. I could tune out my own crazy thoughts and create something for myself, something warm and fuzzy and safe.

When we ultimately broke up, I was just as worried about him as I was upset for myself. I won't say that I handled it perfectly. I didn't even handle it well. I screamed. I cried. I made midnight phone calls to him and everyone else speaking emotional jibberish that almost certainly didn't make a whole lot of sense. However, I managed. I didn't spiral so far into depression that I felt like dying again. I didn't find myself taking hour long cab rides to bang on his door and insist that he tell me he was alive (something I am embarrassed to admit I'd done at least once before during the worst of our combined illnesses). I didn't crawl into bed and stop working and stop answering my door. I did not put a knife on a vein in my arm. I pieced myself together even through the sadness and loss and worry. I stitched a life for myself. Literally, with my hook, stitching into a new day. Sometimes I would desperately want to call him and trigger a conversation that could stimulate feelings in us … and instead, I picked up a crochet hook. Sometimes I wanted to throw myself headlong into the terrible (but comfortingly familiar) arms of depression but I chose colorful yarns that made it hard to be miserable. In the month following that breakup, I made him a wonderful, cozy, beautiful crocheted blanket. I did it because it saved my sanity and it was something that I could give to him even if I couldn't give anything else at that time.

I wasn't exactly this man's caregiver. We were adults living apart and taking care of ourselves as best we could. But I was a key person in this man's life when he was going through really difficult times. I always wanted to take care of him and to be there for him, but sometimes that wasn't the best thing for me. Crochet helped me to get away from the drama of being around someone who is sick. There is nothing dramatic about crochet. It is consistent and soothing. I hope I always remember what crochet can do for me when people in my life get sick as well as when I get sick myself.

And I believe that this is an important tool for all caregivers, regardless of the situation that they find themselves in that causes them to be caring for someone else. So yes, crochet can help the person with early Alzheimer's but it can also help the adult child taking care of that person. Crochet can help the person with depression but it can also help ward off depression and stress-related illness in their loved ones. Crochet can help with arthritis but it can also help to relieve some of the tension that may build up in the caregiver who now has to open a few more jars. Crochet can help in grieving thc loss of someone and it can also help in the mysterious stages of living-grieving that come when you care for someone in the last stages of their life. Crochet, in my humble but honest opinion, can help everyone. As a caregiver, it is your job to figure out how to put yourself first. I give you crochet as an option.

In Summary: Mind Body Health

How can I wrap up a book like this when it feels like starting to crochet for health is just the beginning, not the ending, of a big chapter in life? What I come back to again and again in my own health story is that it is always better to take a preventative approach to health problems than to have to cure them after the fact. It is better to brush and floss every day than to have cavities filled. It is better to eat healthy than to have to ask a doctor why your weight keeps going up. It is better to ask for help early on than to spiral so deep into a depression that it's almost impossible for someone to help pull you out. The best approach to health is a holistic mind-body approach ... and crochet benefits both the mind and the body.

I'll reiterate something that Margaret Mills shared in her interview:

> "I tend to believe the claims made for the health benefits of crocheting – it is good for stress management, strengthening the immune system, regulating blood pressure. I can only testify to its help with depression, but as a cancer survivor, I consider continuing to crochet part of my general health plan. I'm all for anything that strengthens the immune system! I have also found, as an unexpected bonus, that crocheting taps into an unrealized artistic vein. Creative ideas start with a new yarn project, then spill over into house decorating, gardening and even my writing."

And I'll repeat something that Shelli Steadman shared:

> "All three aspects (planning, doing and completing a project) of the crochet process contribute to its health benefits. The planning and excitement that surrounds finding the perfect project to do next is uplifting. Actually crocheting the project is meditative. Having the end product completes the circle and feeds my need to accomplish something worthwhile.

Healing isn't an all or nothing venture. It's an ongoing process that changes with your needs. Crochet is a flexible activity that you can match to your current physical abilities. If you're having a tough day physically, you can crochet something simple that doesn't require much on your part other than repeating an easy stitch. On better days, you can work on something more intricate. I truly feel that crochet can be an outlet for someone in need of healing.

Crochet is a relaxing, meditative art form. It's also portable! You can take your crochet projects with you just about anywhere. Crochet is something you can do for someone else. Any activity that takes your mind off your own troubles to help others aids in your own healing."

And let me share one more thought from someone else ... Kelly from the blog Shorty's Sutures did an October 2011 article about how she spent a bad, grumpy day learning a new crochet technique, frogging her work and making and meeting new craft goals. I loved the sentiment she shared about crochet at the end of this post and think it's appropriate to share here:

"It helps me turn a murky day into a brighter one. It lowers my blood pressure and it brings me peace. Even when I have to start over and begin something totally new I feel better. Even when I have to acknowledge that a simpler stitch is the right way for me to go I feel better. I hope that crochet, or some other form of hand stitchery, can bring you that same type of feeling."

In my opinion, crochet can heal you during your worst times of almost any type of illness. But it can also be a part of a well-rounded, creative, healthy life. You certainly don't have to be sick to crochet!

Is it really true that crochet can improve your health? The fact is that I don't know for sure, at least not in any well-researched, measurable way that I could test and report on and publish in a psychological or social or medical journal. But I do know in my heart that it can. And I know for sure that it is worth a try. I have experienced its healing benefits and I have met many people along the way who have said the same.

Remember this important aspect of the craft the next time you wrap yourself up in that old afghan granny gave you or pick up a handmade scarf at a craft booth. Remember it when you are having a tough time and are seeking relief. Remember it when life gets just a little bit rough and you recognize that you need something that's just for you to help breathe freshness into your days. And if crochet doesn't work for you, take the chance on some other creative endeavor until you find something that does help you heal because that something is out there. What I know for sure, what I can say for certain and without a doubt even though it may sound to others like an exaggeration, is that crochet saved my life.

Appendix A: Mindfulness Exercises for Crocheters

In this book's chapter on depression, I shared the concept of mindfulness and offered an exercise for crocheters to help practice that concept. In this appendix you'll find five more exercises that a crocheter can do to enjoy mindfulness.

Exercise One: Notice Every Aspect of the Stitch

One of the simplest exercises to explain (although it can be surprisingly difficult in practice) is to try to be mindful of every single part of every single stitch that you create in your work. Instead of just working a single crochet, try to pay attention to every micro-motion involved in working it ... from the slight twist of your wrist to the way that you are holding your fingers to the almost imperceptible friction between the yarn and the hook. How many little actions can you notice in just a single crochet stitch? With each stitch, try to notice one more action. Notice your breath as you work. Notice the slight split of the yarn fibers. Notice the contrast between your hook color and yarn color. Be truly mindful of the tiniest parts of your work and you can't help but become completely immersed.

Exercise Two: Mantra Crochet

Exercise two is more for meditation than mindfulness, per se, but it offers the same benefits of relaxation and immersion in your project. You will need to do two things to prepare for this exercise. The first is to choose a project that doesn't require you to count your stitches. The second is to select a short mantra that you will say as you work.

Ideas for projects that do not require you to count your stitches include:

- Any scarf or blanket that uses a repeating stitch (such as a simple single crochet) and won't have any increases or decreases. You can start the project before doing your mindfulness exercise so that the chain and first few rows are done.

- A crochet project worked in the round without any joining or increases. Again, you'll want to use really simple stitches that you don't have to think about to create. I like the half double crochet, personally.
- A large granny square. If you're familiar with the way it's worked then it will come naturally to you without having to focus on the stitch work.
- Any crochet pattern or stitch repeat that is so familiar to you that doing it is like second nature.
- A freeform crochet art project that doesn't have any specific pattern so that you can do whatever you like with it.
- A project you're going to frog anyway. The process is more important than the product when it comes to mindfulness exercises.

The idea here is that you should not have to focus on your stitches because you're going to be focusing instead on repeating a mantra as you work. So, now you have to choose a mantra. You want to choose something really short and simple. Some ideas include:

- "Om." This single syllable widely used in meditation can be repeated over and over for a calming effect.
- "I am." Repeating this phrase over and over can be astoundingly powerful. It may make you think about what you are or how you came to be or it may just be soothing and relaxing. You can also add a descriptive word to this phrase if there is something specific that you want to focus on in your life, such as "I am strong" or "I am loved".
- "Mindfulness." This single multi-syllabic word can be remembered and repeated easily to help you focus on exactly what you're supposed to be doing with this exercise. An alternative is "I am aware" or "I am present".
- Nam-myoho-renge-kyo. This is a common Buddhist mantra that people say to get themselves in touch with their own Buddha nature, which basically means their own inner strength, connection to the wider world and compassion for self and others.

Note: if you don't feel comfortable with the word mantra, think of this as a saying, affirmation or prayer.

Now that you've done the groundwork, the exercise is easy. Place yourself in a comfortable position with your crochet project. Make sure that it is quiet and relaxing in your environment. Now, do your automatic stitching and with each stitch repeat one word of your mantra. Repeat it over and over again until you are feeling completely calm. Any time that your mind starts to wander, come back to your mantra. Remember why you've chosen this mantra and then focus on repeating the sounds over and over.

Exercise Three: 60 Second Observation

This is a great exercise because you can practice it any time that you are crocheting, whenever it comes to mind to do so. Simply pause anywhere in your work and stay still for sixty seconds. During that time, consciously observe your project. Just look at it and take in the saturation of the yarn's color, the details of the stitch work, the overall project and how it breaks down into its small components. Notice what you can see through the holes of the stitches and what it feels like to switch your gaze from the work to the point beyond the work through those holes. Just sixty seconds of mindfulness practiced regularly as you crochet can be very healing.

Exercise Four: Increased Breathing Triangle

In this exercise, you will crochet a triangle and as you do so your breathing will get deeper and deeper.

First you'll start your triangle. Here are the basics of making a triangle:

- Chain 2, sc in second chain from hook, turn.
- Chain 1, turn, increase, chain 1, turn.
- Now, for each subsequent row, you will increase in the first and last stitch and will just sc in all of the other stitches.

The breathing part is what brings you to meditation. For each odd numbered row, you will inhale throughout the row. For each even numbered row, you will exhale. So you'll inhale as you start the triangle, then you will exhale on row two, inhale on row three, exhale on row four, etc. You want to start the breath on each turn and continue it all the way through to the end of the row. You will always be exhaling for a beat longer than you inhaled on the previous row. Eventually, you will reach a row where you can no longer exhale or inhale to the end of the row. That's when the mindfulness exercise is complete.

Exercise Five: Choose a Mindfulness Cue

A mindfulness cue is something that you keep in mind as a thing that will always bring you back to your mindfulness practice and the current moment that you are in. For example, some people get cued whenever they feel an itch and scratch themselves. They train themselves that any itch is a cue to come back into the present moment and to focus on the breath, their feelings, the sounds in the room, etc. Eventually, this becomes automatic and they find themselves regularly brought back to mindfulness. You can choose a cue that relates to your crochet. Maybe it will be every time that you use a crossed double crochet in your work. Or maybe it will be whenever it's time to increase rows. Or perhaps it will be each time that you work with a red yarn. Or maybe it will just be the habit of coming back to mindfulness each time that you start a new project. Pick something you do frequently but not excessively so that it becomes a ritual but not a hassle.

Appendix B: Hand Stretches and Exercises

In the chapter on crochet as a form of occupational therapy I noted that there is some risk of hand injury or pain when crocheting because of the repetitive movement of the craft. This can be prevented in large part by taking breaks from crochet to exercise the hands. Most resources I've checked out recommend taking a break from crocheting approximately every thirty minutes to do some brief exercises. This appendix provides some examples of simple hand stretches and exercises that you can do to avoid repetitive strain injuries from the craft that you love! You can do these exercises any time and anywhere. *Important note: These are exercises that I've seen in yoga classes and various online articles over the years and things I've done myself. However, I'm not a doctor so always take precautions and listen to your own body as you do your stretching!*

Exercises for the Fingers

- Place both of your pinkie fingers on the edge of a table. Press down on the table with your pinkie fingers, gently raising and lowering your hands a few times. Repeat for each of your other fingers.
- Hold your hands palms up in front of you. Now curl your fingers so they touch the bottom of your palm. Release and curl them so they touch the middle of your palm. Release and curl them so they touch the front of your palm (as close to the base of the fingers as possible).
- In any position, spread your fingers as far apart as you can then bring them together and then spread them out again.

Exercises for the Thumbs

- Hold your right hand up in front of you, fingers pointing to the sky. Gently grab your right thumb with your left hand. Pull your right thumb gently away from the finger next to it. Hold the stretch then gently release it. Repeat a few times on that side and then repeat the process with your left thumb.

- Make a fist with your thumb pointing upwards. Bend your thumb as far backwards as is comfortable. Hold the position and then reverse to bend it as far forwards as possible.
- Use the thumb and forefinger of one hand to massage the web of the thumb on the other.

Exercises for the Wrists

- Sit comfortably at a table. Place all of your fingers together at the edge of the table (thumbs and palms hanging off the side). Press up on to the tips of your fingers and then slowly lower your hand down as far as possible while still pressing into the table. Spread your fingers slightly apart and repeat. Spread your fingers still further apart and repeat again, stretching out your wrist each time.
- Hold your arms out to the sides, palms down, fingers together. Draw circles with your hands by moving only your wrists.
- Hold your arms straight out in front of you, palms up. Bend them at the elbow so your hands are facing you. Now rotate your arms so that the palms are facing away from you. Lower the arms back so that they are facing straight out in front of you (palms should now be down). Repeat a few times.

Resources

I have compiled this list of resources for crocheters. It is by no means a comprehensive list to all of the resources that are out there but I hope it gives you a good start into learning more about crochet, health and online communities.

Online Communities for Crocheters

Here are some forums, chat rooms and social networking sites for crocheters:

- Ravelry: http://www.ravelry.com/
- Hookey: http://hookey.org/
- Crochetville: http://www.crochetville.org/forum/
- Etsy Crochet Lounge: http://www.etsy.com/teams/7011/etsy-crochet-lounge
- iYarny: http://crochet-with-cris.blogspot.com/p/iyarny-group.html

If you are interested in finding an in-person craft group then you might want to check out the Directory of Knitting and Crochet Clubs on the Lion Brand website. It's a searchable database.
http://www.lionbrand.com/cgi-bin/lionbrand/charitySearch.cgi?type=club

Online Crochet Classes

Here are some places online where you can learn crochet skills of varying levels:

- Craftsy: http://www.craftsy.com/
- Crochetville: http://www.crochetville.org/forum/classes.php

- Designing Vashti: http://www.designingvashti.com/events/designingvashti-online-classes.html
- Craftyminx Crochet School: http://www.craftyminx.com/2011/11/crochet-school-.html/

Professional Organizations

- Crochet Guild of America (CGOA): http://www.crochet.org/. The CGOA is a non-profit organization for the advancement of crochet.
- The National NeedleArts Association (TNNA). http://www.tnna.org/. This is an organization for needlearts businesses.
- TAFA List: http://www.tafalist.com/. This is an online marketing and networking organization for professionals working in fiber arts

Crafting For Health

- Knitting and Health Article Series on The Compassioknitter: http://www.thecompassioknitter.com
- Crafting Health (Australian holistic healer who teaches crafty stress management courses): http://craftinghealth.com/
- Craft for Health (a blog filled with creative ideas): http://www.craftforhealth.typepad.com/

Crocheting for Charity

There are many options to explore if you want to crochet for charity. These are just a handful of my favorites:

- Remembering Rowan Project: http://rememberingrowan.blogspot.com/ (This is the project by Laurinda who shared her story in this book.)
- SIBOL: http://sunshineinternationalblanketsoflove.blogspot.com/ (Sue, from the UK, collects handmade afghan squares from around the world, makes afghans and donates them to nursing homes.)

- Bridge and Beyond: http://homelessbridge.blogspot.com/ (This OH based organization accepts handmade items to donate to the homeless and people living in shelters).
- Project Linus: http://www.ProjectLinus.org. (This group donates handmade items to children in need in hospitals, foster care, etc.)
- Gift of Life: http://www.donors1.org/donors/wrapped. An organ and tissue donation center that accepts handmade wraps to give to the families of donors.

Other Interesting Websites

The websites that I've listed as resources here are related to crocheting or crafting plus a specific health issue like addiction or fibroymalgia.

- Knitting for Quitting in UK: http://www.ukhandknitting.com/knitting_for_quitting.php
- Fibromyalgia-Crochet Yahoo! Group: http://groups.yahoo.com/group/Fibromyalgia-Crochet/
- Knitting Heretic Blog (a knitting blog from a fibromyalgia sufferer): http://modeknit.com/
- Immunosuprressed Knitter (blog of a post-transplant knitter): http://immunosuppressedknitter.com/
- Guide to Making Polymer Crochet Hook Handles: http://hooksandyarns.blogspot.com/2011/02/crochet-hooks-re-post.html (these handmade fat handles may be more comfortable for people with various hand conditions such as carpal tunnel)

Selection of Recommended Books

- *Comfort* by Ann Hood (a true story of losing a child and getting through it by knitting)
- *The Knitting Circle* by Ann Hood (a novel based on the true story of losing a child; although it's about knitting it's probably the most powerful fiction I've read on the healing powers of needlecrafting)
- *Passing for Normal: A Memoir of Compulsion* by Amy S. Wilensky. (Although unrelated to crafting it's a great memoir if you're interested in OCD and Tourette's syndrome).

- *Prozac Nation* by Elizabeth Wurtzel. (Likewise, this book isn't related to crochet but is a good memoir for understanding depression from the inside out).

Note: I have not included a list of just-crochet blogs here. I read more than 200 of them on a regular basis so including them all here would be absurd. However, I link to all of my favorite crochet-related blog posts from the week on my own blog, www.crochetconcupiscence.com, each Saturday morning, so that's a great place to start if you want to find quality crochet blogs to read!

References

Author's Note: My favorite part of the research for this book was doing the interviews with people who had actually used crochet for healing. However, I did also do extensive research into crochet, crafting for health, and the specifics of different health conditions. If I referenced an author or article in the main text, you should find it here in the references. I apologize that some of the URLs are long ... I did a lot of the research online and have given the specific page to locate the articles I've referenced. I tried to stick loosely to APA style for this reference list although I was more concerned that you as a reader be able to locate the information you were seeking than in making sure that the exact format of the citation was correct!

(1949, November 29). Man Finds Crocheting Ends Ulcers. *Oxnard Press Courier.* Retrieved July 21, 2011 from http://news.google.com/newspapers?id=QgNLAAAAIBAJ&sjid=TCINAAAAIBAJ&pg=6952,7298128&dq=crochet&hl=en.

(1979, October 25). Crochet as Career ... And Hand Crochet as Therapy. *Boca Raton News.* Retrieved June 5, 2012 from http://news.google.com/newspapers?id=2AxUAAAAIBAJ&sjid=tIwDAAAAIBAJ&pg=3773,4434163&dq=crochet+therapy&hl=en.

(2009, February 9.) Knitting and Crochet Offer Long Term Health Benefits. *Fave Crafts Press Release.* Retrieved December 1, 2011 from http://www.prlog.org/10179509-knitting-and-crochet-offer-long-term-health-benefits.html.

(2009, February 9.) Knitting and Crochet Offer Long-Term Health Benefits. *PRLog.* Retreived August 1, 2011 from http://www.prlog.org/10179509-knitting-and-crochet-offer-long-term-health-benefits.html.

(2010, June 29). The Fine Art of Pain. *Rows Red Blog.* Retrieved June 5, 2012 from http://www.rowsred.net/?p=2655.

(2010, May.) Chronic Lyme Disease. *Lyme Info.* Retrieved June 5, 2012 from http://www.lymeinfo.net/chroniclymedisease.html.

(2011, January 22). Fibromyalgia. *Mayo Clinic.* Retrieved June 5, 2012 from http://www.mayoclinic.com/health/fibromyalgia/DS00079.

(2011, June 7.) Crochet Benefits for Body & Soul. *Talking Crochet, Vol. 8, No. 12).* Retrieved on August 10, 2011 from http://www.crochet-world.com/newsletters.php?mode=article&article_id=1742.

A.D.A.M. Medical Encyclopedia. (2010, February 7). Schizophrenia. *U.S. National Library of Medicine.* Retrieved September 1, 2011 from

Arthritis Crochet Tips. *FreePatterns.* Retrieved August 1, 2011 from http://www.freepatterns.com/content/content.html?content_id=381.

An Incomplete List of Cognitive Skills. *Serendip Website.* Retrieved June 12, 2012 from http://serendip.brynmawr.edu/local/Diversdiscov2/cogskills.html.

Azeemi, Samina T. Yousuf and Raza, S. Mohsin. (2005, December 2.) A Critical analysis of Chromotherapy and Its Scientific Evolution. *National Center for Biotechnology Information.* Retrieved on May 1, 2012 from http://www.ncbi.nlm.nih.gov/pmc/articles/PMC1297510/.

Bipolar Disorder. National Institute of Mental Health. Retrieved on May 20, 2012 from http://www.nimh.nih.gov/health/publications/bipolar-disorder/complete-index.shtml.

Bissell, Julie Crites and Mailloux, Zoe. (1981, June). The Use of Crafts in Occupational Therapy for the Physically Dsiabled. *The American Journal of Occupational Therapy.* Retrieved June 2, 2012 from http://www.pediatrictherapy.com/images/content/199.pdf.

Black, Kelly. (2011, October 4.) How to Feel Peaceful in Minutes. *Shorty's Sutures blog.* Retrieved October 10, 2011 from http://www.shortyssutures.com/2011/10/04/how-to-feel-peaceful-in-minutes/.

Bouchez, Colette. Serotonin: 9 Questions and Answers. *WebMD.* Retrieved on June 20, 2011 from http://www.webmd.com/depression/recognizing-depression-symptoms/serotonin.

Brichford, Connie. (2009, March 25.) Coping with Schizophrenic Halluhttp://www.everydayhealth.com/schizophrenia/hallucinations-and-delusions.aspx. cinations and Delusions. *Everyday Health.* Retrieved on August 1, 2011 from http://www.everydayhealth.com/schizophrenia/hallucinations-and-delusions.aspx.

Bureau of Labor Statistics: Occupational Therapists. Retrieved June 5, 2012 from http://www.bls.gov/ooh/Healthcare/Occupational-therapists.htm.

Burt, Mary Pinkas. (1989, November 13). Former Smoker Enjoys Life More Now That She's Quite Cigarettes. *Schenectady Gazette.* Retrieved June 5, 2012 from http://news.google.com/newspapers?id=0nIhAAAAIBAJ&sjid=hYgFAAAAIBAJ&pg=1036,3480091&dq=crochet+health&hl=en.

Carol. Fog Magazine. Retrieved December 1, 2011 from http://www.fogmagazine.com/a-yarn-about-crocheting/.

Carper, Jean, (2010). *100 Simple Things You Can Do To Prevent Alzheimer's and Age-Related Memory Loss.*

Color Meanings. *Paul Goldin Clinic.* Retrieved on May 1, 2012 from http://colorgenicstest.com/color-meanings.html.

Corkhill, Betsan. (2007). Therapeutic Knitting. *Knit on the Net for the Independent Knitter.* Retrieved on September 1, 2011 from http://www.knitonthenet.com/issue4/features/therapeuticknitting/.

Corkhill, Betsan. (2008, April). Guide to Our Theories So Far. *Stitchlinks.* Retrieved on June 1, 2011 from http://www.stitchlinks.com/pdfsNewSite/Theories%20so%20far1%20A4.pdf.

Corkhill, Betsan. (2009 April). Crochet to the Rescue! *Stitchlinks.* Retrieved February 2, 2012 from http://www.stitchlinks.com/pdfsNewSite/your_health_matters/Crochet%20to%20the%20rescue.pdf.

Corkhill, Betsan. Why do we need the research? *Stitchlinks.* Retrieved May 1, 2012 from http://www.stitchlinks.com/pdfsNewSite/Whyresearch.pdf

Cowen, Mark. (2009, January 20). Occupational Therapy Benefits Schizophrenia Patients. *MedWire News.* Retrieved on May 22, 2012 from http://www.medwire-news.md/52/80543/Consumer_Health/Occupational_therapy_benefits_schizophrenia_patients.html.

Crochetbug. (2011, October 2.) Crochet for Weight Control. *Crochetbug Blog.* Retrieved January 2, 2012 from http://www.crochetbug.com/crochet-for-weight-control.

DMiller413. (2011, September 22). Homeopathy for Bipolar. *Life Love and Bipolar Forum Board.* Retrieved December 1, 2011 from http://www.lifeloveandbipolar.com/node/80.

Dow, Merrell. Understanding and Responding to Symptoms of Schizophrenia. *Schizophrenia.com.* Retrieved August 25, 2011 from http://www.schizophrenia.com/family/delusions.html.

Duffy, Kathryn, M.S.S., L.C.S.W. (Winter 2008). Knitting Through Recovery: One Stitch at a Time. *Sequel Youth and Family Services.* Retrieved June 5, 2012 from http://www.sequeltsi.com/files/library/Knitting_and_Recovery.pdf.

DukeHealth.org: Katherine L. Applegate, Phd. Retrieved June 5, 2012 from http://www.dukehealth.org/services/weight_loss_surgery/physicians/katherine_applegate and http://www.dukehealth.org/repository/dukehealth/2007/08/22/10/37/20/3027/2007LifestyleWorkshops.pdf.

Edyn. (2012, January 24). Creativity=Meditation. *MD Junction Bipolar Support Group.* Retrieved May 5, 2012 from http://www.mdjunction.com/forums/bipolar-support-forums/general-support/3415537-creativitymeditation.

Fairbanks, Amanda M. (2010, January 4.) The Neediest Cases; Through Ups and Downs of Illness, Creativity Endures. *The New York Times.* Retrieved December 5, 2011 from http://query.nytimes.com/gst/fullpage.html?res=9B06E5DB1731F937A35752C0A9669D8B63.

Fawcett, Jan, Golden, Bernard and Rosenfeld, Nancy. (2007). *New Hope for People with Bipolar Disorder: Your Friendly, Authoritative Guide to the Latest in Traditional and Complementary Solutions.*

Ferguson, WJ and Goosman, E. (1991, August 30). A Foot in the Door: Art Therapy in the Nursing Home. National Center for Biotechnology Information. Retrieved May 1, 2012 from http://www.ncbi.nlm.nih.gov/pubmed/10114781.

Fiedler, Chrystie. Stressed Out? ... Slow Down. *Natural Health.* Retrieved June 5, 2012 from http://www.naturalhealthmag.com/health/stressed-outslow-down?page=3.

Freeman, Thomas, Cameron, John L. and McGhie, Andrew. (1958). *Chronic Schizophrenia.* Tavistock Publications Limited. P. 117-120. Online version retrieved May 22, 2011 from http://books.google.com/books?id=W2wWyjOJ7foC&pg=PA117&lpg=PA117&dq=schizophrenia+treatment+knitting&source=bl&ots=WfGdRrBCuG&sig=MHu_FUMaZ6j9ww3RcJMdvhj6qOA&hl=en&sa=X&ei=DIK9T_jePOmfiAKUpfmgDg&ved=0CGcQ6AEwAQ#v=onepage&q=knitting&f=false.

Gail. (2011, June 6). Knitting and Health – Gail and OCD, Tourettes, ADHD, Depression. *Compassioknitter Blog.* Retrieved August 25, 2011 from http://www.thecompassioknitter.com/2011/06/knitting-and-health-gail-and-ocd.html.

Generalized Anxiety Disorder. *Anxiety and Depression Association of America*. Retrieved on May 12, 2012 from http://www.adaa.org/understanding-anxiety/generalized-anxiety-disorder.

Gleason, Kathy. (2011). *Obsessed: A Tale of OCD, Knitting and Inappropriate Men.* (A Kindle book).

Gonser, Amanda. (2011, September 17). Six Billion Others: Kelso Grad Feels Pulse of the World at Spain Exhibit. *TDN.com.* Retrieved October 1, 2011 from http://tdn.com/lifestyles/article_d5c4815a-e193-11e0-

9dea-001cc4c03286.html.

Gormely, Sara C., OTS. (2008). The Art & Science of Crafts: Treatment of Physical and Cognitive Disabilities. *StuNurse Magazine.* Retrieved June 11, 2012 from http://www.stunurse.com/features/art-science-crafts-treatment-physical-and-cognitive-disabilities.

Goulette, Candy and LaGrossa, Jessica. (2006, November 27). Crafting Care. *Advance for Occupational Therapy Practitioners.* Retrieved on July 2, 2011 from http://occupational-therapy.advanceweb.com/Article/Crafting-Care.aspx.

Green, Michael Foster. (2003). *Schizophrenia Revealed: From Neurons to Social Interactions.*

Harris-McCray, Chandra. (2011, July 19.) MS Diagnosis Inspires Mom's Crocheting Business. *Knox News.* Retrieved June 10, 2012 from http://www.knoxnews.com/news/2011/jul/19/ms-diagnosis-inspires-moms-crocheting-business/.

Hart, Carol (1996). *Secrets of Serotonin: The Natural Hormone that Curbs Food and Alcohol Cravings, Elevates Your Mood, Reduces Pain and Boosts Energy.* Online version retrieved on May 20, 2012 from http://books.google.com/books?id=VNdm9yRcQwQC&pg=PA230&lpg=PA230&dq=Secrets+of+Serotonin+knitting&source=bl&ots=CvB2vYpDzS&sig=ESxtejXrT8ZoHfzmkOODciyBLGc&hl=en&sa=X&ei=otK6T7jAJLHZiQLtrqCgDA&ved=0CGQQ6AEwAA#v=onepage&q&f=false.

Herr, Laurie. (2011, July 11). Managing Stress with Bipolar Disorder. *Yahoo! Health.* Retrieved December 1, 2011 from http://health.yahoo.net/articles/bipolar-disorder/bipolar-stress-relief-tips.

Hochman, Andee. (2004). Creative Prescriptions. *Time Inc. Health, Pub. 2004-10, Volume 18, Issue 8, Pages 189-195.*

Hood, Ann. (2008). *Comfort: A Journey Through Grief.*
http://www.ncbi.nlm.nih.gov/pubmedhealth/PMH0001925/.

Ilana. (2009, December 3.) Can You Crochet Away Depression? *Lion Brand Yarn Blog.* Retrieved on August 5, 2011 from http://blog.lionbrand.com/2009/12/03/can-you-crochet-away-depression/.

Jacobs, Barry. Case Study: What Causes Depression. *Princeton University Department of Psychology.* Retrieved on July 1, 2011 from http://psych.princeton.edu/psychology/research/jacobs/case.php.

Jamison, Kay Redfield. (1999). *Night Falls Fast: Understanding Suicide.*

Jones, Steven and Hayward, Peter. (2004). *Coping with Schizophrenia: A Guide for Patients, Families and Caregiver.*

Kam, Katherine. Asthma, Stress and Anxiety: A Risky Cycle. *WebMd.* Retrieved July 5, 2012 from http://www.webmd.com/asthma/features/asthma-stress-and-anxiety-a-risky-cycle.

Kamps, Louisa. (2010, June). DIY Therapy: How Handiwork Can Treat Depression. *Whole Living.* Retrieved on June 15, 2011 from http://www.wholeliving.com/134137/diy-therapy-how-handiwork-can-treat-depression.

Katatikarn, Gungsadawn. The Importance of Perception to Schizophrenics. *Serendip.* Retrieved August 6, 2011 from http://serendip.brynmawr.edu/bb/neuro/neuro98/202s98-paper1/Katatikarn.html.

Kindle, Lois. (2011, August 24.) Riverview Woman's Life is Repurposed Through Service. *Tampa Bay Online.* Retrieved June 11, 2012 from http://www2.tbo.com/news/community-news/2011/aug/24/1/brnewso24-riverview-womans-life-is-repurposed-thro-ar-252157/.

Krzywoszyja, Sonya. (2011, April 18.) Stitching, Twitching and Social Anxiety. *Lip Magazine.* Retrieved on May 22, 2012 from http://lipmag.com/opinion/switching-twitching-and-social-anxiety/.

Lang, Monique. (2007.) *Healing from Post Traumatic Stress: A Workbook for Recovery.*

Law, Bridge Murray. (2005, November). Probing The Depression-Rumination Cycle. *American Psychological Association,*

Monitor, Vol. 36, No, 10. Retrieved online on May 20, 2012 from http://www.apa.org/monitor/nov05/cycle.aspx.

LeBlanc, Gary Joseph. (2011, June 1). Idle Hands. *Fischer Center for Alzheimer's Research Foundation.* Retrieved on May 1, 2012 from http://www.alzinfo.org/06/blogs/idle-hands.

Lil. (2011, August 6). Lack of Diagnosis. *Idiocratic Mind Soup blog.* Retrieved May 1, 2012 from http://wireddifferently.wordpress.com/2011/08/06/lack-of-diagnosis/.

Littman, Margaret. (2009, June). Make Needlework Finger-Friendly. *Arthritis Today.* Retrieved Jun 22, 2011 from http://www.arthritistoday.org/daily-living/do-it-easier/around-the-house/arthritis-needlework.php.

Mascia, Jennifer. (2009, December 3). Artistic Program Provides Therapy for Mentally Ill. *The New York Times METRO.* Online version retrieved December 3, 2011 from http://www.wearebcs.org/bcs/Press/neediest_cases/archive_09_10/attachment_25.pdf.

McColl, Melissa. (2011, December 6). Rita's Story – Crocheting Through Grief. *Close Knit.* Retrieved on May 10, 2012 from http://torontocloseknit.blogspot.com/2011/12/ritas-story-crocheting-through-grief.html.

Mental Illness: Seasonal Affective Disorder. *National Alliance on Mental Health.* Retrieved on July 1, 2011 from http://www.nami.org/Template.cfm?Section=By_Illness&Template=/TaggedPage/TaggedPageDisplay.cfm&TPLID=54&ContentID=23051.

Mills, Margaret. (2010, August 23.) The Healing Arts and Crafts. *I Heart Art: Portland.* Retrieved on July 10, 2011 from http://iheartartpdx.com/2010/08/23/the-healing-arts-and-crafts/.

Mitchell, Deborah. (2010). *How to Live Well with Early Alzheimer's: A Complete Program For Enhancing Your Quality of Life.*

Morton, Erin. (2011). The Object of Therapy: Mary E. Black and the Progressive Possibilities of Weaving. *Utopian Studies, Vol. 22, No. 2, Special Issue Craftivism, pgs. 321-340.* Published by

Penn State University Press. URL: http://www.jstor.org/stable/10.5325/utopianstudies.22.2.0321

Nixon, Robin. (2012, April 25). Playing Tetris May Treat PTSD, Flashbacks. *LiveScience.* Retrieved on May 1, 2012 from http://www.msnbc.msn.com/id/47176735/ns/technology_and_science-science/t/playing-tetris-may-treat-ptsd-flashbacks/#.T7xUKO0YQ2Z.

O'Connor, Paul. (2005). *Multiple Sclerosis: Everything You Need to Know.*

Obsessive-Compulsive Disorder (OCD). *Mayo Clinic.* Retrieved August 5, 2011 from http://www.mayoclinic.com/health/obsessive-compulsive-disorder/DS00189.

Palevsky, Stacey. (2007, January 26.) Knitting Offers Physical, Mental Threapy for the Aging. *J Weekly.* Retrieved June 12, 2012 from http://www.jweekly.com/article/full/31474/knitting-offers-physical-mental-therapy-for-the-aging/.

Pearce, Nancy. (2007). *Inside Alzheimer's: How to Hear and Honor Connections with a Person who has Dementia.*

Peele, Stanton. (2004). *7 Tools to Beat Addiction.*

Pereira, Robert B. and Stagnitti, Karen. (2008). The meaning of leisure for well-elderly Italians in an Australian community: Implications for occupational therapy. *Australian Occupational Therapy Journal, 55, p. 39-46.*

Pollanen, Sinikka PhD. (2009, May – August). Craft as Context in Therapeutic Change. *The Indian Journal of Occupational Therapy, Vol XLI, No 2., pgs 43-47.*

Pregnancy and Sleep. *National Sleep Foundation.* Retrieved June 5, 2012 from http://www.sleepfoundation.org/article/sleep-topics/pregnancy-and-sleep.

Purse, Marcia. (2008, September 5.) Flat Depressive Episode: I'm Bipolar Journal. *About.com Bipolar Disorder.* Retrieved December 1, 2011 from http://bipolar.about.com/od/whatme/a/080905_crochet.htm.

Restless Legs Syndrome. *WebMD.* Retrieved June 5, 2012 from http://www.webmd.com/sleep-disorders/guide/restless-legs-syndrome-rls.

Rice, Elizabeth. (2009, February 9.) Exercise Your Brain to Prevent Memory Loss. *Mayo Clinic News.* Retrieved May 1, 2011 from http://newsblog.mayoclinic.org/2009/02/09/exercise-your-brain-to-prevent-memory-loss/.

Rockett, Christine. (1999, June 28.) Needwork: A Tool to Teach Occupation Based Therapy. *Advance for Occupational Therapy Practitioners.* Retrieved June 5, 2012 from http://occupational-therapy.advanceweb.com/Article/Needlework-A-Tool-to-Teach--Occupation-based-T.aspx.

Rodgers, Donna. (2009). Crochet .. The Perfect Solution for Anxiety. *Comin' Home: Sharing the Art and Heart of Homemaking.* Retrieved August 1, 2011 from http://thehomemakingarts.blogspot.com/2009/12/crochetthe-perfect-solution-for-anxiety.html.

Rosberg, Jack. (1999, May.) Jack Rosberg's Model, May Newsletter. *SchizophreniaRecovery.net.* Retrieved September 1, 2011 from http://www.schizophreniarecovery.net/newsletter/may99.htm.

Schwartz, Jeffrey. Dr. Jeffrey Schwartz's 4 Steps. *Westwood Institute for Anxiety Disorders.* Retrieved September 1, 2011 from http://hope4ocd.com/foursteps.php. (This online version used as a source Schwartz's 1996 book called Brain Lock.)

Shoman, Mary. (2011, May 6.) How I Quit Smoking: After Several Tries, I Was Able to Quit Cigarettes for Good. *About.com Thyroid Disease.* Retrieved May 21, 2012 from http://thyroid.about.com/od/symptomsrisks/a/quitting-smoking-thyroid.htm.

Social Anxiety Disorder. *Anxiety and Depression Association of America.* Retrieved on May 12, 2012 from http://www.adaa.org/understanding-anxiety/social-anxiety-disorder.

Squires, Nick and Allen, Nick. (2009, April 8.) Italy Earthquake: Elderly Woman Knitted as She Waited for Rescue. *The Telegraph.* Retrieved on July 20, 2012 from http://www.telegraph.co.uk/news/worldnews/europe/italy/5120197/Italy-earthquake-elderly-woman-knitted-as-she-waited-for-rescue.html.

Stone, Katherine. (2012, February 6). Knit One Purl One: A Story of Postpartum Depression in the 60s. *Postpartum Progress.* Retrieved on May 5, 2012 from http://postpartumprogress.com/knit-one-purl-one-a-story-of-postpartum-depression-in-the-60s.

Strong, Peter. (2009, December 6.) The Mindfulness Approach: Therapeutic Techniques That Work. *Pscyhology Today.* Retrieved on May 25, 2012 from http://www.psychologytoday.com/blog/the-mindfulness-approach/200912/what-color-is-your-depression-overcoming-depression-mindfulness.

Tull, Matthew. (2012, January 29.) Coping with Flashbacks. *About.com Post Traumatic Stress (PTSD).* Retrieved May 1, 2012 from http://ptsd.about.com/od/selfhelp/a/flashcoping.htm.

Werley, Judy. (1975, July 28). Crocheting Afghans "Best Therapy Ever." *The Evening News.* Retireved June 12, 2012 from http://news.google.com/newspapers?id=tm1RAAAAIBAJ&sjid=AjQNAAAAIBAJ&pg=1717,3982803&dq=crochet+therapy&hl=en.

What is PTSD? *United States Department of Veterans Affairs: National Center for PTSD.* Retrieved May 1, 2012 from http://www.ptsd.va.gov/public/pages/what-is-ptsd.asp.

Giving Thanks

I had intended to include a dedication at the beginning of this book but then I realized just how long the list of people I wanted to acknowledge was. This book is really close to my heart and although it came out of my own hard work, there have been many people along the way who helped me get to the point where it could happen.

First, there's the family. Thanks to my mama for being the first one to teach me to crochet, for immediately taking me to the store to buy hooks and yarn when I said I wanted to learn the craft again and for being the person who I know will promote this book more than anyone else. Thanks to my sister for crocheting with me through good times and bad, for spending months with me in my home when I was at my most depressed and for being the person with whom I can always be the most honest. Thanks to my dad for listening to me say five million times that I was having doubts about my ability to write this book, for never hesitating to tell me a story about something I wanted to know more about during my research and for just being there. And thanks to my brother for never failing to ask how the book was going, never making me feel like a fool for constantly changing my mind about how I feel about writing and always providing an escape when I need one.

Then there are my closest friends, most of whom probably don't even remotely understand my crochet obsession but humor me anyway by asking about my craft and accepting crazy handmade items with a smile. Thanks to Rafael for being the steadiest, most stable person in my life, listening to me go on and on endlessly about hysterical nonsense in the throes of my depression. Thanks to Adam for consistent love and support and never failing to tell me that my writing is good no matter how many times I got convinced that I'm a terrible writer and could never do it. Thanks to Kelly for craft nights, creative conversations, unwavering support and belief in me and for just being basically the coolest girl I know. Thanks to Amy, who may not know it but the time that she showed up at my house when I was just on the verge of a breakdown and showed me that a friend will be there for you was really a turning point in my life. Thanks to the rest of "Sunday Dinner" for providing consistency in a life filled with change. Thanks to Anna whose own creative path and constant pursuit of knowledge has been an inspiring example for me in living my own life. Thanks to Julie whose nice comment about how excited she was to see this book reinvigorated my work on it after it had stalled out a bit and who serves as a great example of an inspiring, motivated, creative woman in my life. Thanks to Michael for being the kind of supportive friend who understands why I'm a writer and not a lawyer. Thanks to Bill for being that person that I can go ages without speaking to and yet we pick up the conversation exactly where we left off. Thanks to Jeanette who may be a new friend in my life but who has already shown awesome support for my creative work.

Next are the professionals who helped me in my life and my work. Thanks to Dr. Wells, my psychologist, for shining a hopeful beam of light into my life when my life was feeling anything but hopeful and light. A second thanks to Julie because she was not only a good friend but also the photographer for the cover of this book. And thanks to Kurt who makes every problem I encounter with my blog and website seem simple to understand and easy to fix; he is like an elf working tech magic while I sleep and things are always well with my site when I wake up in the morning.

But finally, and in many ways most importantly, thank you to my crochet community. There is no way that I can list by name every crocheter who has supported me in my craft, my blog, my book, my dreams. Thank you to everyone who has ever left an encouraging comment on my blog and social networking accounts about my crochet and / or my writing, for subscribing to my blog updates and email newsletter, for following me on sites like Twitter and Pinterest. Thank you to the crocheters who are putting out magazines and books and articles and blogs and video tutorials that help me in developing and sharing this great craft. Thank you to the crafty folks who keep my crochet momentum going by sharing their work that I've seen in craft groups and yarn stores and public spaces. And thank you, especially thank you, to the many wonderful women who shared their stories with me about the way that crochet has helped them heal. To the women in this book, and the women that weren't interviewed for the book but who mentioned their experiences to me over time, this book literally wouldn't exist without you.

A Note To My Readers

I wanted to give a special and separate thanks to all of you who have chosen to read this book. I hope that it has resonated with you in some way.

Please know that I'd love to hear from you. If you have a crochet story that you want to put into words, my inbox is open. Crochet healing stories are always something I want to hear. I find them interesting, powerful and beneficial to learn about. I encourage you to drop me a line using the contact form on my website: www.crochetconcupiscence.com. Feel free to share your story with me; I want to listen.

Also I'd like you to know that this book is entirely self-published and was a true labor of love (and hard work). If you enjoyed it, you can help me out by spreading the word. Tell a friend about it, encourage your local yarn store to carry it, put out a mention on Facebook or your blog, pick up an extra copy for someone you love. Every little bit helps add some buzz and lets people know about the power of crochet.

About the Author

It seems a little bit silly at this stage to include an "about the author" page when you've already learned so many details of my life but here it is ...

Kathryn Vercillo is a San Francisco based freelance writer, blogger and crochet lover. She is the author of two previous books (Ghosts of San Francisco and Ghosts of Alcatraz) and has been a contributing author on other book projects. Her work has been published in magazines including Latina Magazine and Skope Music Magazine. Kathryn has worked as a professional blogger for numerous websites including PC World, Dial-a-phone, SF Travel, and Houzz. Her online articles about crochet have been published around the web on sites that include Crochetvolution, Crochet Liberation Front, SF Indie Fashion and Handmadeology. Her Crochet Concupiscence blog was voted one of the top 5 2012 craft blogs in Inside Crochet Magazine and was a 2011 runner-up for a Flamie award from the CLF. You can visit her crochet blog at www.crochetconcupiscence.com or learn more about the author at www.kathrynvercillo.com.

Printed in Germany
by Amazon Distribution
GmbH, Leipzig